This book is dedicated to my favorite teachers:
my parents,
my husband, Michael,
and my children, Sarah and Rebecca

Career Imprints

Monica Higgins

with a foreword by Ed Schein

Career Imprints

Creating Leaders Across an Industry

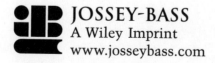

JOSSEY-BASS
A Wiley Imprint
www.josseybass.com

Published by Jossey-Bass
A Wiley Imprint
989 Market Street, San Francisco, CA 94103-1741 www.josseybass.com

Jossey-Bass books and products are available through most bookstores. To contact Jossey-Bass directly call our Customer Care Department within the U.S. at 800-956-7739, outside the U.S. at 317-572-3993 or fax 317-572-4002.

Jossey-Bass also publishes its books in a variety of electronic formats. Some content that appears in print may not be available in electronic books.

Library of Congress Cataloging-in-Publication Data:

Higgins, Monica C., 1964-
    Career imprinting : creating leaders across an industry / Monica C. Higgins.—1st ed.
        p. cm.
    Includes bibliographical references and index.
    ISBN 0-7879-7751-9 (alk. paper)
    1. Leadership. 2. Executives—Training of 3. Career development.
4. Corporate culture. 5. Baxter Healthcare Corp.—Personnel management. I. Title.
    HD57.7.H528 2005
    658.4'092—dc22   658.4092   2004030568

Printed in the United States of America
FIRST EDITION
HB Printing 10 9 8 7 6 5 4 3 2 1

Contents

Acknowledgments

This project spanned a period of nine years and included the support and assistance of many people. In part, this is due to the range and scope of the project, but even more so, it is due to the generosity of so many who helped me develop, shape, and produce the ideas presented in this book.

First, I am deeply indebted to the senior executives who were interviewed extensively for this research. Although the career history interviews that form the basis of this book took the interviewees back many years to when they were ramping up in their careers and extremely busy, I know that for most the pace of their work lives has barely slowed; this makes the time and attention they so generously gave me all the more precious. I thank several alumni of Baxter, the healthcare company of primary focus in this research, in particular: Stan Erck, Gabe Schmergel, Bob Carpenter, Henri Termeer, Steve Chubb, Jim Tobin, and Elliott Hillback, who all spoke with me on numerous occasions, provided rich details about their work lives at Baxter, and indulged my questions with patience. Gabe, in particular, was in many ways an "expert informant" on this project—that is, he provided me with incredibly valuable detail, not only about his own career but about the context in which this study took place. I am extremely grateful to these individuals as well as to all of the Baxter alumni who told their stories in such rich detail. Without their participation, this project would never have happened.

In addition, I thank those who came from other healthcare companies who were interviewed for this book. Several individuals, particularly from Abbott, Johnson & Johnson, and Merck, met with me extensively and answered both my informed as well as naïve questions. They also opened doors for me and gave me access to historical company documents, which helped me triangulate what I was hearing in the interviews.

Another important perspective was that of intermediaries, including venture capitalists, executive recruiters, lawyers, and consultants, who were all engaged in deals or projects during the formative years of the biotechnology industry. In particular, I thank Brook Byers, Bob Higgins, Bill Holodnak, Pitch Johnson, and Leon Schor. These informants and their colleagues met with me on the West Coast, on the East Coast, and followed up with documentation as well. They provided a different and yet critical perspective in this research, and so I thank them for their time and insights.

On the home front at Harvard Business School, I am indebted to many individuals who have worked with me both formally and informally over the years. During the early stages of this project, the primary activity was collecting, classifying, and coding career history data from the final prospectuses of biotechnology companies that had gone public. Suzanne Purdy was the first research associate engaged in this activity. Her enthusiasm and dogged attention to the details in these early years was critical; I thank her for getting this project off to a good start. John Galvin followed Suzanne as my research associate on this project and remained on this project long after he was promoted beyond his research associate position. I can not say enough about John's contributions to this project. He has remained loyal over the years, assisting with collecting and analyzing data as well as overseeing the research activities of others. No question was too big or too small for him. I will always be deeply indebted to John.

During the final months of the project, James Dillon stepped in as my research associate to tie up the project's many loose ends. The research quests were varied and disparate, but James engaged in each with a high level of intensity and curiosity. He was both persistent and careful, and I am grateful to him for all of his support. I also thank the many others who have provided excellent research support over the years, including David Kwan, Christine Teebagy, and

Paul Nguyen. Each person stepped into the project midstream and picked up the reins with dedication and care. And, while these were the official "research associates" on the project, I also called on the assistance of many others in Harvard's superb library research staff. I thank Chris Allen and his team not only for the data they were able to track down but also for their insights on what was and was not "gettable."

For all but the earliest years, Lisa Pode managed the administrative side of this project. From transcribing interviews to producing tables and figures for the book to tracking communications with key participants, Lisa's assistance was invaluable. Every task was treated with warmth and a smile, for which I am truly thankful.

Earlier on, several others tended to this project's administrative tasks. I thank Jean Powers, who will be forever known for her creative designs and figurines which became constants in my conference presentations, and I thank Brenda Senecal, who helped me organize the vast amounts of data I was collecting from the start.

Although this book bears one name as its author, it is the product of the insights, time, and attention of many wonderful colleagues and advisors. I am thankful to Teresa Amabile, Kathleen McGinn, Krishna Palepu, and Joel Podolny, who served as my research directors since 1996 and who provided thoughtful guidance as well as sponsorship during critical phases. I am also extremely grateful to the instrumental and financial assistance of Harvard Business School's Division of Research, which made this research possible.

I am also grateful to Kim Clark, who has been dean of Harvard Business School since the project's inception. From simple questions such as "how's the Baxter Boys Project going?" to requests to read drafts of the manuscript, I thank Kim for his interest in and support of my efforts throughout. I also thank Len Schlesinger, former senior associate dean, who inspired me to pursue this project from the very start.

Throughout the project, I benefited greatly from the comments, criticisms, and suggestions of a wonderful group of colleagues, both at Harvard and beyond. Within Harvard Business

School's Organizational Behavior (OB) Unit, Nitin Nohria, Linda Hill, Jay Lorsch, David Thomas, Mike Tushman, and Tom Delong all read the entire manuscript and provided constructive feedback, often not on one occasion but on several. I deeply appreciate their feedback and recommendations all along the way. I also thank Joel Podolny, Paul Lawrence, Mike Beer, Tiziana Casciaro, Rakesh Khurana, Joshua Margolis, Laura Morgan Roberts, and Boris Groysberg, all who read critical chapters and/or helped me work through important conceptual issues. I am grateful as well to the advice of several former OB Unit faculty members, including Bob Eccles, Herminia Ibarra, and Morten Hansen, who each provided direction during the early years. And, I thank my former dissertation chair, Richard Hackman, who greatly influenced my understanding of helping behavior, without which this research project might never have begun.

Outside the OB unit, Teresa Amabile, Joe Bower, Chris Bartlett, Ben Esty, Amy Edmondson, Rosabeth Moss Kanter, Joshua Lerner, Stacy McManus, Gary Pisano, Bill Sahlman, Bob Simons, and Debora Spar were extremely helpful and in different ways—by either offering constructive feedback on the manuscript itself, providing useful insight into the human resources practices of specific healthcare firms, or advising me on the methods and research design employed. Each of these individuals had a unique perspective to bring, such as Gary's understanding of biotechnology and Chris's understanding of Baxter; they challenged me in important ways for which I am truly thankful. I also thank several doctoral students, including Shasa Dobrow, Wendy Smith, and Jerry Kim, who were resourceful in hunting down data or research sources and who offered kind inspiration at key moments.

I am grateful as well to many colleagues in the larger academic community. Ed Schein, Denise Rousseau, Tim Hall, Kathy Kram, Mike Arthur, Barbara Lawrence, and Yehuda Baruch reviewed early drafts of this work and provided pointed feedback that was extremely valuable to the development of the ideas presented here. In addition, a number of colleagues served as sounding boards, particularly early on in the project, including Ranjay Gulati, my coauthor on several related academic articles; Jenny Chatman, one of the early supporters of the term *career imprinting*; and Candace Jones and Hugh Guntz, who share my interests in mesolevel career research. I would also especially like to thank seminar participants at the Sloan School of Management at MIT, Boston University's School of Management, the Wharton School at the University of Pennsylvania, Berkeley's Haas School of Business, New York University's Stern School of Business, Darden Business School, the European Group and Organization Studies Conference, and at Harvard for their comments and questions; engaging in open dialogue around these ideas was a powerful source of learning for me.

There are editors and then there are developers and then there are those who serve both roles. Regina Maruca did all of the above for me and for this project. Regina was at the same time enthusiastic as she was critical, at the same time curious as she was intentional throughout the revising of the original manuscript. Her editing improved the flow, the readability, and the logic of the book. She was a pleasure to work with, and I thank her deeply for her assistance and her understanding throughout. At Jossey-Bass–Wiley, Kathe Sweeney managed the entire publishing process with great care and attention to timeline and detail and to the audience perspective.

Warren Bennis was the grand editor and coach in bringing this work to the public's eye. Warren coached me in a way that was both provocative and patient. I learned a great deal from Warren's leadership on this project and am honored to have this book as part of his leadership development series. Most of all, I thank him for stretching me to new heights in my own professional development.

Finally, I am grateful to my family, which has been enormously supportive of this book project. Michael, my husband, has worked in the biopharmaceutical arena for many years and so was able to offer support on a host of dimensions. From introducing me to people, to answering questions about how to read a final prospectus, to always encouraging me to "go for it," whether that be a research trip or a conference presentation, I am deeply thankful to Michael. I thank my parents for following this research and my own career so closely and for caring about me amidst these quests. Along the way, I found that having a father as a publisher and a mother as a human resources professional placed me in, yet again, a unique and wonderful position in bringing this project to completion. I thank them for all of their support. Finally, I'd like to thank my daughters, Sarah and Rebecca, who have been so patient throughout. From accompanying me to the library to bringing me coffee in the early morning when I was already up and working to the many small "surprises" they'd have waiting for me after late nights at work, I am forever grateful. I treasured their loving company, curiosity, and encouragement throughout the entire journey.

Foreword

by Ed Schein

One of the persistent problems of organization studies is to explain over time how individuals and organizations interact—how each evolves. How do individuals develop and evolve their career anchors, and how do organizations and industries create and evolve their cultures? How does cultural DNA move from one organization to another, and how do we explain the similarities in culture of whole sets of organizations in the same industry?

In introducing and developing the concept of "career imprinting," this book provides a crucial new link to help us understand individual, organizational, and industrial evolution. In focusing on the *career*, the concept is firmly anchored in the lives of individuals, but in showing how organizational cultures *imprint* themselves during the early and midcareer stages, the concept is firmly anchored in studies of organizational phenomena.

The dynamics of career imprinting that are elaborated in fascinating detail in this book show the reader how cultural elements move from one organization to another, how such movement when it involves a group of individuals from one founding organization can help to spawn a whole industry, as was the case of Baxter described in this book in relation to the biotech industry and Digital Equipment Corporation in relation to the computer industry (Schein, 2003).

As the saying goes, the "devil is in the details." What makes this book powerful and relevant is that career imprinting is explained and exemplified in great detail with fascinating accounts of the individuals who moved from Baxter, how they were imprinted, and how they took their new skills, insights, and values into new organizations. This book should launch a whole new era of research on career and organizational evolution.

Preface

This research began with a phenomenon and has ended with an idea. The phenomenon is the preponderance of Baxter company alumni in the biotechnology industry. The idea is career imprints—the shared set of capabilities, connections, confidence, and cognition that are cultivated at a particular employer at a particular point in time.

My observation of the phenomenon began when I was a doctoral student in Harvard's Ph.D. program in Organizational Behavior. This is a joint degree program of Harvard's Graduate School of Arts and Sciences and Harvard Business School. As part of my doctoral training, I was studying "helping relationships" in the Psychology Department at Harvard. It was during this time that I first witnessed the "helping behavior" among alumni of Baxter International that became the genesis of the present research.

It was 1992 when I began the doctoral program, and my husband, Michael Higgins, who was then chief financial officer (CFO) at a start-up biotechnology company in Cambridge, Massachusetts, was preparing to take that company public. This was an extremely busy time in both of our lives. Michael and I would often work late and on the weekends, and I generally went over to his office to work off-hours, taking any empty seat that was available out in the bullpen area of the office.

Michael and I had become friends with the CEO, Stan Erck, whose office was also right in that area. He would work with doors wide open during some of those evenings, and, inevitably, we would hear snippets of each others' conversations. Immersed in research on helping behavior, my ears pricked up one evening when I heard Stan say something like, "Any chance you could lend us a couple of hundred thousand for a month until the public financing closes?"

Over the years, I became aware of many ways that CEOs of start-up biotech companies were providing help to one another. Beyond financial assistance, help-giving and receiving came in many forms, including instrumental help, such as advice about investment bankers, and psychosocial help in the form of encouragement. I also witnessed face-to-face helping behavior; one of Stan's good friends, Bob Carpenter, would periodically show up at the office to offer encouragement or to act as a sounding board.

It became clear to me, over time, that one common denominator in these helping relationships was that all of these men (all of them were men) had worked together in the past at Baxter, a major healthcare firm located in the midwestern United States. At parties and social gatherings, I often found myself introduced to "so-and-so who also worked at Baxter." I began to think and write about this Baxter connection as something I called "institutional capital," a kind of social capital that is based upon a common institutional affiliation.[1]

Also over time, as I watched this young company struggle to go public, I became more and more convinced that these Baxter relationships were critical not just in terms of the career advancement of the top managers, but also in terms of the performance and survival of their young firms. I began to believe that these relationships, and the help that flowed across them, might be critical to the firms' ability to get to the point at which they *could* go public.

Unfortunately, however, I couldn't figure out how to study this helping behavior or its consequences. What kinds of data could I possibly collect? Even the most obvious form of help-giving—that is, loans of cash—was impossible to track since private companies aren't required to report such transactions. Furthermore, I wasn't entirely convinced that there was indeed a "real" phenomenon out there. That is, perhaps these Baxter relationships were simply part of a small-world phenomenon consisting only of my husband's boss's friends. Perhaps this Baxter network didn't extend beyond my own small window on the biotech industry; perhaps there wasn't any "impact" to speak of at all with respect to this group of people who had left Baxter for opportunities in biotechnology.

Although I couldn't figure out how to capture the helping behavior I had witnessed, I did realize that I knew of one public source of data that might prove useful—at least with respect to identifying the employment affiliations of top executives in biotechnology firms: the career history data in the prospectuses of firms that had gone public. Since my husband had spent considerable time writing and rewriting the prospectus for his firm, I knew that young U.S.-based firms are required by the U.S. Securities and Exchange Commission (SEC) to report on the last five years' experience of each and every managing officer and board member of the company. Here was a source of career history data. It seemed like a good place to start.

After completing my dissertation, "When Is Helping Helpful?," which was based upon a laboratory study, I joined the faculty at Harvard Business School in 1995. It was as an assistant professor that my research in biotechnology and in the "Baxter Boys Project," as I had begun to call it, was reinvigorated. Although my interests had since extended into other forms of helping relationships such as mentoring and social networks, I remained curious about the "Baxter Boys," and so collected data on the career histories and employment affiliations of biotechnology executives. I was hoping to find out whether or not (and if so, to what extent) these Baxter-based affiliations were indeed important to firms in this industry. This data-gathering project, which resulted in a database of the career histories of over 3,200 biotech executives who took companies public between 1979 and 1996, took several years to build.

The data that form the basis of this book are described below. The bottom line is that the analyses of the data that I collected do indeed show that there is a real phenomenon here; that is, Baxter alumni have had a significant influence on the evolution of the biotechnology industry—not just with respect to firm-level performance, but with respect to the growth of the industry. The principal observation is that Baxter spawned a disproportionate number of entrepreneurs in the biotechnology industry. The details of Baxter's impact are described in Chapter One and in the analyses in Appendix B.

Armed with these analyses, the research project evolved to focus on the next logical question: "Why?" "Why did Baxter spawn so much entrepreneurial activity?" Given my own training in social psychology and organizational behavior and, in particular, my research in the field of careers, I looked for answers through a microlevel lens. That is, I traced the career development of the individuals who made career transitions from Baxter into biotechnology. Although spawning behavior has occurred in arenas other than biotechnology, such as Hewlett Packard's spawning of entrepreneurs in Silicon Valley and Fairchild's spawning of entrepreneurs into the semiconductor industry, the microfoundations of industry evolution have not been thoroughly explored. The career development and, indeed, *leadership* development of individuals who make such transitions have yet to be studied.

Of course, it is important to emphasize that biotechnology has become a significant industry with thousands of firms and thousands of executives. My analysis focuses on a small but important part of that whole. As described below, my analysis is of the managers and board members who took approximately three hundred biotechnology companies public between 1979 and 1996; of those top executives, eighty-one came from Baxter. Of those eighty-one, twenty-one were CEOs or presidents at the time of their companies' IPOs.

It is additionally important to note that larger industry-level factors such as the healthcare climate, regulatory changes, and equity market conditions are also critical in providing a complete understanding of this phenomenon. And, although I control for equity market conditions in my quantitative analyses and account for the historical context in which this spawning took place in my qualitative analyses, I do not claim to provide a complete or exhaustive explanation.

What I do provide is a new lens on this important phenomenon and, in the process, I offer a new concept that I have come to call "career imprints"—an idea that has implications for senior executive mobility and influence beyond the specific spawning phenomenon examined here. It is worth clarifying the definition here: organizational career imprints derive from patterns in the career paths of a group of individuals working at a particular company at a given point in time. There are different kinds of organizational career imprints, as we will discover, such as an "entrepreneurial career imprint" or a "scientific career imprint" that derive from career patterns within different kinds of companies. Thus, the full term *organizational career imprint* refers to a particular company—such as Baxter or Merck—and so, we can talk about "Baxter's career imprint" or "Merck's career imprint" but not, in this sense, about "Monica Higgins' career imprint." Therefore, as described more fully in the next chapter, this is an organization-level phenomenon, rather than an individual-level phenomenon.

Following is additional information on the quantitative and qualitative data collection that forms the basis of my exploration into the connection between Baxter and biotechnology and the emergence of the idea of career imprints, along with an organizing framework for this book.

The Present Research

This research spanned a period of nine years, beginning in 1996 with the compilation of five-year career histories of more than 3,200 senior executives who took biotech companies public between 1979 and 1996. These senior executives were either managing officers or board members of these young biotech firms. In this context, senior executive mobility stemmed from three major sources: big pharmaceutical or healthcare firms, such as Eli Lilly; large biotech firms, such as Genentech; and well-established educational institutions, such as MIT.

The data collection for this book occurred in two phases. In the first phase, the objective was to explore the possibility of a connection between senior executive employment affiliations and organizational performance. This data collection led to the conclusions regarding Baxter's influence on biotechnology. As mentioned, to this end, the biotech-executive career histories were collected. All of the employ-ment affiliations and prior career experiences of these executives were coded according to the type of employer (e.g., a pharmaceutical or healthcare company versus an educational institution such as MIT) along with the prominence of the employer for each of the IPO years in the dataset.[2] In addition, each of the executive's previous job posi-tions (e.g., titles) as well as functions and board positions was coded along with the executive's age and tenure with the company.

Data were also collected on the biotech firms themselves. The sample frame for this study includes U.S. biotechnology firms that were founded between 1961 and 1994. Of these 858 firms, 299 went public between 1979 and 1996. Approximately 86 percent of the pub-lic firms specialized in the development of therapeutics and/or human diagnostics; the majority of the remaining firms specialized in agricul-ture and/or other biological products, generally with the explicit intention of developing therapeutic applications in the future.

Data were compiled from both published and unpublished sources, and every effort was made to be as thorough as possible, while also remaining focused on true, dedicated biotechnology firms. The main list of public biotechnology firms was obtained from the *BioWorld Stock Report for Public Biotechnology Companies* in 1996 (n = 281). Unlike other sources (e.g., BioScan), this listing does not include large corporations (e.g., General Electric) that participate tangentially in the biotechnology industry; hence, this is a narrower definition of biotechnology than that employed by other researchers[3] and is in line with more recent research on the industry.[4]

Further, to guard against sample selection bias, information was collected on firms that went public in the same time frame but that did not survive in their original form by 1996 (n = 18).[5] Informa-tion was also collected on biotechnology firms that were founded in the same time period as the sample but that did not go public by 1996 (n = 468) from the 1998 edition of the Institute for Biotechnology Information (IBI) database. Added to this list were private biotechnology companies that had been listed as "dead," merged, or acquired in the first three editions of the *Biotechnology Guide USA*,[6] and that had a founding date in the same time period as the core sample (n = 91). Combining these private firms with the sample of firms that did go public yielded a final combined sample size of 858 firms.

In the second phase of the project, interviews were conducted with the objective of understanding why Baxter had a disproportionate impact on the biotech industry. To explore this question, approximately seventy-eight career history interviews were conducted with a variety of people: people who worked at Baxter and then transitioned into biotechnology; people who worked at Baxter and did not transition into biotechnology (people who either remained with Baxter or transitioned into other fields); people who did not work at Baxter and transitioned into biotechnology (e.g., people who worked at another healthcare firm such as Abbott and then later at a biotechnology firm); and people who did not work at Baxter or another pharmaceutical or healthcare firm but could provide valuable insight into the transitions (e.g., venture capitalists at that time). I conducted the vast majority of the Baxter interviews face-to-face, and the interviews were transcribed shortly thereafter. The process resulted in thousands of pages of transcripts along with hand-written notes. The core career history interviews ranged from one and a half hours to approximately fourteen hours (the latter over a course of seven sessions). Interviewees welcomed follow-up questions, phone calls, and visits, and numerous follow-ups were conducted.

These data, along with the quantitative career history data, enabled me to develop the central ideas presented here regarding career imprints. Further details of this research design are provided in Appendix A.

Additionally, information was obtained through conversations in casual settings as well as in formal settings, such as celebrations in which groups of Baxter alumni gathered. Interviewees also provided an abundance of secondary materials such as letters, company memos, pictures, announcements, annual reports, and alumni lists over the course of several years that described the historical context in which this spawning phenomenon took place. Finally, in addition to these secondary materials provided by the interviewees, the present research is based upon secondary materials regarding Baxter as well as the biotech firms these individuals transitioned to, in the form of analyst and investment reports, case histories, and books and articles written about Baxter and about biotechnology more generally. This information was critical to understanding the business and scientific context in which these career transitions took place. These data form the bases for the conclusions drawn in this book.

The Organization of the Book

This book has three core sections, or Parts, (I) Setting the Stage (Chapters One and Two), (II) The Career Imprinting Process (Chapters Three through Six), and (III) The Consequences of Career Imprints (Chapters Seven through Nine), and ends with some conclusions and questions in the final chapter (Chapter Ten). (Figure P.1, shown here, provides an organizing framework for the material discussed in Parts II and III.)

In Part I, Chapter One introduces the central idea of career imprints and its relationship to the phenomenon in question—the spawning of senior executives from a well-established firm such as Baxter into a new industry such as biotechnology. Chapter Two introduces the "Baxter Boys'" own stories to provide the foundation needed to understand career imprinting in the context of the present research.

Part II focuses on analyzing the three factors that affect the origins of career imprints: the *place* as a breeding ground, the kinds of *people* hired into that breeding ground, and the career *paths* or opportunities provided to these people.

Certain organizational conditions can amplify career imprints or make them stronger, such as a strong corporate culture. Chapter Three explores these factors associated with *place*.

Figure P.1 An Organizing Framework.

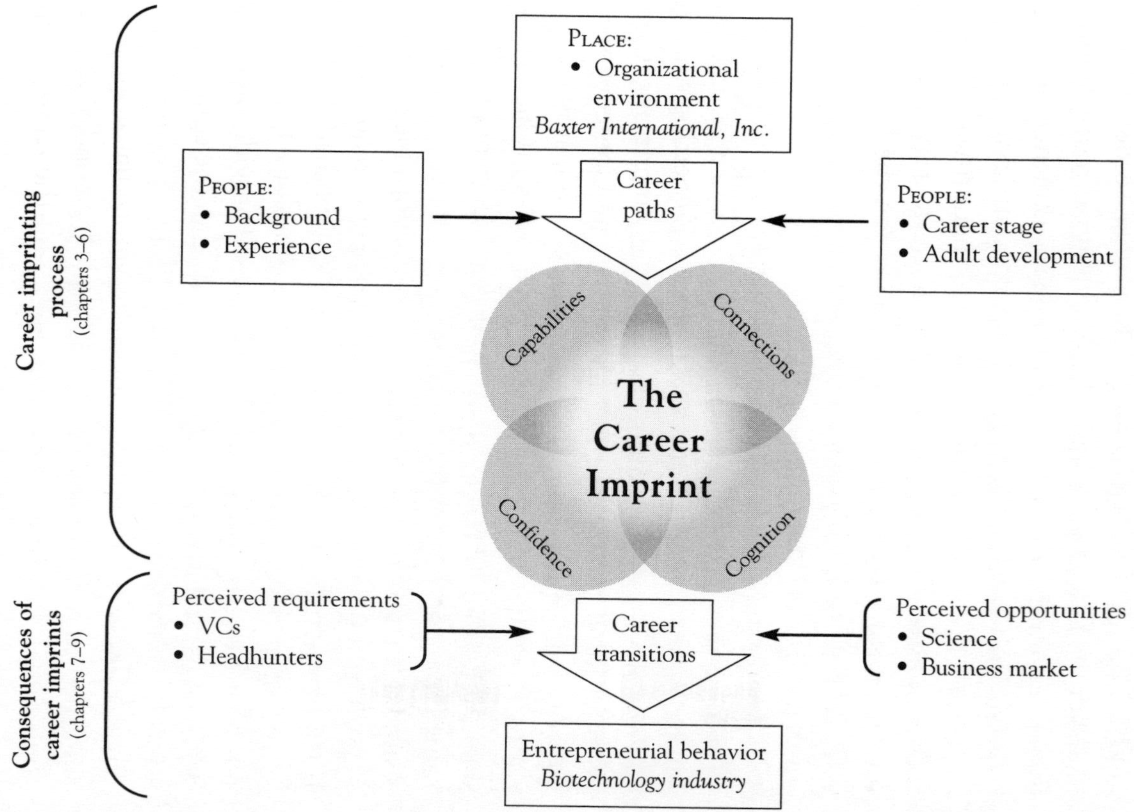

PEOPLE:
• Career stage
• Adult development

Perceived opportunities
• Science
• Business market

PLACE:
• Organizational environment
  Baxter International, Inc.

Connections

Cognition

Career paths

The
Career
Imprint

Capabilities

Confidence

PEOPLE:
• Background
• Experience

Career transitions

Entrepreneurial behavior
Biotechnology industry

Perceived requirements
• VCs
• Headhunters

Career imprinting
process
(chapters 3–6)

Consequences of
career imprints
(chapters 7–9)

Additionally, certain individual-level factors, such as a person's age and career stage, can increase the strength of an individual's cultivation of an organization's career imprint. For example, individuals who are in earlier stages of their careers tend to be more impressionable, and so are more likely to pick up an organization's career imprint. Factors associated with the *people* hired into similar positions are explored in Chapter Four.

Chapter Five turns to the type of career imprint cultivated at Baxter by examining the career *paths* followed by individuals hired into Baxter during the mid-1960s and, in particular, during the 1970s. The data in this chapter suggest that Baxter developed an "entrepreneurial career imprint."

Chapter Six juxtaposes Baxter's entrepreneurial career imprint with the career imprints of three other healthcare organizations—Merck, Johnson & Johnson (J&J), and Abbott. As described, whereas all of these organizations had developed relatively *strong* organizational career imprints during this same time period, the *types* of organizational career imprints were different.

In Part III, the focus turns to the consequences of career imprints for industries, for organizations, and for individuals, again using Baxter and the entrepreneurial career moves this company spawned as the central case example. It also offers insight into the opportunities presented by organizational career imprints and the inherent tripwires.

Chapter Seven explores the consequences of career imprints for industries. The focus is on how and why Baxter's career imprint was seen as a relatively good match for the emerging opportunity structure of the biotech industry at the dawn of the industry. This chapter draws heavily upon interviews with venture capitalists, since they played a huge role in facilitating these senior executive transitions, and since they compared candidates from Baxter with those from other potential sources such as Merck, J&J, and Abbott.

In Chapter Eight, the focus turns to consequences for the organizations these managers joined in the biotech field. The central idea here is that as individuals leave organizations, they take their previous employer's career imprint with them. Further, if the career imprint they take with them was strongly cultivated, as was the case at Baxter, it can have a lasting impact on subsequent organizations by affecting the design choices of those who go on to lead other companies. The example of Henri Termeer, a Baxter alumnus who joined and became CEO of Genzyme (a major biotech company headquartered in Cambridge, Massachusetts), is one such illustration. In keeping with a comparison model, this case is juxtaposed with that of Jim Vincent, who came from Baxter's major competitor, Abbott, to head up Biogen at roughly the same time period as Termeer transitioned to Genzyme.

Chapter Nine discusses the opportunities that open up with an understanding of career imprints and points out the risks of organizational career imprints as well. Chapter Nine also offers lessons from the present research for corporate executives, human resources managers, and intermediaries such as headhunters, who are engaged in senior executive career transitions.

Finally, the last chapter, Chapter Ten, discusses how the findings of this research might stimulate and guide future research agendas.

Part One

Setting the Stage

Chapter One

Introduction: Career Imprints and Senior Executive Mobility

Baxter International, a global medical products and services company based in Deerfield, Illinois, has spawned a disproportionate number of top managers in the U.S. biotech industry. In fact, the company, through those managers, has had a significant influence on how the thirty-year-old biotech arena has evolved and grown. Consider: former Baxter managers were on the IPO teams of nearly one-quarter of all of the biotechnology companies that went public between 1979 and 1996. What's more, Baxter generated a disproportionate number of entrepreneurs in the field—that is, people who went on to lead and manage biotech firms after their time at Baxter.

Why has this one company had such a significant effect on the biotech industry?

Headhunters for years have used the mantra, "if all else fails, pick a senior executive from GE," meaning essentially that they couldn't go wrong picking an executive developed by such a company. Yet a fair number of former General Electric (GE) managers have had a tough time in their post-GE careers. As one 1998 headline from *The Wall Street Journal* summed up, "A Jack Welch Disciple Finds the GE Mystique Only Takes You So Far."[1]

Why is it so hard to predict the relative success of a senior executive's move from one company to another?

The answer to both questions is something I call "career imprinting." In the first instance, career imprinting is a reason Baxter alumni have had such an impact on the biotechnology industry. In the second, it is a reason that a pedigree from a company like General Electric doesn't guarantee a good "fit" for senior executives at their next job in a different organization or industry.

In a nutshell, an organizational career imprint is the set of capabilities and connections, coupled with the confidence and cognition that a group of individuals share as a result of their career experiences at a common employer during a particular period in time. After a time at Baxter, a significant number of managers were "imprinted" with the qualities sought after in the biotech field just as it was starting a steep growth curve. The Baxter organizational career imprint, which was imbued with entrepreneurial spirit, was a relatively good match with what venture capitalists perceived as the requirements for running a biotechnology firm; the "career imprint" also influenced a significant number of Baxter managers to look to biotech as a possible next step in their careers.

But it is important to understand that a career imprint can be perfectly suited to one type of job or industry, while clashing irrevocably with another. Organizational career imprints can bring with them both opportunities and constraints, depending upon the organizational context into which they are imported.

Consider the case of GE alumnus Larry Johnston, who, in April 2001, became CEO of Albertsons Inc., a supermarket chain with over two hundred thousand employees. At Albertsons, the effectiveness of invoking the GE career imprint was anything but obvious. As *The Wall Street Journal* reported:

> [Mr. Johnston] draws on his twenty-nine years at GE in hopes of guiding Albertsons through hard times. It's been a bumpy path, and some employees grumble that the new CEO invokes his old company too often. "I don't care," the 54-year-old Mr. Johnston says. "It's what I know best."[2]

GE alumni at different periods in the company's history have shared similarly strong career imprints and have often been sought after because they were groomed at GE. Larry Bossidy, who joined Allied Signal after spending thirty-four years at GE, provides a classic example. Bossidy exported one aspect of the GE career imprint—a disciplined, bottom-line-focused approach to management—to Allied Signal, where he became a ruthless cost-cutter. Within his first two years at Allied Signal, Bossidy cut the number of suppliers by about one-third, a move that yielded cost savings in the hundreds of millions of dollars a year. And now, Bossidy has taken GE's career imprint on the road to Honeywell and to wider circles, with his book (coauthored with Ram Charan) *Execution: The Discipline of Getting Things Done.*[3]

Career imprints also vary widely by company, and within companies they can vary substantively depending on the time of employment. Managers sharing a career imprint from one organization at a given time, for example, might be inclined to become turnaround experts; managers from that same company at a different time, or managers with another company's career imprint, might instead be "branded" as great marketers. One career imprint may include certain connections—for example, connections with, or particular awareness of, governmental agencies such as the U.S. Food and Drug Administration (FDA)—as was the case at Baxter; other career imprints might include entirely different kinds of networks.

A simplified example of the career imprints of IBM and DEC during the 1970s is telling. Organizational research and historical accounts suggest that a consistent hallmark of IBM's career imprint is an ability to build strong relationships with major customers.[4] People who worked for IBM in management positions during the 1970s in particular were extraordinarily customer-oriented. Managers often rotated through an intense series of sales assignments and so became particularly effective at identifying and servicing core client needs. In contrast, during the same time period, DEC was known for its focus on technology. DEC management's capabilities lay more in identifying new possibilities for innovation and less in servicing existing market needs.[5] Two companies: similar time periods; similar product markets—different capabilities; different career imprints.

In biotechnology, Baxter's entrepreneurial career imprint, which was cultivated primarily during the 1970s, influenced the spawning of a disproportionate number of top managers in biotechnology. The majority of Merck alumni from that same time period, on the other hand, ended up taking on advisory roles in young biotech firms by sitting on their boards while holding scientific positions elsewhere, reflecting Merck's "scientific career imprint."

A manager's career imprint, then, can have an enormous bearing on what that person brings to his or her new post; it can also be a predictor, to a certain degree, of their behaviors and performance. And that means that understanding the origins and outcomes of career imprints has significant implications for senior executive mobility—for individual managers, but also for headhunters, boards and top management teams, companies, and even industries.

Consider how much executives move around. According to recent Booz Allen estimates, CEO turnover increased by a factor of 53 percent in the United States from 1995 to 2001, and 10 percent of big-company CEOs leave their jobs every year.[6] Some of this movement is voluntary, but the fact is that CEOs appointed today are three times more likely to be fired than was the case prior to 1980.[7] Expectations are high for outsiders, and when they are not met within the first few months, boards and investors become impatient. Understanding career imprinting can significantly increase the chances of a senior manager's move being successful.

Consider also where headhunters generally turn to fill jobs in emerging industries. Putting aside for a moment the Internet industry (in which it often seemed as though anyone, no matter what his or her prior experience, could start a dot-com company), most new industries draw upon well-established firms for management talent. Career imprints, then, have enormous implications for the direction and success of new industries. In biotech, it was Baxter. In Silicon Valley, it was Hewlett Packard that spawned a large number of executives for new technology ventures. In the semiconductor industry, Fairchild generated a great number of senior executives who became CEOs of start-up firms.

As these and other examples suggest, senior executive career moves from well-established companies to new ventures can be critically important. A tremendous amount is at stake. For the individuals who make these bold moves, their careers may be at stake; for the young firms themselves, their survival may be at stake; for venture capital firms, their reputations may be at stake, particularly at the start of an industry. And when collectives of individuals from well-established firms such as HP, Fairchild, or Baxter leave to run young companies in a new industry, such senior executive moves can affect the industry's ability to raise funds, go public, and get off to a good start. Finally, to the extent these new industries generate jobs, capital flows, and related services, these kinds of career moves can have important implications for the economy.

This book primarily explores the concept of career imprinting through an in-depth study of former Baxter managers (the "Baxter Boys," as they are called) and the spawning of these executives into the biotech industry. But the greater context is critically important when thinking about senior executive mobility; that is why this book also includes a discussion of career imprinting beyond the Baxter case.

A handful of studies have examined senior executive mobility and the particular phenomenon of well-established firms spawning leaders who go on to influence other companies or industries. However, these studies have done so from a wider-angle lens. Most suggest that phenomena such as spawning are the result of a multitude of environmental factors such as the legal, regulatory, and political environments. Often, the focus is on how these factors all coevolved to create a self-perpetuating ecological system in a particular industry.

In a related fashion, other research has focused on the collocation of such institutional players, leading to explanations that revolve around systems of growth or "regional advantage."[8] For example, research on Silicon Valley suggests that the success of this region, relative to the Route 128 region, hinged on the flexibility of the industrial systems that were built on regional networks and open to experimentation across firms and institutions, rather than confined to learning within dominant firms.[9]

The problem is that focusing on environmental factors like these ignores questions such as "How did these individuals all become general managers and subsequently, leaders of entrepreneurial firms?" and "Why did all of these individuals leave well-established firms to join new ventures at the start of this industry?" Individual career transitions—from generative firms to new ventures—lie at the very heart of this kind of matching process and senior executive career mobility.[10] This book focuses squarely on individuals' career experiences and the resulting imprints on them; the result is thus a different and complementary explanation. This research is the first to explore senior executive mobility through this lens.

A More Detailed Definition

In order to get the most out of the Baxter case and its implications for other companies, industries, and individuals, it's important to have a clear understanding of how organizational career imprints differ from other types of imprints, and how the study of career imprinting differs from other studies of executive mobility.

The Concept of Imprinting

In many respects, the idea of imprinting is not new. Studies in the biological sciences as well as the social sciences have vetted the general term of *imprinting* for decades. For example, the well-known phenomenon of filial imprinting in which newborn chicks imprint or attach themselves to the first prominent, moving object they see—whether that be a living thing, such as their biological mother, or an animate object in a laboratory study such as a bouncing ball—has received close examination in psychological studies since 1935.[11] In organization and management literature, renowned scholar Stinchcombe published a landmark article in 1965 in which he argued that certain kinds of organizational structures vary systematically according to the environmental context and time period in which firms are founded in an industry. Over time, as organizational forms prove effective, certain basic organizational structures become institutionalized, or imprinted, and so come to dominate within industries.[12]

Biological imprinting and the filial studies refer to linkages within the brain; Stinchcombe's work refers to linkages between an organization and its environment. Here, the term *career imprinting* refers to linkages between individuals' careers and a specific organizational context. The notion of a career imprint, then, is a new way of thinking about imprinting and is applied in a different context. Further, whereas prior studies of imprinting suggest that imprints are automatic or even inevitable, here the idea is that since career imprints are associated with an organization, individuals do ultimately have a choice as to how they will respond to an organizational career imprint they picked up at a particular company. As we will see later in the book, although early career imprints can affect the kinds of design choices individuals are likely to make later on as leaders of subsequent organizations, even leaders who have cultivated very strong career imprints from previous employment experiences have latitude in what they do and do not export to another firm.

The Dimensions of Career Imprints in the Context of Management Research

The career imprinting concept reflects the central idea that there are observable patterns in the types of *capabilities, connections, confidence,* and *cognition* that groups of people develop as a result of a common set of career experiences in a particular organization.[13] *Capabilities* refers to the specific kinds of human capital, skills, knowledge, and know-how regarding work and getting work done. *Connections* refers to the kinds of social capital, including both intraorganizational and extraorganizational relationships related to work and getting work done, including the strength and structure of such connections. *Confidence* refers to the types of individual-level efficacy associated with work and getting work done. *Cognition* refers to the taken-for-granted assumptions, beliefs, and worldviews regarding work and getting work done.[14]

When thinking about each of these different dimensions *individually and/or with one individual in mind*, there is a substantial stream of management research to draw upon. Regarding the development of capabilities among senior executives, studies have shown how early on-the-job experiences that involve supervisory responsibilities are critical in developing leadership skills needed later on in their careers. Senior executives frequently cite early career challenges as an important source of learning that can affect their professional development over the long term.[15] In addition, studies of minority advancement emphasize the timing and development of certain competencies such as management and interpersonal skills early on in one's career.[16]

Regarding connections, management studies have focused on the cultivation of particular kinds of early career connections, such as helpful bosses, for the development of high-potential managers.[17] In addition, a substantial stream of research on social networks has examined the ways in which different kinds of relationships and the structure of such relationships affects individuals' access to valuable information and resources that can benefit individuals' career development.[18] Further, studies of mentoring relationships and developmental networks stress the significance of particular kinds of relationships that provide both career as well as psychosocial kinds of support for personal and professional development.[19]

Regarding confidence, scholars, including Warren Bennis, have emphasized the cultivation of particular kinds of confidence such as "hardiness" for leader development.[20] Further, recent research by Kanter explains how the best leaders produce outstanding results by building the confidence of individuals in organizations—activating the firm's talent and producing superior results.[21] Finally, there has been a growing stream of management research on the ways in which individuals' cognition or worldviews shape career development.[22]

Each of these dimensions is important to address when exploring what an individual learns at any one particular organization. However, the notion that *these dimensions taken together may constitute an organizational career imprint* hasn't been explored until now. The concept of career imprints takes these dimensions and suggests that the sum can be greater than any single dimension because the career imprint is an organization-level construct, not an individual-level construct. That's why we can talk about a "GE career imprint" or a "Baxter career imprint" but not a "Monica Higgins *career* imprint." (Although individuals naturally pick up other kinds of imprints in their lives, as a result of shared experiences at other kinds of institutions—for example, among students of certain educational institutions—these would not be "career" imprints.)

Additionally, since career imprints are evident from patterns in the career experiences of *many* individuals, not one, we can examine the implications of career imprints as groups of people make career moves from a single organization, such as a Baxter or Hewlett Packard, and how those moves and the career imprints that accompany them affect growth and change in industries.

In these ways, then, a career imprint complements other career constructs, such as Schein's "career anchor" construct, which focuses on a single person's career history; the idea of a career imprint reflects experiences that are *shared* among individuals who work for a common employer.[23] From observations of *shared* career experiences within a particular organization, we can distinguish among different career imprints of different organizations and can then consider, as well, implications of dominant career imprints for firms and industries. The career imprint construct thus extends the purview of the vast majority of human resources and self-assessment practices, which are often aimed specifically at understanding a single individual's career history.

The Career Imprinting Process in the Context of Prior Research

Career imprints evolve as a result of the combination of three factors: the *place*, including the company's strategy, structure, and culture; the *people* hired; and the career *paths* that people follow at a particular firm. The greater the alignment or match among *people*, *place*, and *paths*, the stronger the career imprint.

Several chapters in this book are devoted to in-depth discussions of these career imprinting factors. For introductory purposes, though, consider the following: when thinking about organizational career imprints and the kinds of capabilities, connections, confidence, and cognition that an individual picks up by working at a particular organization, it is natural to try and pin our understanding on one or another narrow explanation. For example, observing that GE alumni seem to all share a certain "way" or "style," we might attribute this to a particular "personality" and so ignore other psychological aspects, such as developmental stage, that are more dynamic and influenced by the organizational context in which individuals are situated. Stable traits like personality are but one factor that might play a role in the career imprinting process.

Alternatively, it would be natural to sway in the opposite direction and attribute observations about aspects of a career imprint solely to the place or organization in which people worked—positing, for example, that GE was a "talent machine." In this respect, it is tempting to narrow the purview to considerations such as how people are socialized or "learn the ropes" at a particular company.[24] Organizational socialization focuses on certain boundary passages within organizations and how individuals take on new and different organizational roles.[25] At its core, the goal of organizational socialization is to control employees such that they come to share the same norms and values as other members of the organization.[26] Although this linkage is real, it is also misleading because it limits the range of factors that affect the development of career imprints. The career imprinting process is also shaped by elements of the organizational context—including the organization's structure and strategy—that can affect the kinds of stretch opportunities individuals are given at an organization.

Regarding organizational structure, for example, GE's highly decentralized organizational structure shaped managers' norms and values and, specifically, their belief in the importance of delegating responsibility. In addition, GE's structure shaped the kinds of capabilities that were developed—for example, GE managers' skills in tracking and measuring operating results.[27]

Regarding strategy, for example, individuals working in a firm that is pursuing a globalization strategy may, necessarily, pursue different kinds of career paths, affecting not only the kinds of values adopted but also the kinds of capabilities and connections that are cultivated as well. Thus, in addition to factors such as organizational culture and socialization, a company's business strategy and structure are also important factors affecting the career imprinting process.

Situating career development in a firm's larger business context extends traditional management research on careers and organizational behavior, which has tended to focus inward on local aspects of an organization, such as an organization's culture.[28] The assumption here is that the larger business context in which careers in an organization are situated is an important factor as well.[29] Additionally, the assumption here is that people are not entirely passive in this process; people can and do shape their careers and thus the people—including both the backgrounds and stage of adult development of individuals—are also factors that can affect the career imprinting process.[30, 31]

The Consequences of Career Imprints in the Context of Prior Research

The notion of a career imprint encompasses the idea that while career imprints originate from shared career experiences at a single organization, people take career imprints with them as they traverse organizations.[32] Thus, as mentioned early on in the chapter, career imprints may have important consequences beyond what happens in the original company. Executives who leave to join new organizations, and organizations that are founded and/or led by executives who carry with them strong career imprints, have much to gain from understanding career imprinting. There are also lessons in this research for mature companies whose career imprints may be resistant to change, and there are significant implications at the industry level. At the start of new industries, powerful intermediaries such as venture capital firms may prefer certain organizational career imprints over others and so facilitate the movement of collections of individuals from one firm into new industries.

Yet this notion of leaders "exporting" an imprint based on their prior career experiences has received scant attention in management research. To be clear, management scholars have often warned about the problems of selective perception, tunnel vision, perceptual screens, and other forms of myopic behavior and perception.[33] The thrust of these arguments is that managers have limited ability to process all of the information they are exposed to and so selectively attend to information, which can lead to biases that negatively affect their ability to make decisions. However, the idea that such biases may reflect a shared set of career experiences associated with a particular employer has received almost no attention. Further, and of particular importance here, the link between career experiences and changes in organizations and industries has not been examined until now. These consequences are explored in depth much later in the book.

The Impact of Baxter's Career Imprint

The research that forms the basis of this book and the ideas generated regarding organizational career imprints stems from a study of the career development and transitions of managers who worked at Baxter primarily during the 1970s. Baxter was a particularly generative institution for entrepreneurs in biotechnology and so provides a good example of the particular type of senior executive mobility that is studied here—the movement of executives from a large organization to new ventures at the start of an industry. The particular case of Baxter is also compelling because of the significant influence that Baxter's alumni have had on the growth of the biotechnology industry.

In what ways did Baxter alumni ultimately make a difference to the evolution of biotechnology? We can think about the impact of the movement of Baxter managers into biotechnology in three ways.[34] First, Baxter alumni contributed to the growth of the biotech industry by taking a disproportionate number of biotech firms public. As Figure 1.1 shows, from 1979 to 1996, approximately 23 percent of the biotech companies that went public had at least one member of their IPO team who had worked at Baxter. Next in line was Johnson & Johnson, with 19 percent, followed by other companies, including Abbott, Merck, Eli Lilly, and Bristol-Myers Squibb. No matter how these data are sliced, Baxter comes out as the top healthcare/pharmaceutical generator of senior executives of biotech firms that were able to go public during the formative years of the industry. In addition, as we will see, these companies spawned people into different kinds of positions in biotech firms. Baxter was the most prolific spawner of top managers (as opposed to scientists or board members, for example).

Further, as Figure 1.1 shows, these effects hold, even after we account for company size. Baxter was a smaller firm (even after considering their acquisition of American Hospital Supply in 1985) than firms that were also top generators of senior executives for biotech (such as J&J). Thus, Baxter had a disproportionate impact in terms of the sheer numbers of executives generated for the public biotech marketplace.

Second, even before reaching IPO stage, Baxter contributed to the very genesis of the biotech industry by spawning a disproportionate number of entrepreneurial teams. In their study of "entrepreneurial spawning," Gompers, Lerner, and Scharfstein analyzed private company data to determine which companies generated a

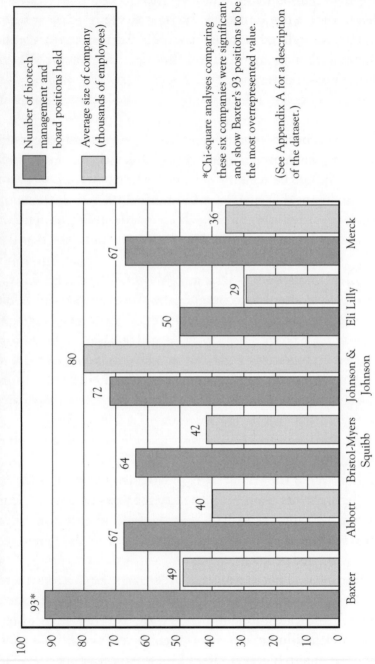

Figure 1.1 Baxter's Overrepresentation in Biotechnology IPO Firms (1979–1996)

Number of biotech management and board positions held

Average size of company (thousands of employees)

*Chi-square analyses comparing these six companies were significant and show Baxter's 93 positions to be the most overrepresented value.

(See Appendix A for a description of the dataset.)

significant number of entrepreneurial teams.[35] And, they did so comparing firms across industries. Their analyses demonstrate that Baxter was a top "entrepreneurial spawner." Baxter was the first healthcare-related firm among their list of top entrepreneurial spawners, following other well-known spawners such as GE and IBM. Thus, Baxter generated a disproportionate number of entrepreneurs—not just businesspeople—who led young firms in this industry.

Third, beyond Baxter's contributions to entrepreneurial activity at the dawn of the biotechnology industry, Baxter-led firms simply performed better early on in the IPO marketplace. Specifically, biotech firms that had Baxter alumni on their senior management teams raised more cash when they went public and were able to attract more and higher-quality institutional investors as well. Not only do these results hold after accounting for the aforementioned market factors, such as the receptivity of the equity markets, these results hold after accounting for the spawning of other generative institutions such as J&J, Merck, Lilly, Abbott, and Bristol-Myers. Appendix B provides additional detail on these analyses.

Taken together, these data provide compelling evidence that the career moves of Baxter managers into biotechnology had a significant influence on the evolution of the biotechnology industry.

Points of Departure

The power of the Baxter story and the contribution of the idea of career imprints as one explanation for this phenomenon are bolstered by comparison. Although many firms spawned executives into biotech, they did so to a lesser extent than did Baxter; further, they spawned people into predominantly different kinds of roles in young firms. That is why this book examines, in a more limited fashion, the organizational career imprints and consequences of other healthcare firms during this same time period. Looking across these firms illuminates what was unique about Baxter's career imprint. It also highlights the facilitating conditions that led to the disproportionate and entrepreneurial kind of spawning we see out of Baxter.

Three particular healthcare firms—Abbott, Johnson & Johnson, and Merck—are particularly useful as points of comparison to Baxter, for two primary reasons. First, interview data suggest that all three organizations were in the consideration set of venture capitalists (VCs) who were looking for business people to run biotechnology companies at the start of the industry. Given the important role played by VCs in these senior executives' career moves, it is therefore critical to compare these companies and their career imprints.

Second, each of these firms was comparable to Baxter in some specific and important way. Abbott was Baxter's fiercest competitor in one major product line, intravenous (IV) solutions containers. Additionally, the two firms were located within ten miles of one another. Stories about their "enemy, Abbott," in the Baxter interviews were extensive, and the reverse was the case for Abbott alumni. J&J was a firm that Baxter's CEO at the time, Bill Graham, often compared Baxter to—not so much in terms of its product lines or strategy but in terms of its decentralized organizational structure. In some respects, Graham appears to have modeled some of his own practices after this much larger firm, and so J&J is also important to consider. Merck, for its part, was one of the quintessential scientific enterprises at the time and so was likely to have managers who were well versed in the emerging science that eventually became known as "biotechnology."

These firms and their career imprints are compared to Baxter (principally in Chapters Six and Seven), after the ground has been set for using Baxter as the benchmark and after the conditions that enable the cultivation of a strong organizational career imprint have been explored in depth (in Chapters Two through Five). As the data will show, whereas all of these firms had relatively strong organizational career imprints, the career imprints that were cultivated were different. Thus, as we will explore in the latter section of the book (in Chapters Eight and Nine), these differences in career imprints have had important consequences—not just for the evolution of an industry, but for organizations and for individuals as leaders and architects of young firms as well.

As a final point of departure, it is important to emphasize that this account of the spawning that occurred out of Baxter and other firms at the dawn of the biotechnology industry does not reflect an historical accident (a "perfect storm" of sorts), nor was this spawning behavior "bound to happen." The theory of career imprints counters that position. The movement of Baxter managers into biotech was heavily influenced by the actions of powerful intermediaries. Venture capitalists had a plethora of top managers to choose from to lead these new biotech companies. And reduced to the essentials, Baxter's career imprint most closely resembled the VC perspective of what was seen as required for the industry at that point in time. Thus, the idea that Baxter's career imprint matched the evolving requirements of the industry reflects much more than pure circumstance or functional fit. It reflects also the role of proactive players such as VCs who recognized and then made the matches possible. It is thus important to emphasize that without Baxter or its major competitor, Abbott, for example, the biotechnology industry may well have "happened." However, the early leadership of the industry and the shape and character of some of the early firms could arguably have been quite different.

To gain a better understanding of these Baxter managers as individual people, and the context in which they began their careers at Baxter, the next chapter tells the story of one particular exemplar who made the move from Baxter to biotechnology, Gabe Schmergel. In addition, Chapter Two sketches the experiences of the other members of the first wave of managers who left Baxter for biotechnology during the late 1970s and very early 1980s and thus provides a sense of this group of individuals, the "Baxter Boys," as a whole.

Chapter Two

From Baxter to Biotechnology: The First Wave of Baxter Boys

Your impact on the [biotechnology] industry was much more significant than just leading a successful company. Before you went to Genetics Institute, nobody at Baxter—or practically anywhere else—imagined a divisional president leaving to run a small biotech start-up, let alone one with no products and an uncertain future. Your decision inspired a wave of managers from Baxter and other companies to leave secure, prestigious jobs in order to advance patient care more directly. As a result, former Baxter people wound up running a substantial portion of U.S. biotech companies. If you had not paved the way, this infusion of talent into the biotech industry would never have occurred, and a host of live-saving therapies might never have been developed.

—Jim Tobin, addressing Gabe Schmergel, when Schmergel received the prestigious 2003 Golden Door Award for his outstanding contributions and leadership in the field of biotechnology. Tobin and Schmergel were colleagues at Baxter long before Schmergel left the company in 1981 to join Genetics Institute.

For Gabe Schmergel, moving into the biotech field (which wasn't even called "biotechnology" at the time) required quite a leap. As he recalled, "Frankly, I wasn't sure about this new industry. At that time, no products were approved. There was no business model. We couldn't look at Genentech; they were there, but they weren't a proven company." Yet he made the move, and, as Jim Tobin's quote implies, his departure from Baxter and subsequent success in biotechnology inspired many more managers to make similar career moves, cumulatively having a significant effect on the evolution of the biotech industry.

In order to gain a robust understanding of career imprinting in the present context, it is important to first get to know Gabe Schmergel and his colleagues. That is why this chapter is devoted to their case studies. Their personal stories provide the foundation for the analysis of career imprinting offered in Part II of this book. Schmergel's case is featured in more detail because he was an exemplar in making the move from Baxter to biotechnology.

Gabe Schmergel's Story

Gabe Schmergel was born in Hungary in 1940. In 1956, at the age of sixteen and with Hungary in political turmoil, he left with his family for the United States in search of a better life. Schmergel began his work life in the United States that year as a penniless refugee, washing dishes in Long Island eating establishments. He attended high school in Long Island, where his family had settled, and later received a bachelor of science degree in mechanical engineering at Rensselaer Polytechnic Institute (RPI), also having joined the ROTC program.

Schmergel's ROTC commission from RPI took him to Germany, where he served for two years as platoon leader. Following his tour of duty, Schmergel was accepted to Harvard Business School. Schmergel graduated among the top of his Harvard MBA class in 1967 and, during the recruiting season, received a broad range of offers. Although he interviewed with engineering-based companies such as Dow Chemical and WR Grace, he found these less exciting than hospital-supply companies such as Baxter, Abbott, and American Hospital Supply, which were all growing spectacularly. Healthcare was seen as a "glamour" industry during the late 1960s. In Schmergel's eyes, "It was the place to be."

Baxter, in particular, was attractive, Schmergel felt. When he interviewed there, Baxter had over $70 million in annual revenues and was growing at a handsome clip. (See accompanying box on the following page for a history of Baxter.)

Schmergel's offer was to be assistant to the head of the International Division. As Schmergel recalled:

> The company was already public. It was a medium-sized company but very fast growing. So it really had a reputation as a prestige company. The whole company had $70 million in sales. And the International Division had sales of $10 million.
>
> The offer was to be assistant to Charlie Schwartz, who was head of the International Division. Then, if I performed well, I would be sent abroad to run a subsidiary. It was a general management track that was promised but not guaranteed. Promised but not guaranteed.

Starting at Baxter

During his first year as assistant to Schwartz, Schmergel took on a variety of business projects, many of which included financial analyses and interaction with line management. His first line-management experience was in Central America. Schwartz told Schmergel to assess Baxter's factory operations in Costa Rica, which were losing money. Schwartz temporarily removed the general manager and sent Schmergel and his family down to live in the general manager's home so that Schmergel could "run the operation" and "find out what's really going on." As Schmergel recalls:

> The general manager was probably suspicious, but he had no choice. I didn't speak a word of Spanish, but I said, "I'm the boss temporarily for the next two months—July and August." I got to know all the people, traveled around Central America, and visited all the distributors [in] Nicaragua, El Salvador, and Guatemala. I went out to the field with the salespeople, and I spent a lot of time in the factory in San Jose.
>
> At the end of the summer, I sat down and wrote my report. [My recommendation] was that we should shut down the operation—that we couldn't possibly make money there. And we should just

A Brief History of Baxter International

Baxter was founded in 1931 by Dr. Ralph Falk as Don Baxter Intravenous Products, Inc., after the physician who developed the first commercially prepared intravenous solutions. One year later, the company signed an exclusive distribution agreement with American Hospital Supply (AHS). (The relationship between Baxter and American Hospital would eventually lead to the acquisition of AHS by Baxter in 1985.) In 1935, Dr. Falk purchased Don Baxter's interest in the company and became its CEO, and the company was subsequently renamed Baxter Laboratories, Inc.

The 1930s and 1940s marked a period of tremendous technological growth for Baxter. In 1939, for example, Baxter developed the Transfuso-Vac, the first sterile vacuum blood collection and storage unit that enabled the storage of blood for up to twenty-one days. Two years later, Baxter's Plasma-Vac product enabled the separation of plasma from whole blood. In 1944, Dr. Willem Kolff invented the first artificial kidney machine, which was later licensed to Baxter in 1954. Baxter significantly improved upon this original technology to produce the first marketable artificial kidney machine in 1956. In 1948, Dr. Carl Walter, a renowned Boston surgeon and cofounder of Fenwal Laboratories, invented the non-breakable Blood Pack plastic container. Following Baxter's acquisition of Fenwal in 1959, Baxter was able to make significant improvements over its glass containers that previously had been used for blood collection and storage. (A figure depicting highlights of Baxter's products is shown in Appendix C.)

During the 1950s, while Baxter continued to improve upon its early innovations, the emphasis began to shift from innovating new products to producing quality products. Baxter grew considerably in its manufacturing capabilities during this time period and, at the same time, strengthened its financial position substantially. In 1950, Baxter opened its second manufacturing center in Cleveland, Mississippi. One year later, in addition to signing a new ten-year contract with American Hospital Supply, the company made its initial public stock offering and

(Continued)

began to trade on the over-the-counter market. In 1952, Baxter's focus on product diversification led to the purchase of Hyland Laboratories, the company's first acquisition. Hyland Laboratories was a leader in the production of commercially usable human plasma and so was directly related to Baxter's core focus on the collection, separation, packaging, and storage of blood products.

In 1953, William Graham, a patent lawyer who had joined Baxter in 1945 as a vice president, succeeded Ralph Falk as president—a position he would retain for twenty-seven years. The following year, Baxter opened operations in Belgium, marking the beginning of Baxter's strategy of local manufacturing (versus exporting) in international markets and, simultaneously, the decentralization of many of Baxter's operations. Baxter's strong performance led to the listing of Baxter's stock on the New York Stock Exchange under the symbol BAX in 1961. Also during this decade, "Travenol" was added to the company name (Baxter Travenol). Many of Baxter's products were known within the industry by this name, a derivative of the term inTRAVENous sOLutions. Further, some of Baxter's products became strongly associated with company divisions; for example, as one informant explained, Baxter's Fenwal name became so well known that "Fenwal was to blood packs what Kleenex is to tissue." (Appendix C also shows a timeline of Baxter's business highlights and milestones.)

From the 1950s through the 1960s, Baxter's expansion, first into Europe and Latin America and later into the Far East, created tremendous opportunities for young managers to run subsidiaries. During the mid-1960s, Graham began to recruit actively from top-tier business schools to take on the company's significant business growth opportunities and challenges. The MBA hiring spree continued through the 1970s, with cohorts as large as fifteen. Baxter's CEO Bill Graham—"Mr. Graham," as he was called—personally interviewed recruits, often by traveling to the leading business schools. Graham selected his recruits from the top of their classes, whenever possible.[1]

serve the market by exporting from our factory in Mexico . . . and keep the distributor network [and] let the general manager go. A decision like that would go all the way up, obviously up to Graham.

So they brought the general manager back and said, "Well, here is Gabe's recommendation. Here's his analysis. Do you think it's wrong? Can you convince us that Gabe is wrong?" And he couldn't come up with a plan of action. There were so many structural problems; there wasn't enough business there, and the prices were low and there was no hope of prices increasing, etc. . . . [W]e shut down the operation.

Schmergel also did some "standard business school reports" for Schwartz, including, for example, analyses of whether Baxter should enter markets in countries such as Japan. Many other MBAs from Schmergel's cohort were working on similar projects. Among the cohort of twelve MBAs hired the same year, some became friends and others became rivals, particularly since only a handful of positions opened up overseas each year. Still, overall, there was a shared sense of excitement among his cohort:

There was the general sense that the opportunities were great; the company was growing very fast. We were gaining growth of 20 percent—over 20 percent! And, geographical expansion! Within International, the organization was geographically based. So there were country operations, factories outside the U.S. As Baxter developed different areas—the Latin American area, the European area, the Far Eastern area—with country subsidiaries, there was an opportunity to become a general manager. And be on your own— sink or swim. That was very clearly the philosophy: sink or swim.

General Manager of Germany

Schmergel had been waiting for a country to open up when Schwartz asked him to take over Baxter's troubled operations in Germany. Schmergel had been with Baxter less than two years. He was twenty-eight years old. There was a large manufacturing operation in Belgium that served most of Europe, but in terms of sales and marketing, Germany was Baxter's largest overseas subsidiary. This was Schmergel's first significant general management (GM) opportunity:

Charlie said, "Would you like to be general manager [GM] of Germany?" I said, "Sure." I didn't have to think for a minute. So he said, "Well, Gabe . . . I talked to Bill Graham and why don't you just fly over to meet [the GM], fire the guy, and install yourself. I am going to give you a letter that you can give him. I'm going to give you a phone number where you can call me if he wants to hear the word from me directly. And you are authorized to negotiate his settlement. . . . Try to do what's best for the company. Just get him out of the office." So, I get on a plane with my wife and infant son. We arrive on the weekend and get a hotel room. I remember that my son was six months old.

Monday morning, I show up in the office. [The current GM] didn't know why. He figured, "Here's another guy from headquarters with some stupid project." I show up in the office, and he said, "Herr Schmergel, what can I do for you while you are here?" I said to him, "Look, sorry to tell you, but I'm here to let you know that you're being terminated, and Mr. Schwartz is very sorry that he is unable to be here, but he had to go to Japan for a joint venture." . . . And I remember this guy's looking at me—and he's twice my age or so— [like], "Who are you?," you know? "You are nobody! Who are you?!" I give him a copy [of the termination letter]. . . . "Let's do this in a friendly way. But it's got to be done today. . . . We would like you to go home today and turn things over to me." . . . He said, "I don't believe this!" So I said, "OK, here, please call Mr. Schwartz. . . . It must be now 4:00 in the morning, but he said call him anytime." . . . An hour later, he says, "I talked to Charlie, and I'm going to go home now. . . . I'm not going to give you a hard time."

[That same day], I said [to the marketing director], who was very unhappy that he did not get the GM job, "I want to have a sales meeting. Call in all the salespeople. What's a good location— a central location?" He said, "Frankfurt." "OK. Call in all the salespeople for tomorrow or the day after tomorrow. A sales meeting. . . . I want to really understand what's going on." . . . I said to [the marketing director], "Meet you in the airport tomorrow. Be on this flight." So, I'm sitting in the airport. I'm probably there an hour before the flight. This guy does not show up! And I'm sitting there. I'm waiting, waiting, waiting. He still doesn't show up! I get on the plane. I fly to Frankfurt. The meeting is at the airport hotel, and this guy is not there either. Can you believe that?! So, I have to introduce myself! I speak German, but not fluently, let's say 75 percent. Later, I become fluent. These salespeople don't speak English. . . . That evening I fly back. Next morning, I call this guy. He's at home. And I said, "Why weren't you at the airport?" He said, "I'm sick." I said, "Look, I don't buy this." [He said], "I have a doctor's certificate." I said, "I don't care if you are sick or not. You were not there for me. Therefore, I don't need you anymore. Don't bother to come to work." So, he went crazy: "You can't do this to me!" I said, "Sure I can. You let me down. The worst thing is you let me down. You are fired." So, I fired the guy. On the spot.

Schmergel learned from that experience the importance of "moving quickly" to "fire a couple of key people if they don't play ball with you . . . then, everybody else knows you mean business." As Schmergel described:

> Removing the former general manager and then the uncooperative marketing director of a troubled subsidiary gave me the chance to appoint my own management team from among the best people there. This formed the basis of what eventually became a major success for Baxter in a flagship country. The point is also that Baxter trusted a selected young person, after two years at an entry-level assistant job, to "parachute" into an important country and make decisions.

Schmergel was GM of Germany for approximately two years. During his first year abroad, he reported to Vern Loucks. At that time, Loucks was VP of Europe. In 1970, during Schmergel's second year in Germany, he reported to Bill Gantz. Gantz had taken over Loucks's position as VP of Europe and Schwartz was now edging toward retirement.

Running Operations in Belgium

After only a little more than two years in Germany, Gantz asked Schmergel, "How would you like to come and run the Belgian operation?" The Belgium operation was a factory with approximately five hundred people at that time. In many respects, Belgium was at the heart of Baxter's international operations since it manufactured products that served most of the European markets. Further, significant expansion was planned for Belgium. (Indeed, it doubled in size during the following two years.) Gantz explained that Baxter was going to terminate its relationship with its distributor and sell directly to its customers with its own sales force. As a result, Gantz anticipated that the factory in Belgium would grow substantially, and he wanted Schmergel to take over. Although the offer had come from Gantz, Schmergel said he felt that "behind the scenes, Graham was instrumental in the decision. He was personally involved in all the important appointments. I had a personal relationship with him even though I was not directly reporting to him." Schmergel recalls his reaction to Gantz's query:

> I said, "Bill, I've never run a factory." He said, "No problem." I said, "I don't speak a word of French." He said, "No problem; you will just learn it quickly." I remember, I flew there on a Friday evening, showed up there Monday. Bill saw me; we sat down and discussed who would take over Germany.

During his time overseas, his superiors would visit Schmergel a few times a year and Schmergel traveled back to the U.S. corporate offices in Deerfield a few times a year. The purpose of Schmergel's visits to the States was often routine, to have meetings with the logistics or financial departments. Additionally, these trips to headquarters gave him the chance to meet with Graham:

> I would see Graham for an hour or two. [Often], he would invite me out for dinner. . . . Graham would pressure me with Charlie Schwartz sitting there. He would question me about everything: performance, which product lines are doing well, which are not, how do I see them, what do I see, and whether I see any acquisition opportunities. For a young guy, that was an unbelievable chance to interact with the CEO.
>
> He had a tremendous memory, and he was just a brilliant, brilliant person. Very intelligent, very good strategic thinker. . . . And you were expected to answer any question. Baxter had a lot of products. You were expected to know market shares by product by country for all key products. You were expected to understand the trends in the U.S. market. The company was geographically organized, and only our research and product development was centralized. Everything else was decentralized. We had our own lawyers; we had our own medical department, our own registration . . . so you already understood all the functions. It was a typical general management job with the key exception of research and development. So you were not developed functionally, as in a functional worldwide product organization. You became ambitious to be your own man, to be a CEO.

After about two years in Belgium, Schmergel was tapped again, this time to return to the United States. Gantz told him, "We are grooming you as one of my potential replacements. I'm going to be here for another few years and Bill Graham feels that you should go back to the U.S. for a while to reacquaint yourself with the U.S., understand how the company has developed—get the final polish." Schmergel assessed the situation once again as a promise but not a guarantee. As he emphasized, "It was *never* a guarantee."

Grooming for Senior Management

When Schmergel returned to the States, his first boss, Schwartz, had retired and a newcomer from McKinsey, Des O'Connell, had taken over the International Division. Schmergel reported to O'Connell, who was his fourth boss in five years at Baxter. He described his job in the States as "vague . . . an area director for part of Latin America, also in charge of a couple of functional areas." Schmergel's initial and primary responsibility was to solve political and legal issues that had arisen in Mexico where Baxter had a very large factory.

In addition, he got up to speed on several of the company's core manufacturing processes when he worked for O'Connell. One of Baxter's main businesses was the production of albumin and human Factor VIII, which are critical for the health of hemophiliacs. During this time, these substances were extracted from human blood plasma that was donated at blood banks all over the world. As part of Schmergel's responsibilities under O'Connell, he was put in charge of all of the non-U.S. blood banks.

At about this same time, Baxter was under tremendous pressure from Wall Street to get its inventories and receivables in line. To deal with the pressure from Wall Street, Graham appointed two people to work on a worldwide project to solve the inventories and receivables problems globally. One person was put in charge domestically, and Schmergel assembled a team to work on the problem internationally.

> I assembled a team of about forty people, basically inventory analysts, financial analysts, and logistical folks. A group of forty. And we had to go around the whole world, in every operation, review inventory management and receivables, accounts receivable collection practices, looking at inventory turns, taking write-offs, and reviewing the production scheduling in the factories. We had some tools at our disposal—a lot less sophisticated than what there is today. But basically, we quickly educated ourselves.

VP of Europe

In 1975, Schmergel took Gantz's place as VP of Europe and Gantz was named president of the International Division. Schmergel had been with Baxter for eight years and was now in charge of a major international market for Baxter, which had become a *Fortune 500* company. He was thirty-five years old.

At Schmergel's level, as VP of Europe, he had many occasions to interact with Graham in the mid- to late-1970s. Schmergel felt that he could talk with Graham, even argue with him on major strategic issues. But in the end, Graham always made the final decision.

> I remember one time we were having a conversation about one of my key countries. I was already VP of Europe, and I really felt I knew everything. . . . I was recommending a major acquisition. I could not convince him . . . I'm arguing and I remember, he looks at me, and says, "You know, Gabe, you may be right—you know the German market better than I do. I may be wrong. But I am the CEO. And you're going to have to just accept that I'm making this decision, which is different from what you strongly recommend. . . . Now, Gabe, I expect you to fully support this strategy that I've decided, both day and night. And if you feel that you can't do that, I want you to tell me. And the consequence is that you will have to go and work somewhere else. Maybe we can find you an equivalent job in the company, or maybe you will have to leave the company. And you're going to do that with my full support. But for you to keep this job, you have to tell me that you will implement this strategy that you obviously think is not good with all your usual enthusiasm."

President of International

In 1979, Schmergel was promoted to president of the International Division. Although this career transition was definitely a promotion, it was a bittersweet change. The promotion required that he maintain a home base in Baxter's headquarters, located in

Deerfield, and then travel the world extensively. As Schmergel explained, "My boss wasn't six thousand miles from here. My boss was in the next building . . . I didn't have that same feeling of freedom, of being a big fish." Schmergel became weary of the numerous corporate meetings he felt obliged to attend back in Chicago. He was eager to be out in the field, where he felt the action was.

With multiple obligations both in the United States and abroad, Schmergel found that he was either traveling or "working all the time" and that the traveling from Chicago to the Far East, back to Europe, back to the Far East and back to Chicago was terribly draining, both for Schmergel and for his family. Chicago was not, as Schmergel was quick to recall, a particularly convenient point of departure for international travel. In contrast to this new position, he had fond memories of his experiences as VP of Europe.

> In many ways, I had a better job when I was running Europe with about five thousand people—a whole bunch of factories, sales forces, my own medical group, my own European product development center—not research, but product development. From time to time, I would meet the prime minister of Belgium. . . . I was essentially running my own business in Europe and, from time to time, interacting with Bill Gantz.

In addition to finding this new, very senior-level position exhausting and, in some respects, less rewarding than his prior position as VP of Europe, Schmergel was more and more aware of the limits of his career within Baxter. As he put it, "At some point in time, you look around and you are in your late thirties, early forties, and you realize that realistically speaking, you're not going to be CEO. . . . Baxter just had too many people who had the qualifications to be running the company." Vern Loucks, who had mowed Bill Graham's lawn as a youngster, was the clear heir apparent to the Baxter throne. Loucks appeared to many to be the ideal candidate, given his background: Loucks was a Yale graduate, had served for several years in the Marine Corps as a line officer, had earned his

MBA from Harvard Business School, had experience in a consulting firm, and had broad exposure within Baxter. It became obvious to people like Schmergel that the Graham era was about to end.

At the same time that Schmergel was restless in his big new job and impatient with company "politics," he was also becoming increasingly excited about the new scientific possibilities he was hearing about in healthcare. Though the term *biotechnology* was not yet commonplace, the beginnings of that industry were starting to take root. Baxter's research and development group tended to be skeptical about the new science that was emerging, but Schmergel and several senior managers such as Ted Greene were intrigued.

Some preliminary talks between Baxter and Genentech were taking place at exactly the same time as Schmergel was feeling that the pyramid of the organizational hierarchy was narrowing for him at Baxter. At this point, Schmergel felt the smart thing to do would be to be in touch with the VC community. To break into the VC community, he relied upon an extraorganizational network—not a Baxter network. Some of these contacts were former classmates from Harvard Business School; others were industry or professional contacts.

Transition to Biotech

The initial catalyst in Schmergel's transition to biotech was a junior partner at Greylock, someone just a year or two older than Schmergel himself. The two met when the VC was in Chicago to visit one of his portfolio companies. After this initial meeting, a senior partner from Greylock called Schmergel to discuss a new company he was starting with two "brilliant scientists," Maniatis and Ptashne from Harvard, who were working on genetic engineering. Schmergel was intrigued.

> It wasn't like somebody said "textiles, steel, or semiconductors"—those would not have interested me because my field was and is healthcare. It was genetic engineering! The senior partner said,

"Come out to Boston to meet with me." And I said, "I can't really do that. I can't just fly out to Boston during the week." I was too busy, and I thought I'd get in trouble. The senior partner said, "Well, you go to Europe a lot, right? . . . Why don't you just fly up on a Sunday and just figure out a way to spend Monday here?"

Schmergel made this arrangement work and met with the senior venture partner, who then suggested that he visit the scientists in the Harvard Biology Department.

It was a cold day and I remember Mark and Tom were in jeans, T-shirts, long hair, and sandals! They didn't look like world-class, super scientists! They were about my age. We spent some time talking, and they told me about this vision they had. . . . I got more and more excited, and they said, "Well, we have been talking with Greylock, Venrock, and Whitney, and $6 million have been committed or promised." And when I heard that VCs were already thinking of $6 million, this sounded to me like an awful lot of money—which actually it was in those days.

Beyond the clear support from prestigious VCs and the potential to get in on the ground floor of this industry, Schmergel was attracted to this particular opportunity because it directly addressed a need he had seen at Baxter. As head of the International Division at Baxter, Schmergel had responsibility for selling all of Baxter's product lines and became very familiar with one of Baxter's most important products, Factor VIII, a treatment for hemophilia. Factor VIII is a clotting factor that hemophiliacs do not produce on their own; without it, the slightest injury could literally cause them to bleed with serious consequences. The Hyland Division was manufacturing and selling domestically Factor VIII and Schmergel, under the International Division, was manufacturing and selling this clotting factor internationally. Factor VIII was derived from fractionating human blood plasma that was obtained through blood donations. Schmergel understood the risks and limitations of the currently used technology and the concerns regarding the donation of blood and was convinced that genetic engineering would eventually revolutionize the treatment of hemophilia.

In 1981, having reached the position of president of International and having played an instrumental role in Baxter's worldwide expansion, Schmergel ultimately left what his colleagues described as "a perfectly good job." He had been at Baxter for fourteen years. He left to head up Genetics Institute—a tiny biotechnology venture founded by two scientists and located halfway across the country, in Cambridge, Massachusetts—quite a change from the twelve thousand people reporting to him when he was head of the International Division at Baxter.

The Aftermath at GI

Gabe Schmergel remained CEO of Genetics Institute (GI) for sixteen years. Under his leadership, GI became a fully integrated biopharmaceutical company and developed drugs for the treatment of hemophilia, anemia, bone growth, and cancer. The company went public in 1986 and soon thereafter became one of the few biotechnology companies to become profitable based upon its own internally generated products. Over this time period, Genetics Institute grew to twelve hundred employees with sales of $270 million. In 1997, Genetics Institute was acquired by American Home Products, and Schmergel retired as president and CEO. The buyout transaction valued Genetics Institute at $3 billion, which made it the third largest out of approximately thirteen hundred companies then in the biotechnology industry.

The Rest of the First Wave

Gabe Schmergel's story is remarkable by any standard. He began as a penniless immigrant and became a pioneer in the field of biotechnology. He was one of only a handful of top managers to join biotech firms at the dawn of the biotech industry between 1979 and 1983. Ted Greene, Bob Carpenter, Steve Chubb, and Henri Termeer were also among this first wave of "Baxter Boys" to leave for biotechnology. There are similar threads in each of these "first wave" cases.

Ted Greene

Howard E. (Ted) Greene was born in a suburb of Cleveland, Ohio, and graduated from high school in North Carolina. After majoring in physics at Amherst College, he went directly to Harvard Business School, where he was named a Baker Scholar in his second term and graduated among the top of his class in 1967. His first job was in McKinsey's Chicago office, where he worked for seven years and was placed on several projects for Baxter. One of those projects garnered him the attention and praise of Bill Graham himself:

> I invented a product line . . . [Graham] said it was the finest piece of consulting work he'd ever seen, because not only did I come up with a marketing strategy . . . but I said, "Okay, here's the product you're going to market." Needless to say, when I decided to leave McKinsey, I put out the word to some of my friends who had gone from McKinsey to Baxter to see what the chances were, and within about two hours I had a phone call from Bill Graham, saying, "Can you be in my office tomorrow?"

Like Schmergel, Greene was hired into an assistant-to position right away—in this case, assistant to Bill Jennett, who was Baxter's president at the time, and to whom the Hyland Division reported in 1973. For the first year and a half or so, Greene was basically an "in-house consultant" for Hyland, working mainly on product market strategies. In these project-based assignments, not unlike those engaged in by Schmergel, Greene was charged with diagnosing business problems and selling his solutions to senior management. Within a couple of years, Greene was promoted to international marketing, running all of diagnostic-product marketing outside the United States. Although this was not an international management assignment like Schmergel's, Greene did have the opportunity to manage a significant part of this business, and that included international responsibilities as well.

Greene stayed at Baxter until 1978, when Baxter was dismantling the Hyland operation, dismissing some people, and moving others back to Chicago. Greene was, in his own words, "not playing the corporate game right," and was not going to be moved back to Chicago. "I was fired," he says, which was "the best thing Baxter ever did for me." In this instance, it was apparent both to Greene as well as to Baxter senior management that a large company was not a suitable place for Greene in the long term.

Greene describes himself as more of a scientist than the rest of the first wave of Baxter managers who left for biotechnology during the late 1970s and early 1980s. Greene had begun to hear about the new "genetic engineering technology," as it came to be called, and in 1976 had attended a speech given by Bill Dreyer, a scientist at the California Institute of Technology who was conducting research on antibody labeling and who predicted that monoclonal antibodies would revolutionize medicine. As he was preparing to leave Baxter, Greene discovered that there were several other employees interested in starting a business involving this new discovery, so he and some of his closest colleagues at Hyland incorporated a company called Cytex to develop the technology.

Greene was also contacted by a headhunter for a marketing position within Genentech, which led to his meeting the founding scientists and investors in Hybritech, another monoclonal antibody start-up that promised to be an early competitor of Cytex. Greene continued to pursue funding for Cytex, finally getting interest from a pharmaceutical company, Syntex. However, the senior investor in Hybritech—Tom Perkins of Kleiner, Perkins, Caufield, and Byers—proposed to Greene that his firm had the money, experience, and contacts to help Greene build a successful company much more quickly. Since differing points of view about leadership were emerging in the Cytex team, Greene turned to Hybritech, joined with the original group of six people—a "ragtag group" according to him—and, as CEO, led them to secure their start-up round of funding in 1979.

Greene remained CEO of Hybritech from March 1979 until March 1986, when the company was acquired by Eli Lilly. From there, Greene went on to co-found another biotech firm, Amylin Pharmaceuticals, where he served as CEO until July 1996. In total, since leaving Baxter, Greene has helped establish and/or managed eleven medical-technology companies. Greene currently serves on the boards of Epimmune and Amylin.

Bob Carpenter

Of all the Baxter Boys, Bob Carpenter had the career with the steepest ascent within Baxter. After graduating from West Point with an undergraduate degree in engineering, he attended Harvard Business School (HBS) and graduated with an MBA in 1975. He interviewed with several consulting firms and some computer companies but was strongly encouraged by a favorite HBS professor to consider Baxter. "You gotta be on a production line, making something. Get in the factory," was part of his professor's advice. So when Baxter recruited on campus, Carpenter signed up for an interview.

He ended up with offers for three different positions within Baxter—one in an internal consulting group, and two assistant-to positions, one for Bill Jennett, the president of Baxter, and the other for Vern Loucks, the executive vice president. More interested in Loucks's marketing orientation, Carpenter accepted the position with the then-executive vice president and so, like Schmergel and Greene, began his career at Baxter in an assistant-to position. His first day at Baxter began at 8 A.M., saw him assigned to the task force devoted to improving manufacturing procedures along with colleagues Steve Chubb, Dekle Rountree, and Steve Schaubert, and didn't end until after 10 P.M. In less than six months, Loucks was promoted to president and Jennett was fired. Carpenter continued on project work, typically with three or four projects going on at the same time.

After barely a year at Baxter, he was promoted to director of product planning for Fenwal—skipping the "manager" step in the conventional hierarchy. Over the next two years, Carpenter steadily received more and more areas of the business reporting to him, until Dale Smith, then president of Fenwal, was promoted. Carpenter was made president of Fenwal in October 1978 at the age of thirty-three.

Carpenter's opportunities for upward progress within Baxter didn't stop there, though. After just about two years as president of Fenwal, Gabe Schmergel, then president of International, offered Carpenter the position of VP of International, responsible for the non-European divisions of Baxter's international business. Concerned by feedback from a valued superior that he was being promoted too quickly, Carpenter turned down the job.

At the turn of the decade, Carpenter was well aware of Ted Greene and Gabe Schmergel's departures and, like others, had his eye on the emerging biotech industry. So when a call came from the venture capital firm Sutter Hill (Ted Greene had given the firm his name) with an offer for the presidency of a fledgling biotech company called Integrated Genetics, Inc., Carpenter accepted the offer. In April 1981, not yet six years into his career at Baxter, he left his job as president of Fenwal and began working for Integrated Genetics—a start-up located in a one-room office/bedroom space in a high-rise building off Memorial Drive in Cambridge, Massachusetts. Carpenter was the firm's first employee.

Carpenter served as chairman, president, and CEO of Integrated Genetics (IG) until it merged with Genzyme in 1989. He then remained as executive vice president, CEO, and chairman of the board of IG Laboratories, Inc., at Genzyme until 1991. Since leaving IG, Carpenter has been involved in a string of entrepreneurial ventures in biotechnology. In November 1991, Carpenter cofounded GelTex Pharmaceuticals, Inc., and served as its president and CEO until May 1993. In 1995, Carpenter cofounded and led VacTex, Inc., another biotech company, until it was acquired by Aquila Biopharmaceuticals in April 1998. As of this writing, Carpenter is chairman of Peptimmune, Inc., a biotech company specializing in the development of immunotherapies. He is also president of Boston Medical Investors, a privately held investment firm that he formed in 1994, and he serves on the boards of Genzyme, Cardiac Science, and VitaResc AG.

Steve Chubb

After a stint in the U.S. Navy, Steve Chubb joined the American Can Company in Oakland, California, and worked in a factory for about a year. During that time, he enrolled at the University of California at Berkeley and began working on an MBA at night. After that year, American Can transferred him to the company's R&D headquarters in Chicago, and he transferred his credits to Northwestern University and continued his business-school education there. He soon took a leave of absence to go full time when he and his wife realized that it was more practical for him to quit and finish his degree full time in one year than to continue only at night. When Baxter recruited on campus at the end of that year, though, as Chubb says, "It wasn't even a close call. What I saw as opportunities, but perhaps more importantly, my interest in the products and what they did—it was just no contest. And Baxter didn't even offer the most money." He began working at Baxter in 1974.

Chubb began as assistant to Pete Phildius, who was heading up Baxter's Artificial Kidneys Division. Soon, though, Baxter faced a crackdown by the FDA on its manufacturing procedures, and Chubb was placed on the same task force as Bob Carpenter, Dekle Rountree, and Steve Schaubert and ordered to go from plant to plant and "fix things." He ended up staying in this position that he describes as "quasi-manufacturing" for a little over two years. In 1977, he went to work for Dolph Bridgewater, an executive vice president who was hired from McKinsey, but who left in 1979 to run the Brown Shoe Company. Chubb was subsequently promoted to run Hyland Diagnostics, a fully integrated division with its own R&D, production, quality control, finance/accounting, sales, and marketing, and with worldwide 1980 sales of approximately $50 million.

In October 1980, Chubb read a *Business Week* article about Bob Swanson and learned about Genentech's IPO: "When Genentech went public, I said, 'That's what I want to do. One way or another, I will do it . . . run a company, one that's innovative.'" As Chubb recalled:

> Baxter certainly was innovative, but primarily in the area of devices (artificial kidneys, blood oxygenators, blood collection bags, and IV bags). In the early eighties the emergence of the biotechnology industry was beginning in the areas of molecular biology, cell biology, and immunology (monoclonal antibodies). Thus, the lure was the opportunity to discover and develop truly revolutionary products based upon recently discovered molecular building blocks rather than be confined to mere product enhancements.

So in May 1981, when he got a call from a former Hyland VP who had become a recruiter and was looking for someone to fill a position in a start-up biotech company, he was more than open to the possibility. His only hesitation was the location: the company was in Princeton and neither he nor his wife was interested in moving to New Jersey. One visit to Princeton, however, disabused him and his wife of their stereotypes about New Jersey. As Chubb recalls, "We looked around, and I said, 'God, this looks like Vermont!' This didn't look like the New Jersey Turnpike. 'This can work!'"

Chubb left Baxter in August 1981 and was able to secure funding for his company, Cytogen, in early 1982. About three years later, Chubb left Cytogen to form T-Cell Sciences in the Boston area. At about this same time, scientists at the Massachusetts Institute of Technology (MIT) were making discoveries that could assist in the detection of cancer. In 1987, Chubb transitioned once more—this time to start a new company called Matritech, which was given exclusive license to MIT's new technology for the early detection of a variety of cancers. Chubb has remained CEO since Matritech's inception in 1987 and has served as chairman of the company since October 1993. Chubb also serves as a director of Charles River Laboratories and is a trustee of Mount Auburn Hospital in Cambridge, Massachusetts.

Henri Termeer

Henri Termeer was born in the Netherlands in 1946. After immigrating to the United States, he attended the Darden Business School at the University of Virginia, graduating in 1973. Baxter was his very last interview during the official recruiting season at Darden in his second year. Intrigued by the MBA program at Baxter and, like the others, the possibility of a quick ascent to a general manager position, he accepted Baxter's offer to be assistant to Phil Henderson, the international vice president of marketing. Soon, though, he realized that he "didn't like being 'assistant-to,' and so [he] said, 'I want to have a job.' And within three months, they gave me a job title at my request."

Termeer became the International Planning Manager for the Hyland Division, which made plasma derivatives such as albumin and Factor VIII. Early on, he worked on a project involving Chagas disease, in which an immune reaction in the heart causes the heart to turn on itself. The project was almost solely Termeer's, and he remembers being surprised at the high level of responsibility and authority he was given after less than a year's tenure in the company. Another early project was his appointment as the sole Hyland representative on a five-person task force, headed by Gabe Schmergel and reporting directly to Bill Graham, that was charged with freeing up working capital.

It wasn't long until Termeer was offered his first general manager position—in a joint venture in South Africa. Unlike many other Baxter managers, though, Termeer turned down not only this opportunity, but also his next offer for a general manager position (in Brazil), feeling that neither position represented a good fit with his skills and abilities. He didn't have long to consider whether he would regret these rejections, though, as just weeks after declining the Brazil offer, he was offered the position of general manager of the German subsidiary. "Now they were talking," Termeer says, "because this was the largest sales subsidiary outside of the United States, and it was a big country. . . . I spoke German, and this was something I thought I could really do." He received the offer on a Monday morning after just returning from a week of traveling in Europe. With the same kind of urgency as Schmergel had had with his first major general management assignment, Termeer talked over the possibility with his wife and was on a plane to Munich that same Monday evening.

After about three years, Termeer was called back to the United States to become executive vice president of Baxter's Hyland Therapeutics Division, reporting to Dave Castaldi. Over the course of a few years at Hyland, he gradually ended up with responsibility for all aspects of the business except human resources. Termeer started to fear that Castaldi might not be promoted to a position back at corporate headquarters in Chicago and wasn't sure when his own next promotion opportunity would come.

Meanwhile, he watched Gabe Schmergel, Bob Carpenter, and Ted Greene depart Baxter to run biotech companies and maintained contact with all three. "The early people that left were good people," Termeer recalls. "They had been successful . . . and I benefited from that by getting things offered to me." Eventually, Termeer also decided to leave Baxter and, in 1983, joined a group of eleven people who were beginning to form a business called Genzyme, a firm that had no structure or funding in place. Genzyme at this point was no more than "the beginnings of good people prepared to think together to make something work." Since October 1983, Termeer has served as president and as a director of Genzyme; since December 1985, Termeer has been Genzyme's

CEO; and since May 1988, he has been chairman of the board. As of this writing, Termeer is also a director of ABIOMED, Inc., and a trustee of Hambrecht & Quist Healthcare Investors and Hambrecht & Quist Life Sciences Investors.

From atop Genzyme, a multibillion-dollar biotech company, Termeer looks back on his decision to leave Baxter and join Genzyme with some disbelief: "If I could go back and read what I read when I made this decision, . . . it's unbelievable. There was nothing there."

The Bigger Picture

These career sketches, together with Gabe Schmergel's story, provide a sense of Baxter as a breeding ground, the typical career trajectory in terms of jobs held—from assistant-to positions including project-based assignments to general management assignments, either overseas or at a division—along with a sense of Baxter's performance-based culture during the 1970s in particular. These stories also provide some sense of the magnitude of the career transitions Baxter spawned. As we will discover, the success of this first wave of managers and the strong networks they developed while at Baxter paved the way for those who followed. In the mid-1980s, and in particular, after 1985, when Baxter merged with American Hospital Supply, a second wave of managers, including Jim Tobin, who left much later, joined the biotech field and similarly took on leadership positions.

The accompanying graphic (Figure 2.1) provides a visual map of the historical and economic context of the Baxter Boys cases; it is intended as a locator for the discussion to come.

Phase A

As noted earlier, Baxter was basically in the blood and IV-solutions businesses—including blood and solutions packaging, storage, and collection—and in medical devices, such as artificial kidneys

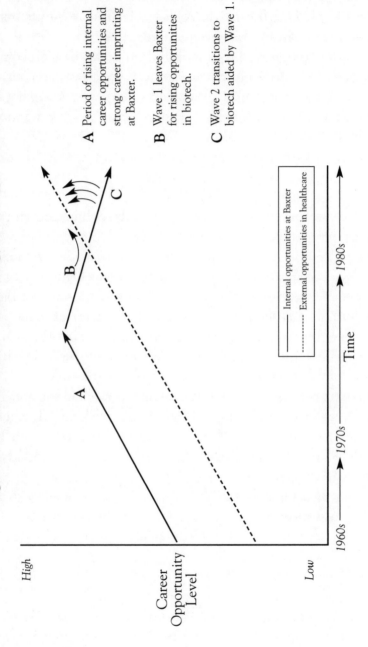

Figure 2.1 From Baxter to Biotechnology: The Bigger Picture

A Period of rising internal career opportunities and strong career imprinting at Baxter.

B Wave 1 leaves Baxter for rising opportunities in biotech.

C Wave 2 transitions to biotech aided by Wave 1.

Internal opportunities at Baxter

External opportunities in healthcare

High

Career Opportunity Level

Low

1960s   1970s   1980s

Time

and dialyses machines. Most of the innovations at Baxter occurred during the 1940s and 1950s. When Bill Graham took over as CEO in 1953 and later, in the mid-1960s, began recruiting at top-notch business schools, his goal was to "professionalize" the company. As the prior stories suggest, the pattern was to hire MBAs into assistant-to or internal-consulting positions and then, within a couple of years, have them try their hand at general management positions. There were thirty to forty general management jobs at Baxter during the 1960s and 1970s, oftentimes overseas. These were stretch assignments for these young men (mostly men) and provided tremendous opportunities for professional development, leading to point A. Although members of the first wave were hired into Baxter in the mid- to late-1960s and the 1970s, we can categorize the career imprinting of interest here as having occurred primarily during the 1970s and the career transitions into biotech as having occurred primarily during the early to mid-1980s. During much of the 1970s, then, when most of the career imprinting that is discussed in this book took place, business opportunities in biotechnology, or "genetic engineering," as it was called, were minimal.

To put this external context in perspective, the Watson and Crick studies in which the double-helix structure of DNA was determined occurred in 1953. Two decades later, in 1973, Cohen and Boyer produced the first recombinant DNA organism. It wasn't until the end of the 1970s, with the founding of Genentech in 1976, that the biotechnology industry truly "began." At the end of the 1970s and during the early 1980s, then, external opportunities in healthcare and, in particular, in the area of genetic engineering picked up momentum.

Phase B

As the science progressed in famous educational institutions such as MIT and Stanford, so too did the media coverage. As Chubb's account suggests, Baxter managers were seeing the early signs of biotech appear on the covers of magazines (such as the *Time* magazine cover shown here) and were intrigued by the new opportunities in life sciences. At about this same time, during the late 1970s, many Baxter managers who had been hired by Graham were also beginning to feel the weight of Baxter's steep pyramid. As

Exhibit 2.1 March 9, 1981 Cover of *Time* Magazine

Schmergel's story suggests, once they had had the experience of working in "mini-CEO" positions, as general managers of Baxter divisions or countries, they were hooked; corporate or staff positions at Baxter, other than the CEO position, became unappealing. Of course, there was only one Baxter CEO position to be had, and that position seemed destined for Vern Loucks. So Baxter managers like Chubb and Carpenter became "available" as well as enticed by evolving opportunities beyond Baxter and so less likely to remain at Baxter.

This was particularly the case after the company underwent some dramatic organizational changes at the turn of the decade. In 1981, Bill Graham, who had personally hired most of these young managers, stepped back and Vern Loucks took over as CEO. Loucks made a number of changes, including centralizing the company, which, as one interviewee put it "took away the farm team." Therefore, internal opportunities started to wane for a variety of reasons at Baxter and good managers started to lift their heads as VCs were searching for well-trained business people to help transform mini-scientific labs into business ventures. As managers from the first wave recall, they were getting a lot of calls from VCs at the end of the 1970s and early 1980s. This combination of centripetal and centrifugal factors led to the first wave leaving for biotechnology, Phase B.

Phase C

Phase C depicts the outflow of Baxter managers to biotechnology that followed the first wave. There was a feedback process that occurred that accelerated the exodus into biotechnology. As Baxter alumni became successful, not only did managers who remained at Baxter begin to consider career changes themselves, but, as Carpenter's story suggests, the VCs who were building new businesses were similarly motivated to go back to Baxter in their search for managerial talent. Further, as Termeer's story reveals, as the first wave became successful, their credibility with recruiters increased, allowing them to assist their Baxter colleagues in making similar kinds of career transitions.

With this overview of the Baxter Boys' story, examples of their career experiences, and an introduction to the idea of career imprints from Chapter One, we turn now to Part II of the book. The chapters that follow explore the factors associated with place, people, and paths that affect the cultivation of career imprints—both at Baxter and at other healthcare firms. As part of this exploration, we will pay particular attention to the conditions that amplify the career imprinting process. For example, we can ask, "What are the conditions that make an organization, such as Baxter, a particularly ripe environment for career imprinting?" We turn to this specific question next.

Part Two

The Career Imprinting Process

Chapter Three

Place: Understanding Breeding Grounds for Career Imprinting

I remember being told that there was a process of bringing people in, MBA types, and giving them a lot of visibility very early. They had jobs like "assistant-to the chairman." Those people were eventually allowed to think up something new or find a division to run. As a result, they were catapulted ahead of the normal organization structure. In doing this, Baxter created a lot of people who gained confidence running a P&L very, very early in their careers. And many of those people left to go run companies.

— *Bob Higgins, venture capitalist involved with healthcare deals during this time period*

Baxter from 1970 to 1980. That was when the healthcare industry was pretty dynamic. HMOs hadn't become restrictive in any way, and so it was a great time to be in healthcare. Baxter was growing at this very consistent rate. They were starving for management talent and so they developed this strategy of recruiting a bunch of MBAs each year. Some years they'd recruit fifteen or twenty. They were bringing these people in, giving them responsibility way beyond what they should have expected at the time. . . . I was given responsibility to start up their operation in Ireland.

I was twenty-five. And I wasn't alone; there were a
lot of guys who got a lot of responsibility quickly,
through the same method.
              — *Doug Scott, an early Baxter MBA hire*

Both of these quotations offer some insight into Baxter as a place
and as a breeding ground for entrepreneurial managers. Clearly,
Baxter had some very consistent ways of bringing people in and
training them, leading to "a lot of guys who got responsibility
quickly," and to producing people who had the confidence of profit
and loss (P&L) responsibility. Years later, Baxter managers became
known for having certain capabilities, connections, confidence,
and ways of thinking about the world that were ultimately deemed
valuable at the start of the biotechnology industry. But what was it
about Baxter, the place, that produced such a strong career imprint?
More generally, what enables any organization to cultivate a strong
career imprint?

The answer, in part, is that the strength of any organization's
influence on employees depends upon the nature of the developmental context at that organization. Although people come to
employers with their own personal bundles of worldviews, skills,
connections, and confidence, management research has long suggested that employers have substantial leverage in how those
assets get shaped and molded. Indeed, management schools are
premised on the assumption that leaders are not just born, but
also made.[1]

Experience on the job is clearly one powerful source of learning for individuals.[2] Indeed, management research has uncovered a
great deal about how certain aspects of job experience such as
assignment variety and time at a particular job or function shape
individual-level performance.[3] But such explanations don't go
far enough to answer questions such as "How can organizations
shape job experiences such that a *group* of individuals come to
share a common set of capabilities, connections, confidence, and

cognition?" and "How can organizations foster the development of a career imprint so strong that it is recognizable by outside parties (such as venture capitalists) and so strong that managers take it with them when they move to other organizations?"

This research suggests that three major factors contribute to an organization's ability to cultivate a strong career imprint:

- Social Reinforcement: The extent to which the company's practices and culture reinforce the sense of commonality among employees' career experiences;
- Stretch Opportunities: The extent to which the company's strategy and structure provide significant opportunities for new hires to engage in stretch assignments, coupled with high expectations from senior management; and
- Demonstrated Success: The extent to which there is demonstrated success, as evidenced in the organization's performance.

These three factors, which are influenced by an organization's culture, systems, strategy, and structure, as illustrated in Figure 3.1, are the focus of this chapter.

Figure 3.1 Place: Factors that strengthen an organizational environment for career imprinting

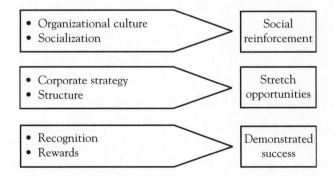

Importantly, the three factors are general conditions with respect to the development of a strong career imprint; although the examples used herein come primarily from Baxter, the conditions are not specific to Baxter or healthcare, and the research cited to support the significance of these conditions comes from different contexts as well. Also, the focus here is on the organizational factors that amplify the career imprinting process at any organization. We will turn to the specific *content* of Baxter's own career imprint and the exact nature of the capabilities, connections, confidence, and cognition that were cultivated at Baxter in Chapter Five, and in Chapter Six we will turn to the specific content of other healthcare firms' career imprints. For now, then, the focus is on the organizational factors that strengthen the career imprinting process.

Social Reinforcement

Since a career imprint is the set of capabilities, connections, confidence, and cognition that result from common career experiences in an organization, the more "common" these experiences are, the stronger the career imprint. The term *social reinforcement* refers to the extent to which organizational systems and practices foster a sense of commonality among employees' career experiences. As we will see, the more the organization's culture emphasizes a collective sense of identity and the more the socialization practices emphasize social comparison and role-modeling behavior, the greater the social reinforcement overall and, hence, the stronger the career imprint.

Organizational Culture and Socialization

Organizational Culture. One reason that some organizations are able to cultivate particularly strong career imprints is that they have very strong cultures. According to Schein, an organizational culture is the "pattern of assumptions—invented, discovered, or developed by a given group as it learns to cope with its problems of external adaptation and internal integration—that has worked well enough to be considered valid and, therefore, to be taught to new members as the correct way to perceive, think, and feel in relation to those problems."[4] A more popular way to think about culture is simply as "the way we do things around here."[5] As a substantial stream of organizational research has established, strong organizational cultures can be a powerful form of social control.[6]

Baxter alumni repeatedly reported that Baxter had a very strong organizational culture. Their career accounts illustrate the existence of pervasive and widely shared norms of behavior, indicative of a strong corporate culture. As Gabe Schmergel described, Baxter's culture was an "up or out, performance-based culture." The "up" represented all of the possibilities for growth at Baxter, which came with assumptions about putting your head down, working hard, and winning Baxter's wars with its competitors, all for the good of the company. This was the collaborative side of Baxter's culture. The "out" represented all of the risks associated with *not* performing up to expectations set by senior management. This was the competitive side of Baxter's culture. In many respects, the following description by a Baxter alumnus of Bill Graham encapsulates the two-sided nature of Baxter's developmental environment:

> Graham is bigger than life, almost. You know, you almost feel that you should bow in front of him because he has a commanding presence. And he has a warmth about him at the same time that is truly a result of driving the business. And, if you're not good, you're out.

The collaborative side to Baxter's corporate culture included a strong sense of collective identity. The concept of identity has a very long history and quite a broad reach across the academic disciplines. Here, collective identity refers to the extent to which a group of people have or believe they share a common characteristic, whether that characteristic be ascribed (e.g., gender) or achieved (e.g., status).[7] In this case, the shared characteristic is an employment affiliation with Baxter. Collective identity has cognitive implications, since people not only share a belief in their membership in a category (e.g., as a Baxter employee) but also a set of beliefs associated with membership. It also has emotional implications, since people can feel affectively committed or close to other members of the same category.[8] Both elements were evident here since people shared beliefs associated with their experience as a group and also felt close to each other.

In some respects, this aspect of Baxter's culture was not unique. The sense of collective identity very much reflected the time in which Gabe Schmergel's story and the career accounts of the others in the first wave took place. During the 1970s, the social psychological contract between employer and employee—that is, what employers and employees expect to give and get in an employment relationship—reflected a tremendous sense of organizational loyalty and commitment in many businesses.[9] This was, beginning in the 1950s, the era of the "organization man."[10] This was the "IBM era" in which people showed their loyalty in a variety of ways, including an attention to dress. And during this time period, employers tended to play a large role in determining the course of individuals' careers. In Japan, laws making it illegal for companies to fire employees or to hire employees from their rivals resulted in a system of lifetime employment that spread to other countries in the 1960s and lasted through the early 1990s.[11] Companies hired workers directly out of high school or college and kept them until the age of mandatory retirement, usually between fifty-five and sixty.[12] Therefore, it is not surprising that other health-care firms during this timeframe, such as Merck and J&J, had similar high-commitment values that characterized their organizations' cultures.

At Baxter, part of this ethos may have also stemmed from the managers' parents' upbringing since, for the most part, managers hired under Graham were children of parents whose families had lived through the Great Depression and World War II. Individuals were committed to a larger sense of purpose during World War II and tried to figure out ways to utilize the workforce more efficiently, and as children of the Great Depression, they were accustomed to dedication and persistence at work. As one interviewee described, "My Dad worked for the same company for forty-eight years. In our family, changing jobs was viewed as a sign of failure. A little bit like divorce or something." As another Baxter alumnus reflected, "This was back in the days when you could make a career with a company."[13]

As part of that psychological contract, spouses were often expected to "go along" with the decisions of the major breadwinner, who was usually male. Indeed, all of the Baxter alumni who left to run biotechnology companies in the first wave were men; in the second wave, only seven of the eighty-one people were women (and none took on CEO roles in biotechnology). Baxter did have women in senior positions, but they were very few and, as one interviewee explained, "they were not in the same league."[14]

Therefore, the social context in which people's careers began at Baxter was characterized by strong norms of organizational loyalty and, in general, limited constraints on intraorganizational mobility. Although several of the interviewees were married at the time they joined Baxter, their ability and motivation to travel was extraordinary by today's standards. Indeed, one interviewee recounted that he had traveled to forty-four countries in his eleven years at Baxter and had moved five times. Additional examples of this propensity for action and mobility will be discussed further, but these brief samples show that the basic value of working extremely hard for the "good of the company," for the good of Baxter, was a key element of the corporate culture at the time most of the first wave entered Baxter.

Further, although managers at Baxter had a sense of "team" and shared identity, ultimately, accountability rested with individuals. Therefore, at the same time that the breeding ground at Baxter supported professional growth by providing guidance, resources, and opportunities for development, the culture was also based upon values that hinged on financial performance, and so there was extreme evaluative pressure to perform. Consistent with Schmergel's description of Baxter's "performance-based culture," in addition to working hard for the good of the company, managers were highly motivated to perform. Expectations for meeting specific goals (such as 20 percent growth) were clearly and explicitly articulated and individuals were constantly evaluated against these goals.

Whereas the aspect of Baxter's culture, its strong sense of collective identity, can be traced back to the organization-man perspective prevalent at that time, the other aspect of Baxter's culture, the emphasis on bottom-line performance, can be traced to Baxter's business context and the types of jobs available within Baxter, particularly during the 1970s. Regarding the latter, Baxter (and Graham, in particular) carved out jobs for the MBAs that primarily entailed developing new markets. These were extremely challenging tasks that were fraught with ambiguity—not uncertainty, but ambiguity—since often, managers didn't even know what they didn't know. For example, in order to build a new country market, Baxter executives had to come up to speed on the geopolitical climate of the country, on currency fluctuations, on healthcare regulations, and on cultural differences in healthcare preferences and infrastructure. These jobs were complex and had many performance dimensions that were difficult to manage, and yet all dimensions were scrutinized closely.

Given these unique business challenges, two key aspects to the performance-based aspect of Baxter's culture were remarkable: (a) a sense of urgency and (b) a sense of fungibility of human capital.

Regarding the former, both of Baxter's key business challenges—developing businesses in new markets and building manufacturing capabilities—were tasks that inherently had a sense of urgency. Either the urgency was to establish a presence in a new market before local competitors, or it was to overhaul a plant's operations swiftly to bring it in line with emerging "good manufacturing practices" (GMPs). Carpenter's earlier account of his first day on the job and how he was immediately assigned to a task force to "fix" Baxter's manufacturing plants illustrates the urgency associated with GMPs that was indicative of early career assignments at Baxter in the 1970s. Similarly, when people were sent out to build new country markets, they experienced a strong sense of urgency along with high expectations for superior performance:

> Baxter turned out, you know, three-year and five-year plans, sure. But everybody knew that you could turn out the greatest five-year plans but if you didn't take care of this year, you were dead. I don't mean dead, but you were in trouble. You had to find a way; your first priority was to find a way to fix what needed to be fixed this year.

The sense of fungible human capital that Graham orchestrated at Baxter meant that security at Baxter was associated with those who "won" or made it through all of these stretch assignments. Therefore, it was a bounded sense of security—security for the chosen. If you performed, you were well taken care of—where "taken care of" meant more challenges and more opportunities, but not necessarily significantly higher pay.[15] That was the psychological contract at Baxter. The rewards were primarily intrinsic, rather than extrinsic, as illustrated in the following account of a salary conversation that former Baxter manager Tim Wollaeger had with Bill Graham:

> Graham said, "Tim, at $40,000 a year, you're making more than the average guy in your Stanford Business School class." And, I said, "But Bill, you wouldn't hire the average guy out of my business school class." And he said, "That's a good point. Okay, would you rather be a financial analyst over at Gould & Co., making $40,000 a year, or running your own show in Mexico for $40,000 a year?" And I said, "Running my own show in Mexico for $40,000." And he said, "Then we're both getting out of this what we want."

Graham was also not shy about reminding people that there were always other eager MBAs waiting in the wings, if one couldn't perform. Thus, Graham's approach combined both the "carrot" in the form of promises for greater responsibility as well as the "stick" in the very real possibility of being let go. One healthcare human resources manager contrasted Baxter's career development strategy for MBAs and its strong up-or-out culture with those at other firms, as follows:

> If you wander into other companies back then, there would have been a more specific career path, rather than, "God, that guy's bright; let's move him out to run a business!" In other words, it was sink or swim. Graham was watching them—these stretch assignments gave Graham insight into who could cut it.

Socialization. In addition to having a strong organizational culture, organizations can affect the strength of career imprinting through their socialization practices. Organizational socialization can be thought of as the ways in which "insiders" transmit the basic norms and values of a company to someone who is just joining a company.[16] Socialization is about learning what is "acceptable behavior."[17] There are many different ways to socialize new employees, ranging from training people one-on-one to putting people together in groups to share a common task or orientation experience. Here, we are concerned with ways in which socialization systems of any kind are "groupy"—that is, we are interested in the tactics that develop a shared or common sense of what's acceptable within an organization. The more powerful the manager's socialization experience, the stronger the employer's career imprint.

At Baxter, organizational socialization occurred through a variety of mechanisms that triggered social reinforcement and so the strength of Baxter's career imprint. First, as Gabe Schmergel's story described, Bill Graham hired people in to "professionalize" Baxter in cohorts—in groups of about ten to fifteen. This set in motion a "general management track," even though there was no formalized training program. Rather, there was a sense of camaraderie amongst members of these cohorts, which, consistent with Baxter's culture, enhanced their collective sense of identity—with the firm and with their cohort as well. This way of hiring also enhanced the likelihood that people would socially compare themselves to one another, leading to a sense of what "should" happen; it thus enhanced the likelihood of managers seeking out and engaging in similar kinds of career experiences across a cohort. Scholars of organizational socialization would categorize this kind of cohort hiring as a "collective socialization tactic" that is bound to strengthen a "custodial view"—that is, a caretaker stance in which individuals basically accept the status quo and don't rock the boat.[18]

Additionally, formal and informal socialization practices involving developmental partnerships can also promote a "custodial view" and so strengthened Baxter as a breeding ground for career imprinting. One obvious way social reinforcement occurred was through the practice of hiring people into "assistant-to" positions in the company, so that people could learn from experience and from more senior managers. Neither Abbott, J&J, nor Merck adopted this practice in the same consistent fashion as did Baxter during the 1970s. This kind of socialization tactic enabled people to "learn the ropes" quickly and strengthened the possibility that people would pick up a common bundle of traits or approaches, such as capabilities and cognition associated with Baxter, the firm.

Another way social reinforcement occurred was through more informal social comparison and role-modeling behavior. In particular, peer mentoring was both prevalent and encouraged within Baxter, which also opened up opportunities for social reinforcement:

> I always felt that you could call up anybody anywhere in Baxter and ask for their help and expect to get it and you would get it. . . . I would be in Australia and I'd call somebody in Puerto Rico manufacturing because I had a problem, and they would help me. I remember one time we had a manufacturing issue, and I called up somebody; he wasn't in International, he was part of the U.S. Division, and he came out on a plane to help me. . . . If somebody called me up and said, "Hey, I've got a problem and I think you

can help me," it's like, "Well, of course, I have to help you, I want to help you."

One reason help-seeking may have been especially prevalent at Baxter is that human resources at Baxter was not a strategically central function, as was customary at other firms such as J&J and Merck during this era. Answers to important questions such as "Is this the right job for me?," lay with Baxter senior management. At Baxter, people were encouraged to seek out such counsel, both from seniors and from peers.

At the same time that these formal and informal socialization tactics enhanced collaboration, there was also a good deal of competition—particularly for the overseas positions, as Schmergel's account revealed. As a result, just like its organizational culture, Baxter's socialization tactics had a paradoxical nature. The following quote by a Baxter alumnus sums this up well:

> There was camaraderie; those guys were all good friends, but they were also very competitive. And they didn't have any hesitation in arraying all their numbers. You would see who was pulling down Europe, and there'd be a lot of commiseration, but in that commiseration, I think there was also a lot of sharing. We didn't have the term "best practice," but people would help each other out, and there'd be suggestions such as, "Why don't you go and talk to Brian Steer about what he's doing in Europe with his program?," and so there was an internal learning process that I think was driven through that team.

A final socialization tactic that can strengthen the extent of social reinforcement is the level of involvement and role-modeling by senior management. Executive actions, including the use of certain language and symbols, can provide strong cues to employees as to what the organization expects and values.[19] Visible actions and even shared perceptions of senior management actions can have a powerful effect on people's sense of what is important in an organization and so reinforce other forms of social control like organizational culture.

From entry into the organization through their first few years on the job, Baxter managers had the sense that "Mr. Graham" was the person behind the scenes charting their career paths. As Schmergel explained, he felt he had a personal relationship with Graham, even though Graham met infrequently with him. Even when Schmergel was tapped on the shoulder by Gantz or Loucks to make a career move, he still had the distinct impression that it was Graham who was orchestrating the changes. This was not a unique impression, by any means. As several interviewees explained, "Everyone felt they had a personal relationship with Graham." Graham was omnipresent at Baxter. One interviewee shared that there was a secret "war room" in the basement of Baxter headquarters in which Graham was "tracking" the career paths of the MBA hires. If you were not on Graham's radar screen, you wanted to be—in a positive way. The following story about an individual's early days in a new position as president of one of Baxter's small divisions highlights this intense focus on impressing Bill Graham:

> [Graham] threw a question at me and asked about a new product, which was the first new product this division had introduced in twenty years. He said, "What's the key? Tell me the manufacturing process." And this was a chemical business with lots of chemical interactions, and I didn't know the answer to that question. And you can bet the first thing I did when I went back was learn that. And believe it or not, and you will believe it, he asked me that question again—in a meeting. And, this time I had the answer down pat. So all of us were trying to impress Graham. We knew that that's what we needed to do. . . . So I went out as a president of the division and took a college chemistry course because I wanted to learn. . . . It's the kind of thing I think people did; they wanted to find a way to position themselves to do their job well.

In sum, strong organizational cultures can make an organizational environment ripe for career imprinting, whether that corporate culture be supportive or "up" or competitive or "out." In the case of Baxter, both the sense of collective identity as well as Baxter's extreme pressure to perform were evident, and strongly so. Even Baxter's performance orientation yielded bonds among these managers; phrases such as "boot camp" and "going through wars together" were used often to describe the commonality of their career experiences at Baxter. Baxter's culture was strong, capable of socially reinforcing the sense of shared experience among people and so the strength of Baxter's career imprint. We also begin to see how this particular kind of strong culture, this "up-or-out" culture and the kinds of responsibilities people at Baxter were given, fed into the kinds of capabilities that were developed—entrepreneurial capabilities that would prove useful later on in their careers.

In addition, socialization practices such as hiring in cohorts, matching people with developmental partners, encouraging peer mentoring, and high involvement by a strong CEO are likely to reinforce socially what people learn and, hence, the strength of an organization's career imprint. We saw these facets emerge from the case example of Baxter but recognize that many of these techniques were not pioneered by Baxter, nor were they necessarily unique to healthcare firms during this time. For example, both Roy Vagelos of Merck and James Burke of J&J were similarly known for being highly visible and engaged leaders. Certainly, other facets of organizational culture and socialization, such as J&J's strong corporate credo, can similarly enhance social reinforcement. Thus, firms have at their disposal a range of tactics that can be used to increase the degree to which people have a common set of experiences and so the strength of an organization's career imprint.

Stretch Opportunities

In addition to social reinforcement, the strength of an organization's career imprint is influenced by the types of jobs that people are offered. As we will see, data from the study of Baxter and other healthcare firms, as well as prior research, suggest that stretch opportunities affect the extent to which individuals are forced to learn new sets of capabilities, connections, confidence, and ways of thinking about the world. More specifically, the more job assignments challenge individuals in ways that they haven't been challenged before, the greater will be the strength of the career imprinting process.

At Baxter, many early career assignments stretched new hires beyond what they had done before. As one Baxter alumnus described:

> You had this sort of confidence that you could go out and make things happen. And it was not a matter of, "I'm only thirty-two, they don't really expect this much." It was, "I don't care how old I am; if I don't get this done, I'm out of here."

These kinds of opportunities forced individuals to learn on their feet. As this quote and the prior description of Baxter's performance-based culture suggest, they had no choice.

In psychology studies, for years, psychologists have tried to pin down a good list of basic human "needs" at work.[20] "Growth is one of them. Alderfer identified "growth needs" as including challenge and independence at work, personal involvement, using one's abilities to one's fullest, and feelings of self-esteem.[21] Here, the idea of stretch opportunities emphasizes the particular dimension of challenge— that is, going *beyond* what one has done or learned in the past. Organizations that offer this kind of growth opportunity allow for exploration beyond one's comfort zone. And, in that stretching, people are likely to pick up new capabilities, confidence, connections, and cognitions, making such assignments particularly conducive to career imprinting.

Similar to the psychology studies, management studies have often found a positive relationship between early job challenges and individual performance.[22] Indeed, management research has shown that "out-of-comfort-zone stretch targets" or stretch

assignments are positively associated with motivation and performance.[23] The assumption has been that when new employees join
an organization, they are unclear about their employers' expectations. In order to reduce this unpleasant anxiety associated with
standing at the edge of an institution, individuals fully engage in
their jobs and, if those jobs are challenging, acquire valuable new
skills.[24] By fully engaging and learning, people move from a stress-
ful "outsider" position to a more comfortable "insider" position and,
in the process, adopt the worldviews of the organization.[25]

Here, the rationale is that if an individual is engaged in a task
he or she already knows, from a prior work experience, for example, then earlier career imprints are likely to be invoked, making
the current organization's career imprint much weaker by comparison. Thus, stretch opportunities should be associated with strong
organizational career imprints.

To a great extent, whether or not an organization offers stretch
opportunities is determined by the organization's business situation
and how that situation—and the organization's response to it in
terms of strategy and structure—shapes what leaders *can* offer their
employees.[26] Here, we explore Baxter's business situation and
subsequent choices regarding strategy and structure with an eye
toward revealing insights about managers' opportunities to "stretch."

Organizational Strategy and Structure

Strategy. Throughout the Graham era, Baxter's competitive
strategy was dubbed the "Willie Keeler, hit 'em where they ain't"
strategy—a niche market strategy in which Baxter derived tremendous returns from identifying a focused market need and then serving that market with a vengeance.[27] As one Baxter alumnus
described Baxter's portfolio and approach, there were "no bedsheets
and bandages, which were commodities. There had to be a place
where there was substantial added value in the making and the
selling of a particular product."

Graham sought out markets in which he could enter with significant comparative advantage, price high, and then, once competitors entered (or reentered) the arena, he would lower manufacturing costs and adjust his prices to compete accordingly.[28] In the 1960s and 1970s, the biggest opportunity for implementing this strategy was overseas. As Dave Castaldi, one of Baxter's early hires recalls:

> Graham had a niche strategy: [he'd identify] a product opportunity that was going to emerge in the future, and then he'd try to shape those opportunities where changes in medicine could take place for the benefit of patients toward growth. . . . Graham positioned the company strategically in growth areas of the hospital-based business, and then executed well on that strategy. . . . Graham clearly had in his strategic vision the reality that many medical businesses are worldwide businesses, not just local geographic businesses. Therefore, he developed an international strategy before many other American companies did, and he started to put in place the infrastructure with people, the Gabe Schmergels and Henri Termeers.

This was also a time of relatively high inflation rates and, in 1973, when the MBA recruiting program was in full swing, it was also the time of the oil embargo. Baxter, like many firms during this time, was trying to squeeze its working capital. Therefore, some of the impetus behind Baxter's move beyond U.S. borders was to reduce corporate taxes and, where possible, to take advantage of favorable exchange rates.

In addition, beginning in the 1970s, dramatic changes were occurring in the U.S. hospital-supply business. Hospitals were facing increasing involvement in medical payments by the federal government,[29] increasing consumerism, and rising costs of complex equipment such that healthcare costs in 1974 were rising twice as fast as inflation (and hospitals were able to recover only approximately 85 percent of the increases).[30] Hospitals, Baxter's primary business customers, were seeking ways to generate revenues and to contain and/or reduce their own costs, placing pressure on their suppliers. Given the increasing constraints facing the health-care markets, there was a significant opportunity cost associated with Baxter's intense focus on growing markets: new product innovation.

From a management development perspective, these business and competitive issues shaped Baxter's internal opportunity structure. In particular, a central challenge for Baxter's business managers was to develop business markets for Baxter's products and core technology. Baxter's technological innovations had largely taken place prior to this time period such that during the 1970s Baxter's business focus turned to marketing, sales, and manufacturing. As one interviewee summarized, "The fifties were a dramatic time of positioning. The sixties were the beginnings of the blossoming of that. And the seventies were the fulfillment of it." Therefore, as a direct result of Baxter's organizational strategy, the people Graham hired in to professionalize the firm were given stretch assignments that entailed building markets for Baxter, particularly overseas. As Baxter alumnus Tim Wollaeger described:

> I'm thirty-two in Mexico, and I'm calling guys [and] it's like I'm call-ing up Don Rumsfeld, and saying, "Hey Don, it's Tim Wollaeger. I'm at Baxter; I'd like to come over and talk to you about the army con-tract for IV solutions." And then you go in and say, "OK, what do I need to do here to make this happen?"

Structure. In concert with an organization's strategy, an orga-nization's structure can also facilitate stretch opportunities by allowing for significant autonomy and responsibility—for example, with a decentralized organizational structure. The primary growth opportunity for Baxter's products was overseas. Since the health-care industry was, at that time, viewed as a locally driven business, Baxter managers who were sent abroad were essentially charged not only with expanding markets but also with creating them—and often from scratch. As one Baxter manager pointed out, "It was much more than growing markets; they were building businesses."

Further, with international differences in manufacturing regulation, employment laws, currency, and cultural expectations (regarding unions, for example), the overseas management experiences could be quite daunting. This key business challenge, launching Baxter products globally, began in full force when the first wave of MBAs were hired. Baxter's globalization strategy and the practice of sending U.S.-hired employees overseas was groundbreaking.

Baxter's direct competitor, Abbott, was not expanding its operations overseas in any similar fashion. Abbott, like J&J and Merck, had a marketing and sales presence overseas, but it was not common practice there to groom people for general management positions overseas. Consider Gabe Schmergel's recollection of his first general management assignment in Germany:

> Bill Graham saw an opportunity to take what was basically a U.S. business international, . . . but to do that we would have to set up our own sales companies abroad, and we'd have to set up our own overseas manufacturing. . . . So that was the vision, and it was really quite clear. At the time, it was very revolutionary in the hospital supply business. Today we accept being a global business. [Additionally, he saw that] "the way I [Graham] am going to do it is, I'm going to take my best people and put them into International. I'm going to take a group of young people and I'm going to train them. And I'm going to launch them out into the international market," which, again, was revolutionary.

As Schmergel's account suggests, an overseas assignment, particularly when one doesn't know the country's language, can be daunting. As some first-wave stories illustrated, this was often a near-break kind of assignment for Baxter managers. Stripped of their ability to communicate, people were required to learn such basic skills as language in order to get by. As recent research by Bennis and Thomas confirms, placement into a foreign territory can be a powerful crucible type of experience for individuals: "Leaders capture the disorientation and weave it into their own experiential tapestry."[31] Other management research similarly highlights that international assignments provide managers with high levels of novelty and uncertainty that stimulates experimentation, exploration, reflection, and, consequently, the acquisition of new skills, networks, and sense of self.[32] Here, Baxter's geographically decentralized organizational structure yielded significant stretch opportunities for its budding managers, and thus, the acquisition of new capabilities, connections, confidence, and cognition.

In addition to building new markets, Baxter's organizational structure offered stretch assignments that were associated with emerging federal guidelines for safe manufacturing practices. People like Carpenter and Chubb were placed on teams to completely reconfigure Baxter's plants—a definite stretch assignment for both of them. To put this into context, in the 1970s, one could see the very early stages of the movement toward Total Quality Management. At that time, quality manufacturing consisted of what the government called "good manufacturing practices" (GMPs). One first-wave pioneer described his assignment to a GMP task force in 1975 on his first day at Baxter—clearly a stretch assignment:

> The government at that time, the FDA, had just started promulgating good manufacturing practices. They had a series of proposed new rules. A small-volume parenterals plant manager said, "Those aren't rules yet. Those are proposals." And the FDA said, "Even though they're not rules, you've got to abide by them." We said, "No, we're not going to do it." They then sent a summons to Mr. Graham, and said, "Show up [knocks on table] in Washington D.C. on the first of July; we want to talk to you about the deficiencies in your plant in Hays, Kansas." And he and Vern Loucks and the other manufacturing guys flew on the company plane to Washington, and were told that they were going to go to jail if they

didn't get in compliance. They didn't want to go to jail. So they flew up and decided to appoint a task force and really get in line.

So Vern said to me, "I'm putting you on the quality control documentation team, because you know about computers, and documents, and systems. We've got a meeting at 6:00 this evening of the group." That evening, everybody's there—the whole corporate executive group, the division presidents, and this group of people that they had fingered out for the task force, the GMP task force, to bring Baxter's plants in compliance with these proposed GMPs. And there were four MBAs in the group. . . . And we had this meeting, which would've seemed to be a little bit like, in the army we used to call it a cluster-[expletive deleted], where you just wandered around not knowing what you're doing.

GMPs extended way back and way forward, you know, even into marketing—keeping track of your drugs all the way through. But mostly, manufacturing was the issue. They [senior management] had shut down Hayes, Kansas. Shut it down completely. And they were debating about what to do about the small-volume parenterals[33] business, whether to stay in it or go out of it. And then, eventually GMPs applied to everything. Hyland, the plasma fractionation plant, and devices where we made all the tubing for IV sets and the artificial organs, everything. But it started out in parenterals. So, they had shut down Hayes, Kansas, and talked about what to do next. The major plants were in Cleveland, Mississippi, North Cove, North Carolina, Mountain Home, Arkansas, and then all the plants in Puerto Rico. We had four plants in Puerto Rico. All making some kind of liquid-filled stuff. The major plants, the IV plants, were where the FDA was attacking.

To address these pressures from the FDA, Graham placed new-hires on task forces to overhaul plants, as illustrated above. Further, Graham decentralized the organization's operations. Unlike competitors such as Abbott, Baxter had many different plants inside and outside the United States. Beyond obvious benefits from a logistical and financial (tax basis) perspective, this provided the organization with an opportunity to cater to local regulations in international markets, rather than simply ship products overseas. From a developmental perspective, it meant that most everyone hired in under Graham received stretch opportunities that included line management positions.

In sum, the nature of Baxter's business and competitive landscape led to at least two central business issues for Baxter managers who joined in the 1960s and 1970s: growing business markets, particularly overseas, and upgrading the quality of their manufacturing practices. Bill Graham's response to these business challenges was to adopt a niche market strategy and to decentralize the organization's structure. Both of these choices of organizational strategy and structure affected the company's ability to offer stretch opportunities, one critical component to cultivating a strong organizational career imprint.

Of course, decentralized organizational structures or niche market strategies are not the only ways to offer stretch opportunities that can augment the career imprinting process. At Merck, for example, a company with a very different organizational structure and strategy, people were given stretch assignments early on that entailed significant responsibility in research development. During the late 1970s, for example, Roy Vagelos brought in hundreds of scientists, increased the R&D budget an average of 17.2 percent each year, upgraded the scientific labs, and created a managerial fast track for new scientists.[34] At Merck, during this time period, the organization was structured like an academic institution, with research as the primary function through which stretch assignments were doled out. As one person who worked for decades at Merck said, "Merck didn't operate like a business at all." So, in contrast to Baxter's strategy of building existing markets overseas, Merck's strategy was scientific innovation. In both instances, the organization's strategy and structure enabled employees to take on significant stretch opportunities that affected the strength of the career imprints that were cultivated at these firms. However, the nature of these opportunities was quite different, yielding, as we will discover in Chapters Five and Six, very different organizational career imprints.

Demonstrated Success

If people believe that the kinds of capabilities, connections, confidence, and cognition they have picked up at an organization actually "work" to produce favorable results, then they are more likely to adopt them and so the career imprint is likely to be stronger. Evidence of "demonstrated success" can occur at multiple levels—at the level of the individual and at the level of the firm. Both appear to have been at play at Baxter.

Recognition and Rewards

At the individual level, small wins provide individual employees with a taste of "success" that can be truly motivating. In her recent book, *Confidence*, Rosabeth Moss Kanter shows that creating conditions for confidence-building is critical to the winning streaks of institutions that range from high-school football teams to major U.S. companies.[35] Confidence creates a self-fueling cycle that, once started, attracts resources and investment from parties both internal to the firm (such as employees) as well as external to the firm (such as investors) that spins that cycle even faster. So too with career imprinting. People are more likely to invest in cultivating certain career imprints when they have confidence that the career imprint "works."

Yet, how can an up-or-out culture like Baxter's work to get such a positive streak of success spinning? Baxter's environment encouraged learning through stretch assignments; on the other hand, the spectre of evaluation, through the involvement and interrogation by the CEO, Bill Graham, was always hovering nearby. Social psychologists have long suggested that learning and evaluation do not mix. That is, if a person is trying to learn a new task and so is in a low self-efficacy position, then evaluating him or her on that learning task will not be effective. Not only might learning not occur, but performance may actually decline despite practice.[36] In contrast, when self-efficacy is high, individuals tend to perform especially well under conditions of evaluation;[37] individuals rise to the challenge because they have the capacity to engage their "best selves" in the task at hand.[38]

At Baxter, it appears that the sequencing of individuals' assignments may have been one reason that Baxter's breeding ground was able to support both conditions of learning and evaluation. The early career, project-based assignments that were characteristic of the "assistant-to" positions were quite effective in generating early wins (i.e., demonstrated success) that enabled the development of self-confidence. Then, later, when individuals were placed in general management positions that were filled with high expectations for high performance, as described, the evaluative aspect of Baxter's breeding ground was effective—even motivating—since these same managers had already built up a sufficient level of confidence in themselves to rise to the challenge. This self-fueling spiral led to the promotion of many people. For those just joining the company, such positive spirals and promotions provided evidence of success. Further, Baxter used these examples of demonstrated success to entice others to join the company. Consider the following account by a Baxter alumnus who used to recruit MBAs:

> We'd say, "OK, here's Gabe Schmergel. He got out of Harvard, and here's what he's doing. Here's Victor Chaltiel, he got out of Harvard Business School, here's what he's doing. Here's Dick Allen, he got out of Stanford Business School, here's what he's doing now. If you think you're that good—that you can handle that kind of responsibility at a young age—then come work at Baxter. And if you don't think you're that good, then don't bother us by interviewing."

That quote brings to light the parallel argument that those who don't succeed don't pick up the organizational career imprint as strongly, a premise that is addressed more fully in the next chapter on *people*. Here, looking at the data from an organizational perspective, we do see that this kind of system of bringing people in and promoting them early to general management positions often "worked" and so affected perceptions as well as behavior within the firm. As one interviewee put it, people aspired to follow in the footsteps of "the Gabe Schmergels and Henri Termeers of the world."

External Competition

In terms of the "demonstrated success" regarding the firm itself, the evidence is more obvious. By the time the first wave entered Baxter, the firm was well on its way to becoming a "Nifty Fifty" company—a company that had been recognized both internally and externally for having achieved phenomenal growth. People knew something was working at Baxter and, as Graham said, Baxter, like other healthcare companies during this time period, became "the place to be." The following two accounts were typical:

> It was a great place to work. Exciting! It was hard charging, you know, twenty-nine years at 20 percent compounded sales and earnings growth. I mean, how many people have got that kind of record, you know?

> This was an exciting company—the *20/20* years! Twenty percent growth in sales and earnings! A "Nifty Fifty" company!

Not only do these accounts demonstrate the motivation that stemmed from the company's success during that timeframe, they also provide a nice illustration of how people connected their own efforts to these performance results. As another alumnus explained:

> Graham set those metrics as targets. And everybody knew those were the targets, and so you better, by God, figure out how to make those targets. You know, either you hit it, or we'll let one of these other guys try. And everybody knew the rules.

Throughout, the references to *20/20* illustrate that the evaluative pressure that Graham typically placed on these managers forced them to focus on hitting their numbers—not just for the sake of their own careers but for the sake of Baxter, to maintain the firm's track record. The accountability was felt at the individual level, while the responsibility was experienced at the firm level. In addition, these accounts show how Baxter clearly tapped into these young managers' appetites for growth and opportunity. Words such as *exciting* were used often in conjunction with *20/20* to describe their career expectations at Baxter. Thus, while these individuals clearly experienced some anxiety associated with whether or not they would "make it," this career risk was also exhilarating for many MBA graduates; those who were not "up for the challenge" self-selected out of this highly charged environment early on—or were "selected" out.

In sum, both in terms of generating small wins during the early stages of their careers and in terms of the bigger picture of the company and its performance, Baxter's breeding ground appeared successful. Abbott, J&J, and Merck were similarly financially successful during this same time period and yet, at Baxter, this was not always the perception. At Baxter, the sense was that what they were learning "worked," relative to their competitors. Over and over again, interviewees spoke of the "mistakes" that Abbott had made—particularly in dealing with the FDA.[39] These comments reinforced the perception that Baxter's whole system—its strategy, structure, systems, and culture—"worked," relative to their competitors'. And, as the following story told by a Baxter alumnus demonstrates, it generated further momentum among employees to dig in even more deeply and to commit to Baxter and the kinds of things they were learning there:

> There was a vicious rivalry between Baxter and Abbott. Abbott had 55 or 60 percent of all the intravenous solution business and the pour bottled business. (Pour bottle is used when you hack somebody open and you want some sterile water to irrigate so you can see what's

there.) And it was all glass. Graham had bought Fenwal, which was the dominant blood collection company in the world because he wanted it. It was a blood business, and it was core to what he was doing. It's far more sensible to collect blood in a plastic bag rather than in a glass container because you don't have to displace the air. The bag just expands. But there was an ulterior purpose—and with Graham there always was—which was that if you could make bags for blood collection out of plastic, you could make them for intravenous solutions. And wouldn't that be much better, because if you have a drip going into someone, that fluid's being replaced by the air in the hospital room. And that's not good because there's a lot of sick people in hospitals—even if you filter it carefully. So he said, "Well, why not have a bag, and as the solution leaves then the bag collapses? And if you drop it, it won't break." So then Baxter goes into a hospital and says, "Look, this whole glass thing is stupid." And they said, "Excuse me?!" They didn't want to be told about replacing glass with plastic. They just did not want to hear it. And as remarkable as that sounds, no one would buy into plastic.

Abbott got into some manufacturing difficulties. There was a [Baxter] guy named John Kimbell who had come out of the Fenwal Division who had an instinct that the FDA was sniffing around at Abbott and that there was going to be a catastrophe. And so he just called down to the manufacturing plants that were making the plastic bags and said, "You run three shifts." And they said, "We don't have any place to put 'em! We've got six months inventory; we've got eight months inventory." Kimbell said, "Rent warehouses, I don't care if you have to put 'em on the roof; do it!" And one day the FDA called and said, "If we pulled Abbott out of the marketplace for pour bottles and intravenous solutions, could you fill the slack?" And so, suddenly, within one quarter, the market shifts for Baxter, which at the time probably had 20 percent, to suddenly having over half! And Abbott was out of the business for a couple of years. Abbott never forgave Baxter. Not that Baxter did anything illegal, but Abbott wasn't making plastic. And so, even when Abbott got back in the business, once the accounts had tried plastic, they would never go back to glass.

Now, unfortunately, some of the people that donate have hepatitis. So the FDA said every single donation has to be tested for hepatitis. Well, Baxter really didn't have an immunology diagnostics capability, and Abbott did. And so every single unit of blood that was collected using a Baxter bag had to be tested with an Abbott test. It drove Graham crazy. He was just so mad he could have spit about that for years. Baxter really wasn't good at diagnostics and didn't belong in the diagnostics business, but Graham bought Clinical Assays. First of all, he thought that Abbott was going to buy them, and so he way overpaid because he didn't want Abbott to rub his nose in it again. And the second strategy was, "Look, we don't want to be paying Abbott a nickel for anything, even if we have to; we'll pay anybody else for hepatitis testing."

As this story illustrates, not only was Abbott a formidable competitor of Baxter's during the 1970s, but the "war" between Baxter and Abbott also created an even more fertile ground for career imprinting. In this instance, Baxter had "won" the war, and stories like this only reinforced managers' collective experience of success. Indeed, research on great groups by Bennis shows how having a common enemy can help a group "rally and define itself (as everything the enemy is not)."[40] Here, although Baxter and Abbott were in close proximity of one another, with headquarters less than ten miles apart, there was rarely any cross-over hiring between them. As one interviewee explained, "Sometimes, the competition defines you."

Summary

Three factors associated with an organizational environment or "breeding ground" for managerial careers can be seen as amplifiers of organizational career imprints: social reinforcement, stretch opportunities, and demonstrated success.

In the first instance, social reinforcement amplifies career imprinting since it provides people with a greater sense of common or shared experience. Social reinforcement can be affected by organizational design choices such as the choice of organizational culture and socialization practices. At Baxter, the culture included both the feeling of a collective identity, consistent with the "organization man" perspective prevalent during this timeframe, as well as a competitive, sink-or-swim atmosphere. Baxter's socialization tactics embraced a similar paradox since individuals were hired in and paired with developmental partners—for example, when hired to work in assistant-to positions—at the same time that they competed with each other for coveted positions overseas and for "Mr. Graham's" attention. In both instances, the organizational socialization tactics and the culture were strong; beliefs and tactics were widely shared and thus socially reinforced the kinds of capabilities, connections, confidence, and worldviews that people were learning at Baxter.

The second dimension, stretch opportunities, forces individuals to expand beyond their comfort zone of what they have done in the past to take on challenging work assignments in organizations. The main reason this kind of opportunity amplifies a career imprint is that it provides a blank slate from which to start; since it is much more difficult to apply earlier career imprints in new and different situations, individuals are much more likely to pick up or cultivate their current employer's career imprint. They have no choice but to learn. The international assignments, in particular at Baxter, to go run a country, provided ample opportunities for individuals to engage in new and challenging experiences.

In contrast to social reinforcement, which can be driven by organizational design choices such as organizational culture and socialization, stretch opportunities are shaped by the organizational design choices of organizational strategy and structure that affect the opportunity structure within a firm. At Baxter, in response to the business competition, Bill Graham chose to adopt a niche market strategy and to expand geographically overseas.

This combination of decisions created many general management jobs that were well beyond anything the people Graham hired into the firm had experienced before and, indeed, stretched these young managers considerably.

Finally, demonstrated success amplifies career imprinting since it instills in individuals the sense that "this works," that the kinds of career paths followed produce desired outcomes. At Baxter, the culture and socialization tactics provided opportunities for early wins (on project-based assignments), generating momentum to help fuel a positive spiral of confidence and success in the company. Further, by using phrases such as 20/20 and by recounting stories of "wars" with their major competitor, Abbott, Baxter created energy around the firm's success that amplified the effects of career imprinting as well.

The flipside is that people who are not able to demonstrate success in their jobs, who are not given stretch opportunities, and/or who don't experience social reinforcement are less likely to cultivate a strong career imprint. People who self-selected out of Baxter's competitive environment early on, or who didn't prove themselves, not only left Baxter, but they did so before much imprinting could take place. This suggests that some minimal amount of time is required for career imprinting to occur, if the people and place are aligned.

It is also important to consider how strategy and structure, culture and socialization, and performance relate to one another. To the extent these factors reinforce one another, as was the case at Baxter, career imprinting is likely to be even stronger. For example, Baxter's socialization tactics of hiring people to work in assistant-to positions generally preceded their general management assignments, which allowed individuals to experience both the third factor—demonstrated success—and then, the first factor—stretch opportunities. This way, they could gather momentum, rather than become discouraged, when given challenging assignments. Therefore, sequencing these components so that they reinforce one another to create a self-fueling spiral can help cultivate a particularly strong organizational career imprint.

This kind of spiral is evident in Henri Termeer's account of his first night as general manager of Germany. The story is telling because it illustrates how someone received a major stretch assignment and felt the effects of social reinforcement and, ultimately, personal success, all of which worked together to create a positive spiral that fueled not just confidence, which Termeer remarks on, but also a certain set of capabilities, connections, and cognition that proved beneficial well beyond his career at Baxter. He had just returned on the weekend from a trip to Europe. That Monday morning Gabe Schmergel had asked him to take over Germany. As Termeer described, this was a "big step," one that he was very excited about. Like many other Baxter stories, Termeer flew out that same night he was tapped for the job. Just like Gabe's story, the presiding general manager was moved out the next day, the same day that Termeer stepped in. Termeer was twenty-nine years old. That first night on the job, Termeer recalls:

> I didn't eat. I drank some wine, and then . . . it hit me, "Here I'm going to run this; this is me." It was a magnificent feeling—[that] somehow, Gabe and Bill Gantz and others thought this was an acceptable risk, to send this young guy and to introduce him for an hour or two, leave, and then let him do it. And it worked. Of course, once it started to work, there's this great experience in terms of your confidence building, you start to think, "Yeah, this is actually OK. I am OK for this. I can do this. And it makes sense, what I'm doing here." That's the Baxter story.

Chapter Four

People: Characteristics and Susceptibility to Career Imprinting

If you scrutinize the real winners—Termeer,
Carpenter, Schmergel, Vincent, who all came from
great B-schools—what came first? The fact that all
these guys found themselves in B-school? Or the
fact that they spent a significant part of their career
at Abbott or Baxter? Certainly, the latter played a
role, but I believe the B-school thread pre-selected
a type of personality who, when given the
opportunity, was able to "step up."

—*Abbott alumnus*

I think they selected competitive, self-driven
individuals, gave them stretch targets and left them
alone.

—*Baxter alumnus*

As these quotations suggest, the process of career imprinting is as
dependent upon the people hired as it is on an organization's strategy, structure, systems, and culture. Even if a company provides
similar kinds of career experiences, certain personal characteristics
and backgrounds have a significant bearing on what an individual
ultimately picks up or learns at work. When thinking about the
career imprinting process, then, it is useful to ask, "What makes
some people more likely than others to pick up or cultivate an organizational career imprint?" Answering that general question is the
focus of this chapter.

Often, the temptation is to point broadly to personality differences to explain a particular career move, success, or failure. "Well, there was a personality fit problem" is a common statement under a variety of circumstances. This tendency is due to our own natural (but flawed) logic system. As the famous fundamental attribution error tells us, people tend to attribute explanations to dispositional factors (like personality) rather than to the particulars of the situation at hand. That is, rather than acknowledging the strength of a situation we find ourselves in, we often rely upon easily identifiable characteristics or behaviors that we can observe and access as explanations.[1]

So too might we simply say that Baxter hired people "who all had the same personality type" to explain why so many left Baxter for biotechnology and/or why they all developed a set of capabilities, connections, confidence, and cognition at Baxter that was different from what was cultivated elsewhere. But again, such a narrow focus on personality is misleading.

Prior research on managerial and leadership development shows that when situations are ambiguous or uncertain, they are ripe for social control; that is, people are likely to acquire the norms and values of a particular corporate culture in ambiguous or uncertain environments.[2] But consider this parallel proposition: when individuals are open and impressionable, they are similarly ripe or "developmentally ready" to cultivate an organization's career imprint. Therefore, just as organizations can employ strategies and tactics to influence employees' openness to organizational influence, as we saw in Chapter Three, so too can organizations select people at times in their lives when they are more impressionable and, hence, "open" to career imprinting.

In particular, two individual-level factors affect the strength of career imprinting: *developmental readiness* and *developmental fit*. Regarding developmental readiness, when people are younger, in early career stages, or in the midst of a transition from one phase of adult development to another, they are more impressionable and, hence, more likely to cultivate strongly an organization's career imprint. Regarding fit, individuals whose background and interests

Figure 4.1 People: Factors that Strengthen an Individual's Cultivation of an Organization's Career Imprint

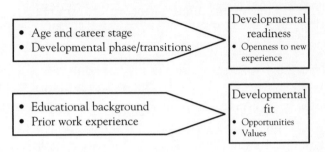

fit with the developmental opportunities a firm has to offer are more likely to cultivate strongly an organization's career imprint. Also regarding fit, when individuals' values are aligned with those of their employer, then career imprinting is likely to be stronger. The central idea here is that the more an organization hires individuals who are developmentally ready and who are a good fit with the kind of developmental environment the employer has created, the stronger the cultivation of an organization's career imprint. Developmental readiness and developmental fit are influenced by individual difference factors such as age and career stage, phase of adult development, including transitions, as well as prior education and work experience, as illustrated in Figure 4.1.

Consistent with the approach taken in the prior chapter on *place*, the two factors explored in this chapter on *people* are general conditions with respect to the creation of a strong career imprint. Further, although the examples come primarily from Baxter, the conditions are not specific to Baxter or healthcare, and the research cited to support the significance of these conditions comes from different contexts as well.

Developmental Readiness

Individuals who are particularly open to new experiences and information are developmentally ready to take in, try out, learn, and adopt the kinds of capabilities, connections, confidence, and worldviews of their employer. Some personality factors, such as "mindfulness," can contribute to an openness to new experiences. People who are more mindful are more open-minded to multiple perspectives and possibilities and so are likely more "ready" to adopt a company's career imprint.[3]

Additionally, at certain times in life, an adult tends to be more impressionable and so much more likely to be influenced by the mechanisms discussed in the prior chapter, such as a strong corporate culture, affecting the strength of career imprinting. Three factors are associated with the extent to which an individual is developmentally ready to take in and cultivate an organizational career imprint: age, career stage, and transition.

Age and Career Stage

Age is the most obvious factor. During young adulthood (mid-twenties), people search to find their place in the adult world, to find a link between what they are doing for themselves and how they will contribute to society.[4] During this time of search and trial, oftentimes, people will seek out help from others such as mentors, and will try to establish a life structure within an institution, such as an employer, in order to "make something of him [or her] self."[5] Since oftentimes there has been generally little life structure or sense of place in the adult world apart from the individual's family, this can be a vulnerable time for social influence—an impressionable time.

In the case of Baxter, managers tended to be hired in at a young age—in their mid-twenties and then moved on into general management positions within a couple of years. Schmergel, for example, was twenty-eight years old when he took over Germany. Therefore, by the time Graham's MBA hires were in their mid- to late-thirties, they had generally advanced to positions of significant responsibility within the organization. As Steve Chubb, one of the first-wave Baxter managers to leave Baxter for biotechnology commented:

The people who were running divisions at Bristol-Myers or Lilly were in their late forties, early fifties. And we were in our early thirties—[Baxter] guys running 20 to 30 percent of the company in their mid-thirties, or late thirties, which just didn't happen elsewhere.

This age difference is reflected in the numbers in the larger dataset of people who served on biotech IPO teams, after their careers at healthcare firms such as Baxter, J&J, Abbott, Merck, Bristol-Myers Squibb, and Eli Lilly. These data show that Baxter alumni were younger by the time they sat on biotech IPO teams; they were the only subset of the dataset with an average age *lower* than 47.5 years—and Baxter's average age was lower by about three years, at 44.5.[6]

Together, these qualitative and quantitative data regarding age suggest that

- First, Baxter hired in people at an early age, which affected how easily the company could influence their leadership development and the career imprinting process.
- Second, relative to other healthcare companies that spawned similarly powerful alumni, the rate of advancement to management at Baxter was faster, affecting the developmental significance of receiving managerial stretch assignments. As Richard Douglas, senior vice president of Corporate Development at Genzyme, who has worked for five Baxter managers, reflected, such extreme fast-tracking was unusual in business at that time:

Baxter brought in very, very bright, very talented, very motivated and committed people into the organization right out of business school, and at a time in Baxter's history where they basically could soak up all the management talent they possibly could need and give them what was, for the relative amount of experience these people had, an extraordinary amount of responsibility early on. So, what you saw was career development and career paths in the first three or four years that were extraordinarily rapid rising to places and positions of authority that were certainly unusual as far as rate of advancement.

This rate of advancement made the Baxter career imprint that much stronger. These individuals were ready for challenge, and, as the previous chapter detailed, they were given it. This synchronization created a self-fueling cycle that led to a stronger imprinting process since, once given responsibility coupled with high expectations from senior managers, most of these young managers became eager for more:

Baxter was going to give responsibility at an earlier age, and give a lot of responsibility. Sink or swim. [Either] you performed or you were out. But you were given that responsibility at a very young age. Sink or swim. And it was given to a lot of people, so it was "go and do it. . . . Just go and do it." So it really gave you the opportunity to perform at a young age.

• Third, if and when other firms also hired people at young ages, they also had the possibility for cultivating strong career imprints; however, those imprints would likely be quite different. For example, at Baxter, people learned how to take on general management responsibilities at an early age; at Abbott, people learned how to take on sales responsibilities at a relatively early age. Since there were only four division-head positions at Abbott, however, general management capabilities could not possibly emerge as a core aspect of Abbott's career imprint. (The content of these other companies' career imprints, as mentioned earlier, will be explored in greater depth in Chapter Six.)

Career stage is also a relevant factor to consider with respect to the strength of career imprinting. Career stage correlates with age. As with early stages of adult development, those who are in early stages of their career tend to adopt a proving mentality such that stretch opportunities are particularly desirable, whatever those opportunities may be. Career studies have found that early career stages are most often associated with periods of trial and early establishment[7] and that early on in their careers, people often seek out information and identification through and with others at work.[8] Thus, those at early career stages are likely to be more easily influenced by factors associated with social reinforcement, such as informal peer mentoring.

Additionally, since at early career stages, individuals have less prior work experience to rely upon, they are simply more likely to be vulnerable or open to career imprinting. This logic squares with research on career development that focuses on how individuals strive to reduce anxiety associated with a new job.[9] Just as newcomers to organizations are often anxious about fitting in, so too are people early in their careers concerned with filling that portion of their life space with something that feels comfortable. They are thus more apt to cultivate strongly an organization's career imprint during early career. This is not to say that people in later career stages aren't susceptible to career imprinting; it is just that earlier on in an individual's life and career, a person is particularly receptive to social cues from his or her organizational environment.[10]

Finally, the opportunity to imprint is also greater early on in career stages simply because little "un-doing" of prior experience is necessary. For Graham's new-hires, Baxter was often either a first or second employer; these managers were at early stages in their careers and so were still in the exploration stages of career development. Such exploration made them much more open to new opportunities and, in many respects then, vulnerable to career imprinting. As Ray Oddi, who was Graham's assistant for decades and very involved in recruiting for Baxter, explained, "They were all ambitious young men who were interested in moving ahead."

Transitions

In addition to age and career stage, career transitions and/or transitions between stages in adult development can be poignant opportunities for career imprinting. Regarding career transitions, management scholars have looked at the ways in which sequential career moves, from one work role to another, entail both psychological and physical transitions.[11] Scholars have examined how career transitions may be almost entirely subjective, such as when individuals maintain their work roles but simply change their orientations to such roles.[12] Scholars have also examined career transitions that are both objective and subjective in kind—that is, entail both a change in work role and organization as well as the belief that change has occurred.[13] All of these kinds of career change open up opportunities for self-reflection, personal development, and learning,[14] and so can strengthen career imprinting.

Many different models of adult development could illustrate the significance of times of transition for career imprinting. Here, Kegan's model of adult development underscores the kinds of transitions that people hired into Baxter were experiencing. Kegan's model is particularly attractive since, unlike some other theories of adult development, it pays as much attention to transitions as it does to "stages" or "phases"; indeed, Kegan prefers the word *balance* over words such as *stage* to indicate the perpetual motion of life.[15]

According to Kegan, there are three "systems of meaning" in adulthood—the interpersonal, the institutional, and the postinstitutional balance. The first two are most relevant for our purposes here. During the interpersonal balance, an individual defines him or herself very much in the interests of significant others; "one's self-definitions, purposes, and preoccupying concerns are essentially codefined, codetermined, and coexperienced."[16] During the institutional balance, an individual develops a more independent sense of self; he or she becomes "more self-authoring, self-owning, self-dependent, more autonomous."[17]

Although Kegan, like most contemporary adult development theorists, claims that age and stage of adult development are not necessarily related, most agree that they are correlated. Young adults (i.e., in their twenties and thirties) tend to be in the interpersonal balance and/or are moving toward the institutional balance. This appears to have been the case at Baxter.

Most all of the Baxter interviewees used words like *mentoring, partnerships,* and *friends* to describe their transition from business school into Baxter and also to describe how they made career decisions within Baxter. These were decisions that were heavily influenced by the behaviors, advice, and perceptions of important others in their lives, reflecting the interpersonal balance. In particular, their recruiting stories about how former classmates lured them into Baxter's general management program suggest a strong identification with important others. For example, Gabe Schmergel described how Wally, a friend from Harvard Business School who was a relatively new hire at Baxter, strongly influenced his decision to contact Baxter, even after the company had already come to campus to recruit.

The way in which these young managers viewed their company provides even more evidence to support the idea that most of these Baxter managers were evolving—quickly—toward the institutional balance. In the institutional phase of adult development, individuals want to feel part of a *larger* system and are eager to defend that system. This system could be a company, a religion, a family, or a nation. During this phase of adult development, individuals strongly identify with the roles and duties associated with a larger institutional system.

In the present context, Baxter was "the larger system." Baxter represented an ideology, one that those in the general management track learned to cultivate and even defend. Across all of the interviews, individuals conveyed very strong identification with their former roles and duties at Baxter. Graham encapsulated these roles and duties. He was the role-model for "the Baxter way," and the people he hired into the general management track identified strongly with the example he set.

Other major healthcare firms, such as J&J and Merck, cultivated similar sorts of total institutional leaders. James Burke at J&J, for example, role-modeled the "J&J way" based upon J&J's famous credo. Like Baxter, people hired into J&J came to identify strongly with and even defend their company's norms and values. Still, given the relatively early age at which Baxter moved people into management, they were likely at an even more vulnerable transition stage in their adult development than their peers at other companies.

Interviews provided three types of evidence of this movement toward the institutional balance. First, Baxter alumni accounts reflected a kind of tunnel vision when it came to their Baxter experience. For example, they often found it difficult to name contemporaries in healthcare firms other than Baxter. This is significant because in "glamour industries" such as healthcare, executives tend to keep an eye on who's moving where, when, and why. The same is true of business school alumni; after graduation, many individuals keep track, at least informally, of their fellow classmates. Yet when the Baxter Boys were asked whether they knew people at Lilly, J&J, Abbott, or Merck that they would consider "peers" during that time period, they generally could not supply names. They were similarly unaware of the organizational structure or systems at other healthcare firms—even Abbott, with whom they competed most directly—and they had astonishing little knowledge of such practices. "I really only know what went on at Baxter," was a common response. More directly, several interviewees described Baxter as "the world."

In contrast, the amount of detail with which they could recount the experiences of their peers *within* Baxter was astonishing—dates, positions, and geography and all in relation to one another were revealed with impressive clarity and accuracy. In an extreme instance of identification with Baxter, one interviewee slipped, early on in our conversation, and proceeded to call his current organization (of more than ten years) "Baxter" for the remainder of the meeting. Abbot alumni, interviews revealed, were far more familiar with Baxter's organizational culture, structure, and practices than Baxter alumni were of Abbott's.

A second manifestation of their progression toward the institutional phase of adult development was the use of phrases such as "life beyond Baxter," which were often used to describe their transitions out of Baxter. Stories revolved around people trying to extract their friends from Baxter, to release them from their myopic view of what they could do with their careers. Phrases such as "I couldn't imagine anything else" were commonplace.

Finally, there was some evidence of the extreme form of the institutional balance during my fieldwork. As an individual moves into the institutional balance, significant others who were once central to the very definition of one's identity in the interpersonal system tend to be placed into supporting roles. Consequently, one downside of being fully engaged in the institutional balance is that significant others often play second fiddle to the priorities associated with building the institution.

This was a common theme in the career accounts; evidently high levels of organizational commitment were expected at Baxter. Their stories, such as Schmergel's account of jumping "on a plane with my wife and infant son" after a day's notice of his international assignment, were commonplace. And only later, once removed from the Baxter environment, was this extreme loyalty questioned or criticized:

> Unless you were having a baby, you went along. . . . But it just didn't make sense! You weren't being paid, . . . and the options were peanuts. . . . This wasn't a start-up! But the loyalty was part of the structure, part of what Graham built.

Back then, being tapped on the shoulder on a Friday to take on a new general management position overseas and moving one's entire young family that very weekend was not uncommon. There were multiple instances in which an individual recalled leaving town (or country) immediately after receiving the nod to go take on a new role and *then*, either en route or *after* arriving in the new location, telling his family about the decision. Even extreme cases in which lives were endangered did not dissuade young Baxter managers from staying on the front line. For example, one

Baxter alumnus recalled the hardships he and his wife went through just trying to set up shop in a new country:

> One day, my wife is sleeping and people are trying to go through the shutters. They are cutting with the scissors—an electric saw—to come into our apartment. . . . So she screamed to the neighbors so that they could do something! Another time, she was thrown on the pavement in the market. . . . Nobody would do anything! They wanted her bag, and we were expecting our second child. It was unreal. And it was a country of contrasts. She was thrown to the pavement in front of the Church where every morning, the head of the communist party was bringing his wife to the Church with a chauffeur. It was a great period. But so, it was, nothing is impossible.

Baxter spouses and other significant friends and family members also related similar stories. After one interview with a former Baxter manager, I was kindly stopped as I was walking out the door and invited back in by the interviewee's wife. She introduced me to their dog, told stories about their grandchildren, and showed me some photographs—addressing areas that the interviewee and I had *not* talked about during the previous two hours. One of her comments was particularly memorable: she told me that her husband had been traveling so much that their daughter, who was five years old at the time, used to point up to the sky whenever a plane flew overhead and remark, "That's where Daddy lives." As I walked out the door for the final good bye, I was reminded to "remember what's important in life."

Although this family seemed perfectly content at the time of the interview, many years after Baxter, it would be misleading to omit this account of what life *had* been like many years earlier. The recollection illustrates, quite easily, the very common tendency for those in the institutional balance to shift the focus—in an extreme sense—toward the building of the institution. And, whether or not one argues that "of course, some kind of sacrifice is inevitable when it comes to work, family, and high-powered careers," these descriptions still fit well with that vulnerable period of transitioning toward an institutional balance.

During transitions in adult development and, in particular, during this kind of transition when individuals are beginning to build their own professional identities, imprinting is particularly likely to occur. These are precious moments in time when companies have the opportunity to exert tremendous influence on an individual's professional development.

Developmental Fit

The general notion of fit or congruence has been central to the study of organizational behavior for decades.[18] A substantial stream of organizational research has examined the particular fit relationship between person and environment as it relates to job satisfaction and performance.[19] Career research has shown that people seek out and select work environments where there is a good fit between their career interests and the career opportunities available; when there is a good match between interests and opportunities, people tend to be more satisfied in their career, and when there is not a good match, people tend to leave.[20] More recently, scholars in the field of organizational behavior have demonstrated that in addition to "interests," individuals whose "values" match the organization's culture are more likely to be committed as well as productive employees of the organization.[21]

Here, the focus is on what is called "developmental fit." The simple proposition is that career imprinting is particularly likely to be strong when there is a good developmental match between the individuals hired and the organization's developmental environment. Data from the present study along with research on leader development suggest that developmental fit can occur in at least two ways: (a) when the organization's career opportunities match employees' developmental needs and interests, and (b) when the organization's values match those of the employees hired. In both cases, the better the fit, the stronger the organizational career imprint.

Fit with Opportunities

In what ways can stretch opportunities provided by a company align with the developmental needs and interests of the people who are hired to fulfill those opportunities? At Baxter, managers were given two kinds of stretch opportunities: general management challenges, which included bottom-line, profit-and-loss responsibility, and process-improvement challenges, which involved fixing manufacturing problems. Looking at the educational backgrounds of these Baxter managers, relative to people at comparable organizations at the time, reveals that there was a good fit here between the particular kinds of people Baxter hired and Baxter, the place, from a developmental perspective. As we'll also see, at other firms such as Abbott, there was also a good opportunity match—however, that match was different in kind, yielding a different kind of career imprint.

Educational Background

Business. Looking across the 3,200 people who eventually took biotechnology companies public between 1979 and 1996 reveals that alumni of Baxter reported having an MBA more often than alumni of other top-spawning healthcare firms, including Abbott, Bristol-Myers Squibb, Johnson & Johnson, Lilly, and Merck. And, although there wasn't a statistically significant difference amongst these focal companies in terms of the proportions reporting executives with MBA degrees, Baxter was by far the most overrepresented company in that area.[22]

In terms of doctoral degrees, these same six companies differed significantly. Further, Baxter was the most drastically *under*-represented in alumni with Ph.D.s of all six aforementioned healthcare/pharmaceutical companies. Baxter alumni reported having a Ph.D. half as often in the final prospectuses of biotech firms they took public than did alumni from other firms; only 16 percent of the eighty-one Baxter alumni reported having received a Ph.D. of any kind. Thus, compared to other firms that generated biotechnology executives, Baxter spawned significantly fewer people with advanced scientific or medical degrees and relatively more MBAs.

The fit between the MBA backgrounds of most of the people Graham hired and the express intent of Baxter's general management track can be described as a good example of what career theorists would call "complementary congruence"—where an individual's skills and talents match the needs of the organization at the time.[23] As discussed in the prior chapter, Baxter was growing at a phenomenal pace and was organizationally designed to enable many people to gain early general management experience. As some of the interviewees described, Baxter provided them with opportunities to essentially try out the lessons they had learned at business school. Phil Laughlin, who spent over eight years running countries overseas, explained, "All of our cases at business school were about, 'What should the general manager do?!' Now, we had a chance to take on that role."

In contrast, other firms that competed with Baxter, such as Abbott, initiated an MBA recruiting program much later, if at all. In the case of Abbott, an MBA recruiting program was not formally put in place until the mid- to late-1970s, and when Abbott did begin to recruit MBAs formally, it hired them primarily for sales positions. Not surprisingly, then, people who left Baxter for biotech were far more likely to have an MBA than those who made similar kinds of moves from Abbott. It is worth noting that there are important exceptions to this trend, however, such as Jim Vincent, a Wharton graduate who eventually ran Biogen after leaving Abbott, and Jack Schuler, a Stanford Business School graduate who became president and COO of Abbott and later joined the board of Medtronic in 1990. Further, Abbott often hired from the military during this timeframe. As an ex-salesman from Abbott who did earn his MBA (at night, while working at Abbott) recalled:

> At Abbott . . . they realized they couldn't get a lot of MBAs, so what
> they did was they hired JMOs, who were, in their mind, the next

best thing—junior military officers. . . . These guys were talented hard-working aggressive soldiers. And the emphasis is on *soldiers* 'cause if you told them to do something, boy they could get it done. But if you asked them to, "OK, now be creative and run a business," they'd look at you and stare. They needed orders.

These Baxter and Abbott accounts clearly show that different recruiting strategies were used to match the different needs these two companies had during this same time period. Linking these accounts back to the larger data set reveals that these different forms of congruence between people and place ultimately affected the kinds of career paths people experienced and so the career imprints that were cultivated at these different firms. Again, the point to emphasize is that in both the Baxter and Abbott cases, career imprints were strongly cultivated. However, given differences in terms of both people and place, *what* was cultivated, in terms of career imprints, was different, as we'll discuss shortly in the next chapters.

Engineering. All of the first wave of Baxter managers had earned degrees in the hard sciences—in engineering (mechanical engineering, most often) or in physics. Moreover, influential second-wave executives such as Tobin had an affinity for the hard sciences as well: as he claimed, "I would have been an engineer if I'd gone anywhere but Harvard." And, Castaldi, who is sometimes thought of as being among the first wave even though he left Baxter in 1986, worked for a family business in precision mechanical spring-making prior to Baxter, which gave him hands-on exposure to engineering problems.

Although at first glance, engineering may seem unrelated to healthcare and so an unlikely pattern to find, in other respects the pattern made perfect sense—it was related to Baxter's business, which, as interviewees stressed, was "basically medical devices, plastics!" During the 1960s and 1970s, following Baxter's major product innovations, as described in the previous chapter, one of Baxter's key challenges was manufacturing—improving efficiency and quality control at its plants. Therefore, not surprisingly, many people, like Carpenter, who came in with engineering backgrounds were given early high-profile project assignments that entailed "fixing" some aspect of Baxter's operations.

Additionally, having an engineering background fit well with the culture of Baxter. As Baxter alumni explained, this was "not a discovery research culture" and so was quite unlike many pharmaceutical companies, such as Merck, at that time. At Merck, by comparison, having a Ph.D. in chemistry would have fit well with the stretch opportunities presented. At Baxter, the scientific mentality was to focus on *applied* problems in the hospital supply industry—not basic research challenges. The key issue was patient usage of Baxter's products, and the orientation toward understanding the needs of the end user was emphasized throughout the company. Therefore, the engineering mentality fit well with Baxter's business and strategy in healthcare.

Fit with Values

The extent to which an individual's values fit with those of an organization can also affect the career imprinting process. The more these values and beliefs systems are aligned or egosyntonic (value congruent), the greater the strength of career imprinting.[24] If the individual's beliefs and values are egodystonic (i.e., not value congruent) with those of the organization, then the career imprinting process is likely to be weaker.

Prior Work Experience

Military. One kind of background experience that can have a profound effect on one's beliefs and values is serving in the military.[25] Not surprisingly, given the time period in which these managers began their adult lives, half of the "first wave" held officer-level positions in the Navy or Army prior to coming to Baxter. Additionally, several Baxter alumni who have been influential in the biotechnology industry but who left later during the second wave, also had prior military experience; for example, Jim Tobin served in the Navy and Bill Gantz served in the Marine Corps Reserves.

In several respects, the beliefs and values that stemmed from the military fit well with both Baxter's stretch assignments and performance-based culture. Further, because of the time spent earning their MBA degrees, new hires at Baxter felt even more "behind" coming out of Vietnam than those at other firms (e.g., Abbott). Many veterans felt that they had been "delayed" and so experienced a sense of "delayed gratification in getting this next job at Baxter." These MBA military veterans were ready for action and, fortunately for both Baxter and these new hires, that was exactly the kind of job Baxter had waiting for them. Baxter had plenty of high-responsibility, high-accountability, line-management jobs during the late 1960s and 1970s. And, for those who did not have that action mentality, Baxter was not a good fit:

> You were expected to be reasonably self-sufficient, and to go for it, and to find solutions, and to build alliances and network, and the real issue was, get it done. You know, don't come back and tell us why you can't do it. You've got to try to find a way to get this done. . . . To try something and not really to succeed perfectly is much better than to sit around and not do it. That was a very clear message.

This up-or-out nature of Baxter's merit-based promotion system was suitable to these individuals who had served in the military. Proving oneself was a reward system they were accustomed to. Two different alumni naturally commented on this aspect of fit:

> That was Graham's program. You knew it was a meritocracy but with a very high threshold of being able to stick around. It was like an accelerated military experience, with promotion-or-get-out kind of thing. That's what happened.

> I remember my Navy background of "the captain is responsible for the ship; if the ship runs aground it doesn't matter whose fault it is; you were the captain." I always had that attitude at Baxter: "If I'm

running this operation and it doesn't perform, I don't care. It doesn't matter whose fault it really is; I'm the boss and I'm accountable." . . . That was the culture.

Finally, in many instances, their prior military experience affected their worldviews. This too seemed to align with Baxter values. As Gabe Schmergel put it, they wanted to "do important things for the world and still make money at it." Although Schmergel did not serve in Vietnam, he had personally experienced a revolution in Hungary and so shared a similar orientation with those who had. As one Baxter Vietnam veteran explained, it was important to join "a company with outstanding performance and a high-growth culture and environment. One that was socially valuable—to save lives," particularly since many Vietnam veterans were being treated with disrespect. As he recalled, this probably played a role in his career decision making out of business school—his decision *not* to pursue opportunities with companies such as Procter & Gamble, Coca-Cola, or Ford, all of which were major recruiters but were in businesses that were less socially appealing, in his eyes. Further, their bias toward "action" and desire for "real work" meant that popular jobs, such as consulting, were not often seriously considered. Indeed, only two interviewees even reported considering working for a consulting firm prior to joining Baxter.

In sum, the military experience of many of these Baxter general managers clearly fit with Baxter's values of meritocracy and saving lives. Moreover, consistent with the previous theme of complementary congruence, their MBA backgrounds and interest in finding a "fast-track" job where they could prove themselves fit nicely with Baxter's performance-based culture.

At other companies, different kinds of values matches were encouraged. At Merck, which hired rising stars in science, employees were given stretch opportunities that fed their high needs for scientific achievement. As several interviewees who worked for Merck during this time period described, Merck was "just like a university campus!" Ph.D.s were often called "Doctor," and Roy

Vagelos, CEO of Merck during this time period, often sported a white lab coat in the office. Different companies: different kinds of values matches, and, as we will see in subsequent chapters, very different organizational career imprints.

Evolving Match: People and Place

Finally, and perhaps most important of all, organizational career imprints are particularly likely to be strongly cultivated when employers choose people and offer opportunities that fit not just for the time of hire, but over time—that is, there is an evolving fit between people and place. This creates a tightly wound system.

The first part of this chapter described how people who are young, in an early career stage, and/or in a period of transition in their adult development tend to be more open to new experiences, strengthening the career imprinting process. Individuals are vulnerable during such times and therefore highly impressionable. Additionally, hiring people whose developmental needs and interests match the kinds of opportunities and values a company espouses can enhance the strength of career imprinting. Pulling these two themes together, we can see how a company that does both—hires people who are at vulnerable times of transition in their own adult development and addresses the developmental needs of both sides of a developmental transition—can, over time, provide an especially strong context for career imprinting.

What is particularly interesting about the Baxter situation is that the kinds of opportunities that were offered as well as the kinds of social reinforcement tactics that were employed met individuals' needs for both sides of their developmental bridge—as they crossed over from the interpersonal to institutional balance of adult development. For example, Baxter's hiring practice of putting people in either "assistant-to" positions or on group task forces early on met their needs for developing close helping relationships with important others. Further, as assignments changed, Baxter's developmental environment grew with them. That is, as people were moving toward the institutional balance, Baxter's stretch assignments—the general management positions, whether running a division or working overseas—capitalized on their needs for a more autonomous, independent sense of self. Other companies at the time, such as Abbott or J&J, didn't allow for both sets of needs to be fulfilled since they didn't hire in cohorts and individuals were not given that sense of autonomy and independence that comes with high-level jobs such as running a division until much, much later (if at all) in their careers.

Summary

The people hired into an organization and, moreover, the match between the *people* hired and the *place*, from a developmental perspective, can have a huge effect on the strength of the cultivation of an organization's career imprint. Two factors can strengthen the career imprinting process, in addition to the factors associated with place described in the prior chapter: the *developmental readiness* of the individuals hired and the *developmental fit* between people and place. With respect to developmental readiness, people tend to be more open to new career experiences and, hence, career imprinting when they are younger, at an earlier career stage, and during particularly formative times of transition in their adult development.

With respect to developmental fit, two kinds of fit are important to consider: fit with the opportunities provided by the firm and fit with the firm's values. Regarding the first kind of fit, the more that the stretch opportunities a firm provides fit with the developmental needs and interests of those hired, the stronger the organization's career imprint. This is not the same as saying that the opportunities a firm offers should exactly duplicate what someone has done before; clearly, that would not amplify the conditions for career imprinting since the assignments would not provide a "stretch" or significant challenge. Rather, certain developmental needs and interests, such as an action orientation born out of an MBA experience, can be more aligned with the kinds of developmental challenges and opportunities a firm has to offer. Similarly, as the Baxter stories also suggest, background factors such as prior military experience can also influence individuals' values and may be more or less aligned with those of an organization, affecting developmental fit as well.

Finally, one reason that Baxter, like many firms that hire people during their mid-twenties, was able to exert such influence was that it hired people during a "critical period" for learning in their adult lives. Just as linguists have long suggested that there are windows for learning foreign languages,[26] there are windows of opportunity for career imprinting. Here, shifting from the interpersonal to the institutional balance in one's adult development opens up a window for learning. At such times, individuals are more likely to pick up the career imprint of a company, particularly a strong-cultured company. Here, it appears that Baxter provided a developmental environment that met such evolving needs—in this case, needs for building close relationships as well as needs for letting go and establishing independence and autonomy. This suggests that not only was Baxter able to take advantage of the managerial talent it hired, but catching people during this transitional phase and providing a culture that supports that transition may have placed individuals in an even more precious window for development, thus making the strength of career imprinting even greater.

Chapter Five

Paths: The Baxter Career Experience and Resulting Career Imprint

Armed with an understanding of the elements of people and place that affect the career imprinting process, it is now possible to explore in more depth how these elements come together to produce a particular career imprint. Identifying an organization's career imprint during any given period of time entails looking across individuals' career experiences within an organization during that period to discern patterns in the kinds of capabilities, connections, confidence, and cognition that were cultivated there. In the present context, the questions, then, are, "What were the specific capabilities, connections, confidence, and cognition that individuals cultivated at Baxter during the 1970s?" and "How, if at all, did Baxter's career imprint differ from imprints of other healthcare companies during this time period?" This chapter is devoted to identifying and exploring Baxter's career imprint; Chapter Six will compare that imprint with the imprints of other healthcare firms during that same time period.

There are many different approaches to studying career paths, ranging in discipline orientation from psychology, sociology, anthropology, and labor economics, to interdisciplinary fields such as organizational behavior.[1] Over the years and across these disciplines, there have also been many different ways to conceptualize *career*, with definitions ranging from associations with particular occupations or professions, to work roles across an individual's lifetime.[2] Here, since the focus is on organizational career imprints, a more narrow organizational behavior definition of a career—"the evolving sequence of a person's work experiences over time"[3]—is warranted to look at the sequence of a person's work experiences within a particular organization.

Additionally, since organizational career imprinting is an interindividual phenomenon, the primary focus of this analysis must be on patterns *across* individuals' career experiences, rather than within any one particular individual's career progression.

Finally, this analysis calls for an understanding of individuals' career experiences from two sides: first, from the perspective of the kinds of jobs and positions held, similar to a résumé; and second, from the perspective of how people *experienced* these jobs within the firm. Career scholars have long suggested that careers are not simply the objective or easily identified positions and salary levels associated with one's worklife; careers are also internally determined by the sense we make of that sequence of experiences.[4] Put another way, it is important to consider both "objective" and "subjective" career patterns in order to identify a career imprint. Both are important in the consideration of career paths and, here, in understanding the career imprint of Baxter. (See Appendix A for details on the interview protocol used during the career history interviews.)

Objective Career Patterns: Jobs Held at Baxter

To cull out patterns in the career paths of individuals who were hired into Baxter under Graham, the interview data were deconstructed into timelines. Individuals' career histories were summarized in a format similar to that of a résumé, one sheet per interviewee, so that dates and positions could be easily identified and compared. Table 5.1 provides one such example, the career path of Gabe Schmergel. In cases where individuals had résumés, these data were used to verify dates given during the interviews. Additionally, follow-up conversations and secondary sources (e.g., Dun & Bradstreet reports) were used to confirm prior information. Then, patterns in timing and jobs held were compared across Baxter alumni.

Table 5.1 Summary of Gabe Schmergel's Career Path

Name:	Gabe Schmergel
Education:	BS in mechanical engineering, Rensselaer Polytechnic Institute, 1962. MBA, Harvard Business School (HBS), 1967 (Baker Scholar).
Pre-Baxter:	Mechanical engineer in power plant design, New York City, 1962–1963. U.S. Army, 1963–1965.
Post-Baxter:	CEO at Genetics Institute, 1981–1997.
	Chairman at Syntonix, 1999–present. Board affiliations post-Baxter: PerkinElmer, IDEXX, Tufts Veterinary School, Common Angels, NE Medical Center, Visiting Committee at HBS, Boston Ballet.

Year	Position/Event
1967 →	Starts at Baxter, assistant to the president of the International Division.
1968	
1969 →	Becomes general manager of German sales subsidiary.
1970	
1971 →	Becomes general manager of Belgian manufacturing/sales subsidiary; retains Germany.
1972	
1973	
1974 →	Returns to Baxter headquarters as area director, a mixed staff/line position.
1975 →	Becomes vice president of Europe, located in Brussels.
1976	
1977	
1978	
1979 →	Becomes president of Baxter's International Division, located in Deerfield, IL.
1980	
1981 →	Leaves Baxter. Becomes president and CEO of start-up, Genetics Institute.
⋮	
1997 →	GI purchased by American Home Products. Schmergel leaves.
1998 →	Joins board of directors at Syntonix.
1999 →	Becomes chairman at Syntonix.

The data suggest that the following general management career path was typical at Baxter during the 1970s: first, upon joining Baxter, an aspiring manager would take on the role of either (a) assistant-to a senior executive within Baxter or (b) consultant within the marketing or finance internal consulting groups. In either case, the person would work on project-based assignments around the firm for one to two years.[5] Second, that person would move out into a general management position, oftentimes overseas for one to two years. Third, he (again, these were, almost without exception, men) would round out the "Baxter education" by changing management roles within the company, often moving laterally to a job that entailed a different general management challenge (e.g., an operations position rather than a marketing position, for example). The individual would repeat the third "step" for as long as he was motivated. Fourth, he would return to the States to a staff position for "the final polish." Finally, unless he was chosen for one of the few very senior-level positions within Baxter, he would typically leave the company. The narrowing of the Baxter pyramid at higher levels of management was inevitable in many respects; still, this final step was never explicitly part of the Baxter plan.

These steps, shown in Figure 5.1, constituted the typical career path for those who were hired as part of Graham's initiative to professionalize Baxter. The interview data suggest that this was also the general pattern for those who did *not* transition into biotech but either remained at Baxter until retirement or ventured elsewhere of their own accord. Thus, this was not a path that was unique to those who left Baxter for biotechnology.

Within this overall pattern, there were minor variations, of course. For example, a couple of members of the first wave, such as Carpenter, remained within the United States for his entire Baxter career and so did not experience Step 4, the "final polish." The same was true for Chubb, given his U.S.-based responsibilities at Baxter's Hyland Diagnostics Division. Even though these two were not placed into overseas general management jobs, however, their jobs, like all Baxter general management jobs, involved substantial

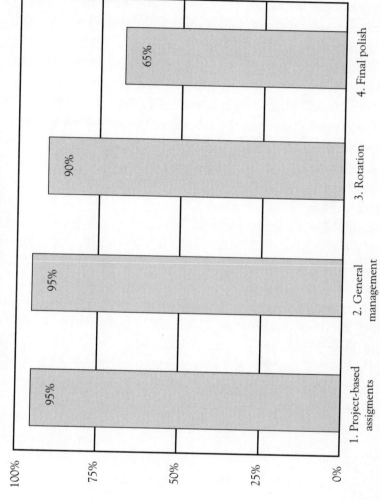

Figure 5.1 Summary of the Baxter Career Path

Percent of interviewees whose career followed each step

international exposure. As will be described in greater detail later in the chapter, even in the cases in which there was some deviation from the norm, the basic career paths and, hence, capabilities, connections, confidence, and cognition that Baxter cultivated were quite similar.

There were also many who did *not* make it all the way through these four steps in the career path and back home to the States for the "final polish"; their experiences lend insights as well. The data suggest two main reasons for a break in this general management career path: either individuals self-selected out of this path, which usually occurred during the first one to two years, or individuals did not perform well at their first significant general management job and were dismissed.

Interviews with people who were fired and/or who worked closely with individuals who were let go indicate two general patterns for early dismissals: either the individual had not "played by the rules," by (a) repeatedly "making excuses for poor performance" and/or by simply missing their numbers for other reasons or (b) by not having good interpersonal skills (i.e., that fit with Baxter's culture). Regarding the latter, stories revolved around disrespectful behavior such as keeping people waiting for meetings, stepping on senior management's toes, or backstabbing. Alternatively, it seems that one could be *too assertive* at Baxter, as one interviewee described:

> So I got up and would say that [X was a "dumb idea"] in these off-site meetings and that wasn't very popular. We were encouraged to speak our minds, which I did, but clearly I was way over here and everybody else was going the other way.

This person ultimately went on to lead several successful biotechnology companies. However, as Gabe Schmergel's account of his conversation with Graham about a potential acquisition, described in Chapter Two, showed, open confrontation had its limits at Baxter. Again, there was a definite competitive edge to the collective sense of identity experienced there.

Patterns in why people did *not* make it to the final polish stage suggest two important aspects of the Baxter career imprint. First, not making one's numbers indicates the discipline one was expected to learn of managing the bottom line, a basic general management skill. Second, stories about "making excuses" along with stories of disrespectful behavior highlight another aspect of the Baxter career imprint—developing strong and respectful relationships with senior management. Those who were not able to cultivate such intraorganizational relationships were invariably let go.

But although the negative stories about why people were let go at Baxter illuminate some aspects of Baxter's career imprint that were valued and reinforced, the positive stories about individuals' career experiences at Baxter reveal, even more persuasively, key aspects of Baxter's career imprint. These aspects of Baxter's career imprint are summarized in Table 5.2.

Following begins a more in-depth exploration of the four career steps at Baxter and the resulting career imprint:

Step 1: Project-Based Assignments

During the first one to two years, Baxter new-hires worked in either assistant-to positions or in one of two internal consulting groups. In either case, the assignments were project based. These projects involved diagnosing a problem and coming up with a solution for senior management either in a written report or through presentations. Preparing and presenting this final deliverable to senior management was one way that individuals learned, early on, the significance of cultivating positive relationships with senior management.

Several key characteristics of these assignments are remarkable. First, with the exception of the assignment to a task force, as was the case with the GMP task force that Carpenter and Schaubert were put on, these were generally independent assignments. Individuals were sent out to a plant, as was the case with Schmergel's

Table 5.2 Aspects of Baxter's Career Imprint Derived from Patterns in Jobs Held at Baxter

	Capabilities	Connections	Confidence	Cognition
STEP 1: Project-based assignments	• Learn by doing • Recognize one's limits ➤ Ask for help	• Extraorganizational ➤ Government based • Intraorganizational ➤ Developmental partnerships (with journeymen)	• To make "no-go" decisions • To learn from others' expertise	
STEP 2: Transition to general management	• General management skills ➤ Exercise influence (rather than execute) ➤ Manage human resources ➤ Negotiate beyond borders • Crisis management—cope with uncertainty	• Extraorganizational ➤ Government based	• Learning-based efficacy	• "Mini-CEO" viewpoint
STEP 3: Rotation	• Broad functional understanding ➤ Marketing, sales, operations, finance • Manage bottom line (not strategic thinking)	• Extraorganizational ➤ Hospital community • Intraorganizational ➤ Broad, peer-based network	• Future-based confidence	• CEO perspective • Results orientation/focus on "the numbers"
STEP 4: The final polish	• Manage politics, power, and influence	• Intraorganizational ➤ Senior management		• Corporate perspective

story of his work in Mexico, or to a division, either abroad or domestic, and told to "investigate" a problem—detective work. Even when paired with a more senior manager for the project, individuals often felt alone, since they were ultimately and independently responsible for delivering their final reports. Further, since these individuals did not yet know the products nor the business markets (recall that having a background in healthcare was not one of Baxter's selection criteria), these assignments entailed "getting one's hands dirty" on the job.

How did individuals learn? All of the interviewees were asked this question. The following response is representative of the types of answers offered across the board: "We all had to learn on the job. Because Baxter was growing so rapidly, you couldn't just go in and learn; you had to go in and do." Gustav Christensen's account of his first year at Baxter echoes this competency, learning by doing, along with some other aspects of the Baxter career imprint:[6]

I went to Chicago as assistant to the president of International, Bill Gantz, who was a fantastic guy to work for. . . . He just let you go. . . . I'd been there a week when he said, "I'd like you to go to South Africa next week with a team of two other guys; we have a problem there." The riots had just started in Soweto, and our plant was a mile away from the main gate into Soweto, so it was a big issue. [Gantz said], "Before you go there, go talk to (he had a special assistant called) Jerry Lacey, an old-timer; he will fill you in." And there was this pile of history of political problems. . . . And I said, "Oh my God, we've got to go into a bees nest," and see, Gantz didn't tell me all this. He figured if I'm smart, I'll work it out on my own.

We did well, so Gantz sent me to Italy, where collections were a huge problem. He always had me work with someone who was more experienced. . . . He gave me one name. I'd start there and work my way around. The Italian government was a year behind on their payments . . . Baxter had decided to leave the dialyzer market because they weren't going to sell dialyzers to customers who didn't pay their bills. The government was now discussing doing the same thing one more time—renew the legislation and pay half the old debt and reset the clock again. So, I went over with a more experienced guy, and [after a couple of weeks] this [more experienced] guy was promoted to general manager in Mexico (he later went to Hybritech) right as I was in the middle of my program, so I was alone with this thing.

I had to stop by Gabe in Brussels and try to explain what we were doing down there in Italy, and I really felt kind of out there. I was also reporting to the special assistant to the chairman, Ray Oddi, with reports as to what was going on. Financially, it was a big decision for Italy. It was very exciting, actually. At that time, you know, you get a little bit more self confidence, a little bit more, . . . but you still don't even know the products you're making in the company. I mean we had a diverse product line. How would you know?! . . . So whatever you happened to work on when you were there on your program is what you'd get to know a little bit about. . . . So, Gabe said, "Hey, when you're done with your year, I think we'd like to get you to Europe to work." . . . So after ten months, I had another project in Scandinavia. And then Gantz told me they had decided to fire the general manager in Sweden, . . . and I was asked if wanted to go be general manager in Sweden. I was ten months into this job.

As this career account highlights, early on in their careers at Baxter, individuals learned how to learn on the job, a critical competency in highly uncertain environments.[7] Further, Baxter was not afraid to put new-hires into positions in which there were complicated extraorganizational relationships to be understood and managed. Unlike many typical functionally based, entry-level positions at other healthcare companies at this time, early career jobs at Baxter entailed dealing directly with governmental authorities. Thus, another key aspect of Baxter's career imprint was the cultivation of extraorganizational, and in particular government-based, relationships.

In addition, as this story and Schmergel's story both illustrate, these early career experiences helped build self-confidence, specifically with respect to making tough decisions. In Christensen's project in Italy, as in Schmergel's story about his first-year assignment with the plant in Mexico, the resolution was a "no-go" decision. Not a "yes" decision, such as the decision to enter a new market, for example, but a "no, let's get out" kind of decision. Nearly every Baxter alumnus I interviewed had an early career story that entailed saying "no," either collectively or individually, in the face of a high-profile business issue. Thus, another key general management capability Baxter careers developed was making tough "no-go" decisions. Baxter senior management was looking for change, and these new-hires were eager to meet the challenge, if they could. And, since these projects were generally high-level projects, neither "no-go" nor "yes" types of decisions were to be taken lightly. As one interviewee told me, he rewrote his final report to senior management seventeen times before delivering it.

Finally, Christensen's career account and the first-year stories of many others interviewed reflect the kinds of developmental relationships that were cultivated as part of Baxter's career imprint. Baxter had a common practice of pairing up an experienced Baxter manager or "old guard" with a new MBA or "young turk" to solve an important problem—or, at a minimum, to provide the younger manager with the necessary "background," as Christensen put it, to analyze the problem. This sort of pairing fostered the development of strong intraorganizational ties. Oftentimes, people talked about these "journeymen" as their mentors. Dave Castaldi's description of his developmental relationship with self-described journeyman Pete Phildius was typical:

> Pete Phildius was old guard, but he was a guy I'd walk off a cliff for. I developed a fantastic relationship with Pete. . . . He taught me how to dress; he taught me so many things that were . . . substantive and

nonsubstantive [such as] how you position yourself for success in this culture. And I mentioned dress. . . . I wore crazy plaid suits. He'd say, "Look at that guy—he's wearing brown slacks and a . . . tan sports jacket that's very light colored, that's made out of a wool fabric. . . ." And I'd be wearing pinstripe suits! He'd say, "Go to Brooks Brothers." And I went to Brooks Brothers for years until I developed enough confidence to be able to choose my own suits. . . . And on substantive matters too, I have tremendous respect for him. So there were those mentor relationships.

Others had similar stories of mentoring relationships that evolved out of informal working relationships during those first couple of years at Baxter. Since Baxter placed people into project-based assignments often with "one name to start," people had both the entrée and the motivation to cultivate valuable developmental partnerships. Further, these types of early career assignments and pairings, as unofficial as they were, taught budding Baxter managers another critical general management capability: to recognize one's limits—to know when you are not the expert. As leadership scholar Linda Hill has shown, becoming a manager often requires learning how to exercise influence through others, rather than relying solely upon one's own skills and knowledge.[8] This was something Baxter new-hires were forced to learn early on.

Step 2: Transition to General Management

Generally after one to two years of project-based assignments, Baxter placed people into general management assignments. The assignments often began as small division or country manager assignments, generally in an area in which they had spent some time during the previous year and/or where they had some basic skills (e.g., spoke the language). Still, having little prior knowledge was generally the norm. Just as Gabe Schmergel's account of his move to Germany illustrates, people were often dropped into these jobs with surprisingly little prior experience.

These general management jobs were coveted. As Schmergel's story revealed, International was where the growth was perceived to be and so, people were generally eager to take on overseas assignments. The perception was that these were opportunities to run "mini-Baxters," an opportunity to "own something," unlike jobs they might find at other companies during the same time period. Indeed, as described in Chapter Three, Graham's strategy of creating lots of overseas general management jobs for bright MBA graduates was a rather unique strategy for healthcare firms during that time period. Elliott Hillback's story of his first overseas assignment illustrates this type of exposure along with several particular aspects of Baxter's career imprint:

> When [my wife and I] looked at Baxter, we looked at this long list of country opportunities—Munich, Germany; Versailles, France; just outside of London in Thetford, England, etc., etc., etc. . . . And she said, "What about this—Castlebar, Ireland?" I said, "That's a manufacturing plant in the middle of nowhere; I'm a finance guy, we're never going there!"

Yet after only seven months at Baxter, Hillback was moved to Ireland as an assistant to the general manager there and, within a year, was promoted to general manager:

> In the end, it was fabulous because I had seen what senior management was thinking in Deerfield and then I got to work very locally down in the Irish plants. I changed the way I dressed and everything—I went local—to tweeds, perpetual raincoats, Guinness Stout, and the whole bit. And I was always in the plant before the local management, every morning.
>
> I did big things like negotiate with the Irish government for huge grants, manage several major plant expansions and numerous new product start-ups, deal with a major FDA inspection, etc. But then it's the "little" things that just happen where you really learn. You know, I tell this story. I don't mean to say it in a negative way, but when a

nineteen-year-old kid drops dead in the plant on the second shift from a heart attack, and the nurse who's on duty can't save him, and she goes off the deep end because she didn't save him, and there's about three hundred women working in the plant, most of them know the kid, and they start fainting and hitting their heads on the terrazzo. . . . They don't teach you that at Harvard. They don't teach you how to cope with that at Harvard. When you run out of water—this is an IV fluid plant. . . . the water came from a lake, almost a pond really, and they had a bad drought, and the lake dried up. . . . We had these huge filtration systems that we used to turn this into sterile water, but we just ran out of water! So what do you do with a plant that you can't get enough water for? Well, you work on the government to try to solve some things real fast and you figure out what you're going to do with your seventeen hundred people for about three weeks! . . . And they don't teach you that anywhere. In fact, Bob Hayes . . . my first-year business school professor, my manufacturing professor, came over while I was in Ireland. He came over to give a talk at the Harvard Club in Dublin, and I went over. And he said, "What are you doing here?" And I said, "I'm running a plant." And he went white, he says, "You?!" "Yeah." I said, "How many courses did I take in operations at Harvard?" He says, "I don't think you took any." I said, "Just the one you taught for three months in the first year—should've taken more."

This account reveals several important aspects of Baxter's career imprint. First, like most general management career paths at Baxter, Hillback's second career step into a general manager role required developing certain kinds of connections—extraorganizational relationships—in particular, with governmental agencies as well as capabilities such as negotiation skills. Second, this example shows Hillback's progression from an individual contributor role to a management role and the complex and important human resources issues that go along with such a transition. As his account suggests, although specific skills one begins to learn in business school, such as operations, are important in a general management role, other human resources skills, such as managing crisis situations, are critical to learn as well.

Third, as this example shows, the general management career assignment fostered a sense of confidence that was based upon stretching oneself beyond one's comfort zone. Rather than self-efficacy based upon well-established expertise, this type of confidence came from knowing you could figure it out—what could be called "learning-based efficacy." Learning-based efficacy concerns confidence in one's ability to learn. It is forward looking, since it has to do with coping with the unknown, the unfamiliar. In contrast, what could be called "expertise-based efficacy" hinges on confidence from the past—believing that one can rely upon what one has already learned. As one Baxter alumnus described:

> It's like the Marines. A few good men, or women. It's, "We've been to war, and we can conquer anything that we've set our sight to, set our will to. Yes, we may not know everything but things will come out fine—we will find out the next day more than we know today." That's maybe *it*. Maybe there is one word to describe our experience at Baxter; Baxter instilled in us a sense of *self-confidence*.

Self-confidence was borne out of learning how to succeed in an unfamiliar and challenging setting. Schmergel, Termeer, and Hillback's stories of their first experiences as general managers reflect a sense of having overcome tremendous obstacles or crucibles, of having achieved beyond what they thought they could, beyond what they learned in business school. As a result of these particular kinds of stretch opportunities, Baxter managers gained important general management skills, extraorganizational connections, and confidence in their ability to learn.

Step 3: Rotation

The next step in the typical Baxter career path was to rotate through a series of general management roles, changing positions

approximately every one to two years. In general, the jobs in this
series were very different from one another. The sense among
interviewees was that Baxter was intentionally exposing people
to multiple functional areas within Baxter. For example, Gabe
Schmergel first transitioned into general management in Germany,
which was, at that time, largely a marketing and sales-driven subsidiary. From there, he was tapped to go to Brussels, which was
largely a manufacturing operation. Hillback's example took him in
the opposite direction: he began in operations and then moved
into marketing and sales. Rotation was expected. As one Baxter
alumnus described:

> Baxter offered people diverse experiences, and people were moved to
> get that. There was a lack of hierarchy. Not a large sophisticated
> HR group in charge. Mr. Graham wanted to optimize the company,
> not optimize a particular unit or sector. So, it wasn't bad to move
> around. No ill will to moving across businesses. There was lots of
> hopping on multiple levels—by business, by geography, by function.

All of this "hopping" helped people develop an understanding of multiple aspects to running a business. Therefore, a core
capability these general management careers developed was functional understanding—not functional expertise, which would
have been the case had these Baxter careers centered on creating
specialists by moving people vertically up through particular
functions. Rather, Baxter careers developed "generalists."[9]

In these general management positions, Baxter managers were
encouraged to build extraorganizational relationships, particularly
within the hospital community. The relationships they had with
doctors and the contact they had with patients were highly valued
at Baxter and, of course, enabled them to make many operational
decisions regarding the marketing and selling of Baxter's products.
So, whereas Baxter managers' expertise was not in knowing the
details of the science behind its products, these career transitions
did enable them to cultivate extraorganizational relationships with

the doctors and other constituencies, so that they could learn and improve upon Baxter's products. As one overseas manager said:

> We were very close to the patients. Very, very close. . . . Every week I was going to hospitals. And I was going along with the salespeople. That was also part of the equation. You don't stay in your office; you really meet your customers. You sense how the sales force is trained, how to market the products. You're going to warehouses; you're going to pharmacies. When I was going to the warehouse, I was known, because every time I would go to the eating room I'd see if there was oil, grease, or things on the floor. That was also another aspect. You are not in your tower; you have to go into the details.

Finally, as all of the interviewees described, the experiences they had in general management continually reinforced the importance of managing one's bottom line—a critical general management skill. As Bill Gantz, who was head of Baxter International for several years, commented:

> Graham's concept was, "I'm going to take a group of executives and I'm going to commit to having a cadre of executives. I'm going to move them back and forth between the U.S. and International, and I'm really going to develop the business." . . . The business was growing 20 percent a year; the company was exploding, and we moved people around a lot. The assignments were interesting—they were fun—and I think people really loved and enjoyed growing the business. So that was one technique. . . . When I was president of International, every Monday morning, we had a two-hour meeting. We would go through what everybody was doing in the company, and I would say we got coached a lot. It was like going into an exam every week.

This "coaching" revolved around business decisions that were often operational in kind. Graham made the major strategic decisions, but individuals were encouraged to bring strategic ideas to him. Graham's hires had "mini-CEO jobs," as they called them, generally within their first few years at Baxter. When running their businesses, emphasis was placed on "making the numbers"—on performance based upon clearly established goals between the general managers and senior management. And, in particular, the "rules" hinged on results. Schmergel's description of a "two strikes, you're out" mentality at Baxter was illustrated often in the interviews. Excuses were seldom tolerated. This disciplined bottom-line capability and mindset were central aspects of Baxter's career imprint.

Step 4: The Final Polish

Those who made it through Baxter's general management ranks and had rotated through a number of assignments were eventually brought home to the United States—unless they were already in the United States, such as Carpenter and Chubb. The other first-wave Baxter managers eventually "retired" to the United States to a VP or staff position. Some of these career moves were motivated by personal issues, such as responsibilities associated with parents or children. However, most often, the idea, as Gantz described, was to "groom executives." This final step, from VP to president, was reserved for the very few. As one Baxter alumnus explained:

> So once you're a VP in a division and there are three or four of you that might have a shot someday of running that division, all of a sudden that's where the ceiling starts to, you know [smacking hands together], you feel it. And that's where a lot of people got to. A lot of people got to be a VP of a division and said, "Oh God, the president's not going anywhere. He's still got kids in high school; he's not gonna leave for a long time." And so, up until that point, more countries, more products, sideways, lots of sideways expansions, new units, new things to do, but they were still under the umbrella of a certain number of presidents, and that [umbrella] expanded some but not at the rate that [other types of opportunities] expanded.

This account illustrates the inevitable narrowing of the Baxter pyramid. Back in Corporate, as Gabe Schmergel's story revealed, people often realized that they had "had more fun" before, when they were running a business. They had had the opportunity to have full responsibility as a general manager; they had had independence (despite the "coaching" Gantz described), and they wanted that back. In many ways, ironically, this fourth career step reinforced the affinity these managers had developed for the kinds of capabilities, connections, confidence, and cognition that were nurtured in the first three steps of the typical Baxter career path. These earlier career experiences (and, ironically, often the fourth step as well) ultimately left Baxter managers with an appetite for the independence associated with running one's own business. Hillback described this well:

> I think Baxter did a lot to move people forward in terms of creating an entrepreneurial environment, a sink-or-swim environment, a perform environment, and a get it done, find a way, practical type of environment—[that was] really entrepreneurial.

Subjective Career Patterns: The Experience of Working at Baxter

In order to understand how people experienced their career paths at Baxter, the interview transcripts were scanned for patterns in the ways people described their career experiences, including repeated stories, phrases, and analogies. Looking at patterns this way is new to the study of careers but is quite common in other domains of organizational research. For examples, as qualitative research by Boje suggests:

> Story performances are part of an organization-wide information-processing network. Bits and pieces of organization experience are recounted socially throughout the firm to formulate recognizable,

cogent, defensible, and seemingly rational collective accounts that will serve as precedent of individual assumption, decision, and action.[10]

Similarly, as Eccles and Nohria claim:

To view management from a rhetorical perspective is to recognize that the way people talk about the world has everything to do with the way the world is ultimately understood and acted in.[11]

Here, a narrative lens provides further illumination into Baxter's career imprint. Patterns in career narratives can help us understand underlying "assumptions" regarding "the way the world is ultimately understood"—here, as it relates to one's career.[12] Therefore, such patterns can lend insight into the final "C" of a career imprint: cognition. So, for example, whereas understanding that Baxter promoted people early and often into positions as heads of overseas subsidiaries lends insight into general management capabilities cultivated at Baxter, the subjective experience of that job—for example, the dedication to Baxter's "20/20"—lends additional insight into their bottom-line, results-oriented mentality to managing a Baxter business.

In addition to the phrase *20/20*, three other phrases—*war, Mr. Graham,* and *nothing is impossible* came up often in the interviews and so, are detailed below. These phrases and the aspects of Baxter's career imprint that they illuminate are summarized in Table 5.3.

20/20

Over the course of the interviewing process, it became clear that the reference to *20 over 20* did not just refer to the company's *demonstrated success*, as discussed in Chapter Three; this phrase referred to a directive about what Baxter managers were expected to achieve and sustain. In nearly every interview with Baxter

Table 5.3 Aspects of Baxter's Career Imprint Derived from Patterns in the Phrases that Describe Career Experiences at Baxter

	Capabilities	Connections	Confidence	Cognition

"20/20"	• Manage top line (growth) and bottom line (profits) simultaneously
	• Operational (not strategic) decisions
		• Intraorganizational
		  ➤ Senior management
			• Risk taking to achieve milestones	• Results focus
				  ➤ Growth
				  ➤ Profits
				• Business focus (not science)

"War"	• Tactics—take market share from competition • Act pragmatically	• Intraorganizational ➤ Peers/"comrades"	• Risk taking to beat out competition	• We/they mentality • Defend turf (Baxter) • Sink-or-swim view

"Mr. Graham"	• Impression management
	  ➤ Manage up
	• Learn business details
	• Manage product quality
	• Prevent unionization
		• Intraorganizational
		  ➤ Authority/high-status relations
			• To learn from others' expertise	• Detail orientation to business
				• Growth focus
				• Quality/safety focus
				• Anti-union

"Nothing Is Impossible"	• Act pragmatically
	• Ask for help
	• Negotiate to get results
		• Extraorganizational
		  ➤ Government
		• Intraorganizational
		  ➤ Senior management
			• Optimism
			• Learning-based efficacy
			  ➤ "Search/find your way through"
				• "Just do it" mentality
				• Forward-looking perspective

alumni, this phrase or some variant of it was used when describing the experience of working at Baxter; it was by far the most oft-repeated phrase. Further, it was often preceded by *you know*, indicating that this was a taken-for-granted understanding or rule with respect to fulfilling one's role at Baxter.

The *20/20* reference demonstrates several aspects of Baxter's career imprint. First, it shows how the kinds of capabilities people developed at Baxter centered around managing one's numbers. People had targets and were expected to reach them. No excuses were allowed.

> Twenty percent growth was the target. You didn't want your finger-prints on not making that happen. You didn't want to be within an inch of letting the company down. We knew the growth streak would come to an end, but we didn't want to be there when it did. It was a function of pride, of pressure, and accountability.

In terms of capabilities acquired at Baxter, the *20/20* reference suggests that Baxter careers taught people how to become highly disciplined managers who were extremely focused on growth and the bottom line simultaneously. Other accounts of the *20/20* aspect of Baxter's career imprint illustrate how Baxter was able to cultivate this capability and orientation—specifically, by giving people latitude for operational decisions but not for strategic decisions:

> There was a very disciplined approach to management. Graham had the strategy, but the operations were done by us. There was strict adherence to budget and processes. Hitting 20 percent growth a year was never an accident! Everyone knew and expected this, so you had managers [learn] good management tools.

Further, references to *20/20* included explanations about how people learned that there were acceptable and unacceptable ways to hit the target. As one alumnus described:

> One of the tough things in business is to figure out how to stretch
> the system in an acceptable way. . . . And when you had business
> practices that were so incredibly divergent from country to country,
> internationally, you had to find ways to be able to do that—to with-
> stand massive currency swings and other things and all in a highly
> volatile environment. Those skill sets Baxter did a very good job of
> developing in people. The art form is, how do you manage results
> within acceptable ranges, throughout your piece of responsibility,
> and in a way that manages results for the entire company? And I
> think that was done pretty well within Baxter.

In sum, the *20/20* aspect of Baxter's career imprint lends
greater insight into Baxter's career imprint. In terms of capabilities, the *20/20* phrase helps us understand that managers learned
how to be "economical, always," as one Baxter alumnus described
it, as well as ethical, as the previous account suggests. Further,
these *20/20* accounts illustrate that the managers' forte at the
time was in managing operations—the implementation side, as
opposed to strategy, which was often dictated by Graham's office.
The *20/20* references also show that another key aspect of Baxter's
imprint was confidence that comes from taking risks, risks that are
associated with reaching specific goals or milestones, such as
20/20.[13] Finally, the *20/20* phrase lends insight into the cognitive
dimension of Baxter's career imprint—into the worldview Baxter
careers cultivated, which was clearly both results-oriented and
business-focused.

War

War was referred to the second-most-often in these individuals'
accounts of their career experiences at Baxter. If not the word *war*,
then *battle*, *fight*, *victory*, or *defeat* were used—all references to

confrontation of some sort. These references were either inwardly directed or outwardly directed. In the former case, individuals referred to competition they felt with one another for certain positions in the company. Still, as described, this was always tempered by references to *camaraderie*. Outwardly directed accounts of war generally referred to a couple of key competitors, as the story of Abbott, told in Chapter Three, illustrated. Generally speaking, these were not small battles in the minds of the interviewees. They conjured up strong emotions; individuals often referred to people or institutions that were "hated" by Baxter people, as in the following instance:

> Baxter hated the Dutch Red Cross because they presented themselves as a philanthropic organization; in fact, they were a cutthroat commercial organization. They sold the same products as Baxter, and they would use their political clout to keep Baxter out— Travenol in those days—and when I was there we were able to break the stranglehold of the Dutch Red Cross in one of their product areas. . . . One of Baxter's international strategies was, "I'm gonna have this local competition, and if you have quality problems (that can result in patient deaths) then, I, Baxter, will be there. I will have top quality, top quality. I will never endanger patients, and eventually my competitors are going to make a mistake, and that's when I go and kill them."
>
> That's how Baxter took the market share from Abbott in the United States. Abbott was the leader. Baxter was there. Abbott made quality mistakes, and we killed them. And that was part of the folklore. You know. We moved quickly and we slit their throats. We did the same thing in the Netherlands. They made a mistake . . . two deaths,[14] and we killed them. Within six months, we had 70 percent share, up from 15 percent. My bosses loved that.
>
> The ultimate, in my career, would be driving Abbott out of business—into the ocean. . . . And it was great when you did. I remember when I went to [my boss] and he said, "BE RUTHLESS!" And so I went to the Netherlands . . . and two thirds of the way

through my stay there, we'd broken through; we'd broken the Red Cross. And the head of the Red Cross, this guy [my boss] hated, had had a heart attack. They were advertising for a job for his replacement, so I cut this advertisement out of the newspaper, and I said, "This advertisement is because Herr So-and-So had a heart attack . . . was that ruthless enough?!" So that was very much the culture. But you loved it. You've got your battle, or a competition, and you got your thrills from winning, either beating your colleagues for the awards or just beating your competition.

This account describes a fierce battle, like the one with Abbott, and how it was won—with patience, with cunning, and with determination. It also illustrates the desire to please Baxter senior management, consistent with the *20/20* rule. Further, it describes this orientation toward gaining market share, in particular, taking market share—taking the hill, as in ground combat. As interviewees often told me at the end of their battle stories, "that was part of the culture": to go to war in defense of Baxter, their company.[15]

These references to *war* and *battle* yield additional insights with respect to the capabilities, cognition, and connections that constituted Baxter's career imprint. With respect to capabilities and cognition, we find that Baxter general managers were extremely competitive and eager to survive in their new marketplaces. Reflecting this "we/they" mentality, another analogy which was used often was "sink or swim." Swimming entailed beating out the competition so that one could make one's numbers—taking market share from local competitors. If not, you "sunk" or were "killed," depending upon the choice of metaphor. In particular, and echoing the insights gleaned from the *20/20* reference, here we see that winning battles entails making smart operational decisions—"moving in for the kill" in a tactical fashion and being ready, as John Kimbell of Baxter was in 1971 when Abbott had quality problems,[16] to take a larger slice of market share.

With respect to connections, these battle stories illustrate how individuals' career paths at Baxter cultivated strong intraorganizational connections—particularly in the International Division. Interestingly, however, as these accounts and others suggested, ties were not necessarily based upon working directly together nor upon frequent communication.[17] Indeed, after being "parachuted into a subsidiary," and having "survived" an important milestone (such as a financial quarter), Baxter managers would come together as comrades:

> It's not as if this was a big group hug. Most of the time you were [competing], but when you got together on a quarterly basis, we'd have great times. I remember midnight swims fully clothed in pools at places; there was lots of camaraderie. . . . You don't have to be in daily contact to have that develop.

Thus, the *war* metaphor illustrates the positive connections that result from surviving challenging or "war-like" career experiences along with the shared mentality of defending one's turf. Sharing battles whether near or far from one another, whether involved in the same "war" or not, enabled the cultivation of a broad range of strong intraorganizational connections.

Mr. Graham

A description of how jobs were experienced at Baxter would be incomplete if we did not consider the influence of Baxter's CEO, Bill Graham—or, *Mr. Graham*. This is a very different kind of pattern in the Baxter career history accounts—that is, how people referred to Bill Graham as *Mr. Graham*. This was the form of address employed whether the interviewee had an MBA, was a journeyman and had no advanced degree, or was someone who never left Baxter and still works there (even though Graham has long since retired). Indeed, in only two cases of all my Baxter interviews did the interviewee never refer to Bill Graham as *Mr. Graham* at all during their interviews.[18] And, in both of these cases, the interviewee referred to Bill Graham using his full name, *Bill Graham*, rather than *Bill* or *Graham*, and often in the very same sentence as the first name of another senior manager. Sentences such as the following, in which a first name was given to one person while the formal salutation was given to Bill Graham, were commonplace: "I was told later that Vern didn't want to do it, and that Mr. Graham did." This formal address was often openly acknowledged as follows:

> At Baxter, the world was Baxter. We knew nothing about the world outside. Except customers. We went to conferences not to look at the world, but to work with our customers. And inside, Graham ruled. I mean someone said "Mr. Graham wants [X]," and you said, "Yes, sir." . . . He was the only person there called by his last name, "Mr. Graham."

This account reinforces the felt sense that Baxter was the institution—a total institution, in many respects, since so much of these individuals' personal and professional lives revolved around their careers at Baxter.[19] In this institution, clearly, *Mr. Graham* ruled. He was omnipresent.

In terms of Baxter's career imprint, this form of address reveals a different aspect of Baxter's career imprint: deference to authority figures. Another interviewee made this quite clear when he described a party that was thrown for Graham in 1999. Apparently, ninety-two of the one hundred invited guests came from all over the world to attend this party in Chicago—most more than a decade after they had left Baxter. At the party, the attendees were supposed to roast Bill Graham. In the end, no one did since "that would have been an audacious thing to do because nobody ever roasted Bill Graham." The closest anyone ever got to roasting Bill Graham was to say, "You know, we've got all these people here, they're heads of companies, and all these wonderful people who've left Baxter. You sure had a hard time hanging on to your good people." As this interviewee recalled, "Graham never forgot that."

In short, *Mr. Graham* seemed to be untouchable. And he always had the final word. Company rituals, such as Saturday morning coffee breaks, reinforced this sense of an authority figure in *Mr. Graham*. Further, through such rituals associated with *Mr. Graham*, young managers cultivated another key general management skill—how to manage impressions[20]:

> Bill Graham typically worked every Saturday morning, . . . and the culture at Baxter was to have a break on Saturday mornings, where everybody gathered in the cafeteria. I don't know, 10:00, whatever the time was. A coffee break. Bill Graham was always there. And those of us who wanted to impress Bill Graham, wanted to be noticed, wanted to go someplace, were there on Saturday mornings working. And we had the opportunity to interact with Bill Graham. You could be at the Bill Graham table! You could be at it with him!. . . . Everybody knew Bill Graham was the one you wanted to impress, the one who was making the decisions.

In addition to impression management, these kinds of stories about encounters with *Mr. Graham* reveal another lesson learned at Baxter—how to lead on the ground floor—including the importance of being visible to valued employees. Indeed, as one alumnus told me, Graham was "managing by walking around" long before there even was such a term.

Further, through these impressionable interactions with *Mr. Graham*, these managers learned how to manage upward. People needed to be able to "answer questions" for *Mr. Graham* without flinching. The story about one young GM deciding to take a chemistry course after getting some tough questions during a dinner with Bill Graham (described in Chapter Three) was a fine case in point. And, like the ritual of calling Bill Graham *Mr. Graham*, this unwritten rule, "know the details about your business," had a lasting effect on the capabilities people picked up at Baxter. Either you learned this rule through the direct experience of Graham "nailing you," or you learned it through vicarious experience—that is, through the experience of your peers being interrogated by Graham. As Jim Tobin, who worked at Baxter for years, first under Graham and then under Loucks, recalled:

> A lot of people were afraid of [Graham]. Rightly so . . . looks like a grandfatherly type, but the man has an intellect to this day that is razor sharp. And he does not suffer fools lightly. He's smarter than everybody else, and he's driven, and if you did or said something that was stupid, he'd make sure you knew it. I've seen very powerful people cringe at a sideways glance from Bill Graham. He could be brutal. Now he never was with me. I'm sure I would remember it. Everybody remembers it when it happens, but I only remember it happening to other people. I don't remember him ever nailing me. But it didn't matter; I still lived in fear of that.

Still, mixed in with this fear of Graham's tough questions was inspiration. Graham's tough questions tapped into these individuals' high needs for achievement. And, Graham's career marked the epitome of that journey; he was their role model for achievement, since he had led the company through a tremendous period of growth. Thus, we find that Baxter's career imprint and, specifically, the management focus on "growth" were echoed in the very reasons people admired Graham and gave him a unique and high-status form of address, *Mr. Graham*. Indeed, people's admiration for Graham stemmed from his ability to "grow the business" and also "grow with the business":

> A man who took a business that was under $2 million, 1945, post–World War II, after it shrank down, and grew with it, and was as commanding a figure at $2 billion as he was at $2 million?! That is rare: a man that can grow with a business from nothing to a big business and still be the right leader, a good leader, a strong leader. And he was able to do that. Just the admiration, the awe, the inspiration, the affection . . . is just astounding.

Finally, there was a remarkable range of emotions attributed to this leader called Mr. *Graham*. People used the words *fear* and *awe* in the same paragraph, and they also remarked on how "passionate" Graham was about patient care. As one businessman commented, Graham's "only rival in his passion for saving lives is Henri Termeer. Henri can make you cry." Indeed, interviewees said that while achieving growth targets was paramount at Baxter, the absolute worst thing you could do was either kill a patient or let your operation become unionized. Graham wanted to maintain Baxter's reputation for high-quality (i.e., safe) products and to maintain control over the company's operations. Through people's fear, awe, and admiration for Mr. *Graham*, they too learned some of these same capabilities and mental models about running a business.

In sum, some of the key aspects of Baxter's career imprint suggested by the accounts of Mr. *Graham* are capabilities that include managing impressions (particularly of those who are in positions of legitimate power and authority), attention to detail in both operations and business markets (though not to company strategy, as that was Graham's territory), and a dogged focus on business growth. In addition, from their accounts of intense dinners and breakfast encounters with Mr. *Graham*, we can infer that Baxter managers learned how to present their ideas clearly and convincingly and with evidence to substantiate their arguments in order to impress Graham.

Additionally, the admiration associated with the way in which managers referred to Graham suggests that people attempted to absorb lessons from Graham's management-style handbook: for example, manage by walking around (e.g., on Saturdays), ask extremely detailed questions, give tough feedback (when appropriate), and maintain control over the strategic decision making of a company. Additionally, this role-modeling behavior suggests that Baxter managers picked up a worldview from Graham that was bottom-line focused and results-oriented. Further, they admired Mr. *Graham* for his business (not scientific) knowledge, which, in turn influenced their cognitive orientation—toward business results, as opposed to scientific prowess.

In terms of connections, their simultaneous fear and affinity for *Mr. Graham* suggests that the Baxter career experience cultivated respect for high-status relationships—those with legitimate or formal authority. Additionally, given their intense interactions with Graham, people also clearly learned how to manage upward and so actively engaged in cultivating such ties. In terms of confidence, Graham's interaction style and, in particular, tough questioning resonate well with the idea that confidence was built at Baxter through learning from others' expertise. People respected others' skills such as "market identification," which was Graham's noted expertise.

More generally, Graham was clearly perceived as a business expert in the area of medical devices. He sat on many local healthcare associations and boards, and, at Baxter, this was often summed up as, "He knew the whole business"; Graham was the "head of Baxter . . . the world," as previously described. Even just being with Graham was treasured. He was "brilliant," as many explained and was "constantly surprising you with his insights." Thus, people came to appreciate that expertise in others, to admire it, which was also reflected in their special form of address, *Mr. Graham*.

Nothing Is Impossible

One more phrase offers insight into an aspect of the Baxter career imprint that has not yet been fully examined. The phrase is *nothing is impossible*, and the aspect of the career imprint that it taps into most clearly is the type of confidence people developed at Baxter.

As described in the first part of this chapter, the typical managerial career path at Baxter fostered learning-based efficacy or confidence in one's ability to learn. Rather than relying upon one's developed expertise in a particular area, such as scientific expertise, Baxter career assignments purposefully tested people's abilities to cope, optimistically, with the unknown—as, for example, building a business in a foreign country. The "nothing is impossible" phrase and the stories that surround it provide additional depth to this observation. Gerard Moufflet's description of his experience building operations for Baxter in Spain (and indeed, later, in Italy) provides a good illustration:

> Ten days after they realized that I spoke Spanish, they sent me to Valencia. Baxter had just completed a minority investment in Spain, and Baxter had nobody. I went there and I ran the budget; there was no budget, there was no nothing. . . . I think the idea was to take very young people, put them in tough spots with responsibility and see what they could do. . . . But I worked eighteen hours a day, and I was going every Sunday from Brussels to Valencia and coming back every Friday, and leaving Saturday, and I did that for eight months. But that was it—nothing was impossible. That was the style.

Moufflet had been assigned to head up Baxter's operations in Spain, where there was a family-run IV solutions business that Baxter had a minority position in. Gantz, who was head of International at the time, believed they needed to increase production. However, since Baxter did not have a majority position in the business, managers had limited leverage; no healthcare company had a majority position. Gantz wanted to change that. He told Moufflet, "We have to do it; we have to find a way to increase our production of IV solutions in Spain." In recounting this story, Moufflet describes how he "searched his way" through what seemed an impossible task.

When dealing with these stretch assignments, people did not wait around for answers. They were expected to step up to the task and take some initiative quickly. And, this was not haphazard stepping up that was going on. As Moufflet recalls, they were very "prepared" when it came time to negotiate with external hierarchies. Indeed, planning and, in particular, goal setting, as the 20/20 phrase suggested, was rewarded at Baxter. Planning at Baxter had a pragmatic orientation to it, which enabled its people to cope with seemingly impossible tasks, as the following two quotes illustrate:

> Part of the Baxter teaching is being pragmatic because if you don't get pragmatic soon, you're gonna sink! Very simple. Start swimming. If you just try to be there and just try to analyze the situation, you're gonna just drop to the bottom of the ocean.

> You better be thinking well ahead and you better have alternatives. If Plan A doesn't work, you better have B and C ready, too, because again, there were no excuses.

Both of these quotes illustrate how the mentality, *nothing is impossible*, and the behavior, *be pragmatic*, were mutually reinforcing. That is, without the sense that *nothing is impossible*, one could stagnate or "sink." Further, the more swimming you did, the more you were convinced that *nothing is impossible*. Baxter gave these managers just enough of a life jacket during their first years at Baxter, with developmental partners along the way, that people could start a positive spiral toward building confidence.

In sum, the *nothing is impossible* phrase lends further insight into Baxter's career imprint—specifically, the type of confidence built at Baxter. The attitude *nothing is impossible* reflects the underlying sense of resilience—that you can figure out what you need to know and need to do, whether that means drawing upon experts from Corporate to help or forging connections with people in the field, as was the case with Moufflet.[21] The excitement at Baxter was often around confidence-building assignments that involved some amount of career risk. Such was the case as illustrated in the career experiences of Moufflet in Spain, Hillback in Ireland, Christensen in Africa, and Schmergel and later Termeer in Germany. The words they used to describe these tasks—feeling that they needed to "find [their] way"—all echo confidence that reflects learning on the job, rather than applying previously acquired expertise.

Summary: Baxter's Entrepreneurial Career Imprint

Looking across both kinds of data—the patterns in the jobs and positions people held at Baxter and the patterns in the stories and analogies people used to describe their career experiences at Baxter—reveal that Baxter cultivated certain capabilities, connections, confidence, and cognition that reflect what could be called an "entrepreneurial career imprint."

First, in terms of capabilities, Baxter careers led to knowledge of specific functional areas such as operations, marketing, and finance. Manufacturing operations, in particular, was at the forefront given the increasing concerns regarding rising hospital costs and the increasing involvement of government agencies in regulating facilities. However, the central capabilities developed over the course of these careers were generalist capabilities—general management capabilities necessary to run a business. These included, in particular, a disciplined focus on managing the bottom line as well as business management skills associated with managing the human side of the enterprise. Technical or scientific expertise was stressed less, as individuals relied heavily upon local country talent and/or journeymen in the firm.

In terms of connections, Baxter careers fostered the development of one or more close developmental relationships, particularly during the early project assignment phase of their careers. These developmental relationships clearly provided both career as well as psychosocial support to these new-hires. In addition, Baxter careers cultivated the development of extraorganizational relationships, particularly with governmental agencies. Their hands-on approach to learning Baxter's products, particularly during the investigative work characteristic of their first couple of assignments, fostered the development of extraorganizational ties with key constituencies in the hospital community.

Additionally, Baxter careers cultivated a sense of confidence that stems from jumping into the unknown and learning through others what was needed in order to get the job done—learning-based efficacy. This contrasts with the kind of self-confidence that stems from relying upon past knowledge or expertise. Baxter managers often described themselves as "really out there" or "alone" and, yet, excited by those opportunities all the same.

Finally, with respect to cognition, the career experiences at Baxter fostered a dogged focus on business results—both with respect to managing the bottom line as well as the top line. The mindset at Baxter revolved around results with respect to business, rather than science, during this time period. Additionally, the career accounts reveal that although "Mr. Graham" played a heavy hand in monitoring progress, the focus was clearly on results, as opposed to process. Later, in the mid-eighties and beyond, once Graham stepped aside, there was a renewed focus on business processes, including the implementation of standardized processes to achieve business targets. But during the time period in question the focus was on business (not science) and on results (not processes).

Patterns in interviewees' stories and phrases such as *20/20*, *war*, *Mr. Graham*, and *nothing is impossible*—employed to describe their career experiences—provide some additional insight into the afore-mentioned categories of Baxter's career imprint and are summarized in Table 5.3. These patterns will become particularly useful as we consider why Baxter's career imprint was deemed appropriate for top-management positions in biotech in later chapters in the book.

Across these four categories, capabilities, connections, and con-fidence, and cognition, there is a common theme—entrepreneurship. Baxter's career imprint was an entrepreneurial career imprint: people learned how to become "mini-CEOs," and, more specifically, gained general management and business skills that prepared them for such jobs. They learned how to build and manage relation-ships beyond organizational boundaries and how to cope with uncertainty with confidence.

And yet, Baxter did not develop scientific entrepreneurs. The term *entrepreneurial management* is often used to describe the situa-tion in which people seize business opportunities with limited resources.[22] *Entrepreneurial career imprint* is used in that sense here.

At Baxter, although people were given financial resources to enter new markets, other kinds of resources, such as connections (e.g., with governmental authorities), confidence (e.g., in one's ability to learn), and capabilities (e.g., managing the bottom line of a business), had to be acquired. Baxter career experiences taught people how to build resources in each of these domains, ultimately yielding an "entrepreneurial career imprint."

Chapter Six

Beyond Baxter: Career Imprints of Merck, Johnson & Johnson, and Abbott

The power of career imprinting becomes increasingly apparent when we can show that similar companies cultivated different kinds of career imprints during the same time period and that these differences matter. To that end, this chapter will compare the critical drivers of the career imprinting process—people, place, and paths—at Baxter and at three other major healthcare firms during the 1970s: Merck, Johnson & Johnson, and Abbott. In the process, it will focus on the "four Cs"—confidence, capabilities, connections, and cognition—which, when shared among a group of employees from the same company, are the signature of a career imprint.

Comparing career imprints in this way allows us to understand that Baxter's entrepreneurial imprint, and the resulting impact that Baxter alumni had on the biotech industry, was not simply a byproduct of "good management" at Baxter. Such a comparison also highlights the extent to which firms have choices in how they develop managers and leaders, which, here, lends insight into what is and is not unique about an entrepreneurial career imprint. Finally, comparing career imprints within a single arena, such as healthcare, provides the foundation for understanding the implications of career imprinting on a broader scale. For example, it illuminates the impact that perceptions of a particular career imprint can have on senior executive mobility or on an emerging industry. We will examine these consequences in Part III of the book.

Merck, J&J, and Abbott were chosen for comparison in part because of their demonstrated strengths in the healthcare sector.

Bill Graham often described J&J as a "role-model company," largely for its decentralized structure. Abbott was Baxter's fiercest competitor in one of its core businesses, IV solutions, and was located within ten miles of Baxter. And Merck was considered one of the quintessential scientific organizations in the healthcare arena. Table 6.1 provides a summary of some of the core character-istics of these organizations, as they existed in 1979, just before Bill Graham stepped aside as CEO at Baxter and just as the first wave began to leave Baxter for biotechnology.

These three organizations were also selected because of their reputation among other constituencies, namely powerful interme-diaries such as venture capital firms (VCs), which were choosing among firms at the dawn of the biotechnology industry. Since one of the ultimate goals of this study is to understand the long-term significance of career imprinting, the VC perspective is significant. From the VCs' vantage point, Merck, Johnson & Johnson, and Abbott were all top-notch breeding grounds for managerial talent and so were often naturally used as points of comparison. These firms were all reasonable recruiting grounds for top-manager positions in biotechnology.[1]

The Unique Career Imprints of Merck, Johnson & Johnson, and Abbott

Returning to the larger dataset provides a good place to start to compare the career paths of individuals at these firms. This dataset includes the five-year career histories of approximately 3,200 exec-utives who were on the IPO teams of biotechnology companies between 1979 and 1996. Of those 3,200, 26 percent spent time in a prominent healthcare firm.[2] These data provide information on the mix of positions held by individuals in various firms *before* leaving for biotechnology as well as information regarding the positions these individuals took on at biotech firms. Since we first want to compare Baxter's career imprint with those of other firms, we will compare in this chapter the kinds of positions individuals held

Table 6.1 Comparative Company Statistics and Characteristics

	Size	Primary Product Lines (1979)	Geography (1979)	Strategy/Structure
Baxter	1970 1979 Sales $0.2 B $1.2 B Employees 11,000 33,000 R&D (1979): $47M, 4% of sales.	Medical care products (parenteral, blood therapy, renal, and urological care products; 99% of sales), instrumentation (1% of sales).	Headquarters: Illinois U.S.: 63% of sales. Int'l: 37% of sales, focusing on Europe but with a presence in Latin America and the Far East.	Focus on bringing to market products with high growth and margin potential; marketing and manufacturing were organized at a regional (multinational) level overseas starting in 1970.
Abbott	1970 1979 Sales $0.5 B $1.7 B Employees 18,394 27,765 R&D (1979): $85M, 5% of sales.	Pharmaceuticals (prescription drugs, nutritional supplements; 49% of sales), hospital and laboratory products (fluids, equipment, diagnostics; 41% of sales), and consumer, animal, agricultural, and chemical products (10% of sales).	Headquarters: Illinois U.S. provides 63% of sales. Int'l provides 36% of sales; Abbott operations cover major markets except East Asia.	Operating divisions organized around major product groups; international expansion typically via acquisitions and joint ventures (often leading to acquisitions). Focus on productivity and cost control (as measured by sales per employee).

(Continued)

Table 6.1 Comparative Company Statistics and Characteristics (Continued)

	Size	Primary Product Lines (1979)	Geography (1979)	Strategy/Structure
Johnson & Johnson	1970 1979 Sales $1.0 B $4.2 B Employees 38,200 71,800 R&D (1979): $193M, 5% of sales.	Consumer products (toiletries, hygenics; 43% of sales), professional products (sutures, diagnostics, equipment; 32% of sales), pharmaceuticals (contraceptives, therapeutics, veterinary; 15% of sales); industrial products (textiles, tapes, fine chemicals; 7% of sales).	Headquarters: New Jersey U.S. provides 56% of sales. Int'l provides 44% of sales worldwide through subsidiary operations in 44 countries.	Decentralized operations, research, and marketing; strong marketing capabilities; demands market leadership for all products; readily licenses or acquires promising products it has not developed.
Merck	1970 1979 Sales $0.7 B $2.4 B Employees 22,300 30,800 R&D (1979): $188M, 8% of sales.	Pharmaceuticals (human health, animal health, agriculture; 84% of sales), and environmental-pollution treatments (16% of sales). Merck offers over 1,000 products.	Headquarters: New Jersey U.S. provides 53% of sales; manuf. centered in NJ and PA. Int'l provides 47% of sales; but most initial manufacturing is done in U.S. and Ireland.	Leading-edge, centralized scientific research; consolidated marketing effort in late 1970s; "committed to growth through innovation and invention" (Merck & Co., 1979, p.14).

Sources: Abbott Laboratories (1970, 1979), Baxter International (1970, 1979), Foster (1986), Jasinowski and Hamrin (1995), Johnson & Johnson (1970, 1979), Merck & Company (1970, 1979), and Pratt (1987).

before they moved into biotechnology. In Chapter Nine, we will compare differences in the kinds of positions that people from Baxter, Merck, J&J, and Abbott ultimately took on in young biotechnology firms.[3]

Merck's Scientific Career Imprint

The career-history data reveal that people who worked at Merck typically held scientific positions before taking on roles in biotech companies, whereas people from Baxter, Abbott, and J&J held management positions. Approximately 70 percent of the total number of people from Baxter, Abbott, and J&J reported holding management positions (e.g., "manager," "director," "vice president"). In contrast, about an equal percentage of people from Merck held scientific positions, such as "senior research scientist," as held management positions (about 35 percent for each) before moving into biotech.

Further, examining the titles of those who held management positions at Merck reveals that 64 percent of these involved some sort of responsibility for a scientific area—"VP of Molecular Biology," for example. Most management positions at the other three firms were either function-based (for example, "VP of Marketing") or product-based (for example, "manager, Cardiovascular Equipment") or geographically based (for example, "VP of Europe"). Abbott was the least representative; only one person in the dataset had a title that included responsibility for any area of science.

Overall then, nearly 70 percent of the people who worked at Merck and subsequently moved on to biotechnology held a position that was science related. This includes people who held straight science positions and those who held management positions within a scientific area at Merck. Exactly the opposite was the case at the other three firms; the predominant model was to move from some sort of management position at these firms into biotechnology.

This pattern reflects Merck's reputation for an intense dedication to scientific excellence, and interviews with people who worked for Merck during this time period corroborate this viewpoint. People talked about Merck as having a "university-like atmosphere." As one person who worked closely with the company during this time-frame described:

> At Merck, people were rewarded for going to professional con-
> ferences and for giving papers. . . . Business was a lower form of
> activity! . . . The problem at Merck was that they had *no* interest in
> business; . . . that was the problem. All they wanted was to do
> science, like in a university!

Merck's emphasis on science was reflected in the company's hiring practices and organizational structure and culture, which in turn affected the types of career paths people pursued. The emphasis on science also reflected the vision and strategy of the company's founders. Merck's dedication to in-house science began in the 1930s with the revolutionary ideas of George Merck (around the same time that Bill Graham joined Baxter). George Merck introduced the idea of doing in-house research by creating top-notch research labs within the company, which, in the 1930s, were primarily oriented toward speeding up the production of penicillin (the company's first product).

Over time, and after Merck merged with Sharpe and Dohme in 1953, the company began to experience a clash of two cultures—the old scientific Merck culture and a new marketing culture. And, during the 1960s, Merck became a much more diversified company. However, under the leadership of John Horan, the company got back on its original scientific track—particularly, with the hiring of an aspiring and talented scientist named Roy Vagelos. Vagelos joined Merck in 1975 and became CEO a decade later.[4] Many accounts credit Vagelos with driving Merck's dedication and success in developing top-notch science during the 1970s and 1980s:

> [Vagelos] revamped the research operation, bringing in hundreds of
> new scientists, creating a managerial fast track for them, modernizing

the labs. . . . He sought—and found, he says—"really better people who wanted to work in drug development." He set up a crash program to ensure that half the new-hires would come directly from universities. Many of them—including all the Ph.D.s—he interviewed personally. Even after he became CEO [in 1985], Vagelos would meet with the senior scientists who were hired.[5]

As described, unlike at Baxter, Merck's "managerial fast track" was fed with people who had scientific backgrounds—not business backgrounds. Indeed, the picking grounds for talent for Merck were doctoral programs, not MBA programs, during the 1970s. And, just as the attraction to "run a business" at Baxter wooed top-notch MBA candidates, the attraction to "do great science" at Merck was similarly enticing to talented young scientists. As one informant explained:

> The science was *so* good at Merck that it truly was a toss-up for top Ph.D.s coming out of their programs as to whether they became scientists at MIT or scientists at Merck!

Another person who also worked closely with Merck during this time similarly remarked:

> If you were a top scientist, there is no other drug company you would have gone to other than Merck. Scientists viewed Merck as having the same values as the great academic labs. So, imagine yourself as a top-notch academic. You haven't gotten your Nobel prize yet. You are at MIT and your mentor says, "Well, you can leave." Why? "Because it's Merck!"

Looking at the kinds of people Merck hired reflects this emphasis on science. Over 50 percent of those reporting advanced degrees at Merck had Ph.D.s, whereas the other three firms reported having Ph.D.s half that often. Whereas Baxter senior management was interested in hiring MBAs to professionalize Baxter, Merck was keen on developing highly skilled *scientific* managers. Both companies offered stretch assignments and social reinforcement in the form of a strong culture, but at Merck, the content of those assignments and values associated with the culture were much more geared toward scientific innovation, whereas at Baxter, it was business expansion.

Merck's innovative culture and hiring and socialization tactics translated into career paths that were much less focused on general management than was the case at Baxter. Unlike Baxter, where people moved laterally to develop a general management perspective and set of skills, careers at Merck encouraged deep knowledge in a particular area—often a scientific area—rather than breadth of business capability. As one interviewee explained:

> Merck was a functional organization and the business came together only at the top. Research was a cost center. Marketing was a revenue center. Manufacturing was a cost center. So, the calculation of profit only came at the CEO's office . . . the first time all of these functions got together.

Therefore, in contrast to the general management skills developed at Baxter, Merck career paths fostered specialization in a particular research domain. Merck did not have the many general management opportunities that Baxter offered. As one advisor to Merck put it, "Merck has just one general manager—the CEO!" Therefore, unlike Baxter, one key aspect of the Merck career imprint was scientific capability, particularly in the areas of chemistry and biochemistry.

Baxter managers did learn about the science behind their products, but the depth of knowledge required was relatively low compared to the depth required at companies like Merck. Merck had a strong tradition of doing "Big Science."

Consequently, unlike Baxter, where status was associated with the size of the country or business one ran, at Merck, status hinged on one's scientific breakthroughs. This too was reflected in the hierarchical structure of the firm, as one person who worked for Merck recalled:

> MRL (Merck Research Labs) had all the power. When they were finished building a drug, they would throw it over the wall to manufacturing and marketing to sell. They just wanted to identify the biggest problems in medicine and solve them!

In contrast, developing scientific expertise, as a core capability, and expertise-based confidence were not cultivated at Baxter during this time period. As a Baxter alumnus explained:

> I don't think that we could be regarded as a bunch of scientific people, but we were curious. We wanted to know, and we had consultants, but Baxter was never known for its big great science, although there were some pretty meaningful inventions.

Further, in terms of connections, Baxter managers were paired with journeymen who knew the technology fluently, whereas Merck managers ended up working on research projects or in labs with teams, yielding different kinds of connections as well. Tony White of Baxter described his process of learning science through his mentor this way:

> Dale Smith was the guy who taught me about R&D and managing risk on the technical side. Dale was the technology guru in the company. When I ran Fenwal, Dale came to me a hundred times one way or the other and said, "Tony, you're not gonna make it if you don't learn this technology—if you don't understand the science." He never thought I knew it well enough, and he beat that into my head. Maybe I never knew it well enough to suit him, but I certainly knew it better than I would have had he not done that. And I knew it well enough to be successful.

As this quote shows, these kinds of close relationships allowed Baxter managers to cover what was a blind spot in the Baxter career imprint but a strength in the Merck career imprint—developing scientific skills and knowledge. At Merck, individuals *themselves* engaged in developing scientific expertise. At Baxter, managers relied heavily upon their strong ties with competent others—not just within the firm, but within the larger scientific community—as a way of learning what they needed to know.[6]

> The key is that while these [Baxter] folks did not have scientific backgrounds, they did have science and medical contacts. For example, through their work with Fenwal and Hyland, Carpenter and Termeer had connections to the academic institutions on the coasts (Harvard, Stanford, Caltech). This gave you the feeling that although you were in the Midwest—Deerfield, Skokie, or Morton Grove—you had a high level of contact with science and the medical community. You had business experience which was valuable plus the scientific connections. So, we knew who to talk to—Bob Carpenter knew who to talk to—at the Red Cross about Factor VIII, for example.

Baxter managers developed confidence in their ability to learn what they did not already know—understanding that, although they weren't the experts, they could figure out what they needed to know and "go do it." Quite the opposite was the case at Merck. At Merck, career paths fostered a sense of confidence from knowing that *you* were the expert. Expertise, and scientific expertise in particular, was cultivated and rewarded at Merck. As Gordon Douglas, former head of the Vaccine Division at Merck described:

> We always criticized Pfizer by saying that a lot of what they did was "me too" drugs, or that they licensed-in. . . . They [at Merck] believe in themselves. They know how to do everything better than anyone else. There's a great deal of confidence that the company has the people, the resources, and the facilities to do whatever it decides is the best course of action.[7]

At Merck, the confidence came from expert knowledge—"how to do everything better." Indeed, in conversations with former Merck employees, people often prided themselves on having this kind of expertise-based confidence and compared themselves favorably on that criterion to their competitors. (Pfizer was a common target.) As one former manager of Merck remarked, "Pfizer grew through M&A activity versus Merck's mentality, [which was,] 'We can do it ourselves!' . . . Merck people had that R&D confidence!"

In terms of connections, career paths at Merck, as at Baxter, fostered the development of strong internal and external connections. Merck employees were encouraged to attend scientific conferences and so developed expert-based extraorganizational ties. Further, given the significance of government legislation, regulation, and shifts in the political landscape for research-oriented drug development companies, Merck, like many large research-based pharmaceutical businesses, was very keen on maintaining credible ties with the regulatory community. As one interviewee explained:

> The emphasis at Merck was also on the sociopolitical sphere—for example, relations with the NIH [National Institutes of Health]. There was really no relationship between the price they charged and the costs of developing the product—it was really what society was willing to let them get away with. So, Merck formed interest groups to try and shape the emerging landscape.

Thus, given the significance of government legislation, Merck managers had to be extremely focused on gathering information and developing sound relationships with key regulatory agencies. To do so, managers often sought leadership positions in industry associations and employees were required to assist in the development of briefs and position papers to help prepare for important meetings.[8] Considering the high costs of developing healthcare products and the company's dedication to drug development, it is likely that the external ties developed at Merck were at least as strong as those developed at Baxter.

However, because Merck employees generally progressed up through a single division and made relatively few lateral moves, internal connections were primarily within one's division and, hence, relatively narrow in scope. Baxter ties were comparatively diverse, since Baxter careers entailed changing assignments, and often geographical location, every couple of years.

Working within a particular division for an extended period of time also enabled Merck to enjoy extraordinarily high levels of organizational commitment. As one prominent venture capitalist who has been involved in recruiting since the start of the biotech industry remarked:

> Merck is a very important company. . . . But recruit out of Merck?! Forget it!! People don't leave Merck. The first person I could ever recruit out of Merck was a medicinal chemist who I recruited out in 1994. It was Roy Vagelos who inspired a corporate culture that kept people there.

Another key difference between the career imprints of Baxter and Merck, then, lies in the types of intraorganizational ties the organizations cultivated. At Baxter, there were strong connections among managers at the senior levels (resulting from the assistant-to roles that new-hires were given) and at the peer levels (from the experience of joining a cohort); yet those ties were not strong enough to keep people from leaving the firm. At Merck, they were. Perhaps due to the frequent career moves people made across divisions and subsidiary boundaries within Baxter, people learned to cultivate relationships that then traveled with them as their careers changed. At Merck, the ties were less mobile—more binding to the firm—as the VC's comment suggests.

In sum, Merck's career imprint was characterized by capabilities that revolved around science and, to a lesser extent, functional expertise in key areas such as marketing. This contrasts with careers at Baxter, in which general management capabilities were cultivated above all else. Second, whereas both Baxter and Merck enabled the development of instrumental intra- and extraorgani-zational relationships, at Merck, the intraorganizational ties were likely stronger, more bound to Merck, and highly interconnected or dense. In addition to connections with regulatory agencies, Merck careers cultivated ties with scientific institutions; at Baxter they were more often associated with hospitals as well as regulatory bodies.

Merck helped build self-confidence associated with know-ing the answer—of building upon one's own expertise—whereas Baxter steered individuals, confidently, toward the unknown. At Baxter, confidence was oriented toward the future—knowing that one can learn; at Merck confidence stemmed from relying on what one already knew. Finally, although the cognitive mindset at both companies was results-oriented, at Baxter, this results orien-tation revolved around the business; at Merck, it revolved around science.

The common denominator across all four Cs—confidence, capa-bilities, connections, and cognition—in the Merck career imprint is the relevance and attention to science: stretch career assignments revolved around taking on more responsibility in a scientific area or division; external connections centered on building a professional and scientific community; and self-efficacy was built around the notion of being an expert—in microbiology, for example—in sci-ence. Thus, the career experiences borne out of Merck's organiza-tional strategy, structure, systems, and culture and the people hired all supported the development of a strong "scientific career imprint."

J&J's Boundary Spanning Career Imprint

Like Baxter, a large percentage of J&J employees who went on to join biotech firms had been managers (as opposed to scientists) at J&J. However, unlike at Baxter and Abbott where the manage-ment track appears to have been pretty uniformly established, at J&J the career paths were quite varied. The progression at both Baxter and Abbott was (after an entry-level position) as follows:

manager, director, vice president, executive vice president, and then president (of a division or function, for example). J&J alumni, as a group, sported pedigrees with more than twice as many title possibilities—senior vice president and/or executive vice president, for example, and executive director and/or group director and/or associate director.

J&J careers, then, were much more diverse than the standard, if informal, "general management track" that was evident at Baxter. Interviews with J&J alumni confirm this: there was no single "program" followed at J&J, informally or otherwise, despite the fact that J&J reportedly had a very strong human resources function and despite the fact that J&J has long been known for its deliberate and thoughtful attention to management development.[9] Without this "groupiness" among people in terms of the kinds of career paths followed, it seems logical that J&J did not cultivate as strong an organizational career imprint as was the case at Baxter, Abbott, or even Merck. There simply wasn't the same kind of uniformity or commonality across the career experiences of people at J&J. Still, as we will see, J&J had other levers, such as its well-institutionalized credo, that affected the commonality of the *experience* of working at J&J (the subjective side of these careers) and thus the strength of J&J's career imprint.

Several organizational design factors contributed to J&J managers' many different titles and positions at the company. First, J&J's size and breadth of products: J&J was a much larger organization than Baxter during the 1970s by a factor of about four, with over a hundred different companies associated with its many product lines. And as then president, James Burke, commented, "Companies in the family were managed as separate entities, each with its own . . . research, marketing, and production departments."[10] Therefore, different organizational strategies and structures were pursued within J&J's different companies, yielding varied titles and positions. Second, J&J pursued a growth-through-acquisition strategy. For aspiring executives this meant that there were many more points of entry into J&J management, in contrast to Baxter's tendency at that time to hire from MBA programs into a common "track," as it was often referred to.

Reflecting J&J's growth strategy and sheer size, J&J's organizational structure affected the kinds of opportunities and, hence, career paths that were possible. Importantly, J&J was highly decentralized. The company had (and continues to have) a large number of decentralized business operations that were organized by product line. Baxter, by contrast, had similar business or product lines but in multiple locations; therefore, Baxter was decentralized *geographically*, whereas J&J was decentralized by *business market segment* and by *geography* and so was more fragmented. As J&J's annual reports during the early 1970s described:

> Johnson & Johnson has typically grown over the years by creating new companies built around a particular technology or group of products. These companies, often previously units of a larger organization, are able to concentrate on a special area of business. . . . [J&J] is organized on the principles of decentralized management and conducts its business through operating divisions and subsidiaries which are themselves integral, autonomous operations. While direct line management of these units is maintained through the Executive Committee of the Board of Directors of the Company, operational responsibility lies with each operating management.[11]

In the late 1970s and early 1980s, J&J had over 160 distinct and separately run business units. These subsidiaries were formally organized into three healthcare businesses in 1986: Consumer Products; Pharmaceuticals and Diagnostics; and Professional Products. The latter was primarily a device business, like Baxter, and accounted for approximately 30 percent of total sales during the late 1970s.[12] The Professional Products segment, like J&J as a whole, grew in large part through acquisitions; the company made approximately thirty acquisitions during the late 1970s and early 1980s, which significantly expanded its product lines.[13] One person who has consulted for J&J for decades said that the company's preference for decentralization was so entrenched in the minds of longtime J&J executives that when these executives sat on the boards of other companies, they would "immediately recommend decentralization!" Another J&J alumnus explained it this way:

> They've taken decentralization and made it a mantra. Now you can make as many cases for why you shouldn't decentralize as why you should, but J&J actually elevated it to a religion. Decentralization is right there with the cradle!

To be clear, both J&J's strategy of growth-through-acquisition and its decentralized organizational structure have "worked" over the last few decades; J&J has not experienced an operating loss in its nearly 118-year history.[14] Further, those who operated at the top of J&J's business units had P&L responsibility and so had to take on a general management role within the company. Indeed, management scholars have written about the benefits of decentralized organizational structures like the one found at J&J for decades—for the very reason that they allow many individuals the opportunity to develop as general managers.[15]

Still, it is important to consider *where* these general management skills were developed; many J&J subsidiaries were acquired companies, as were their presidents. Those who entered J&J in lower-level positions and were groomed (rather than "acquired") for management, tended to do so in functional positions, such as sales or marketing, and then, slowly, moved their way up the ranks within J&J. Both the quantitative and qualitative data suggest that by the time these J&J employees reached senior-level positions, such as head of a division or an area, they were often ten or more years older than those holding equivalent positions at Baxter. Interviews with Baxter alumni similarly reflect this. As Schmergel recalled:

> When I was VP of Europe and would go to these [pharma associa-
> tion] meetings, I would feel like a kid! I would be the youngest by
> far, by ten or fifteen years, compared to the people running J&J
> Europe or Pfizer or other pharma companies.

One of the consequences of J&J's strategy and structure was a
sense of independence within the organization and across its subsidiaries. Indeed, J&J's subsidiaries were so autonomous that the
transfer of products across the subsidiaries represented less than
10 percent of total sales.[16] And one result of J&J's acquisition strategy, as reported, was that it did *not* foster the same kind of "just
do it" entrepreneurial mindset, as was the case at Baxter. As a long-
time J&J manager explained:

> J&J bought company after company, product line after product
> line. . . . So, there was not a huge entrepreneurial spirit at J&J. If a
> division is being spun off, it's unlikely that it's because of their expe-
> rience at J&J; it's more likely J&J acquired those people, and those
> people said, "OK, time to move on, but it is nice having J&J on my
> résumé."

J&J's choice of strategy and structure also yielded very different
kinds of management opportunities for people hired into J&J during this timeframe. J&J new-hires did not have the same kinds of
opportunities to build markets, as was the case at Baxter. However,
J&J *was* able to place people into functional positions such as sales
or marketing and then provide broad exposure across a number of
divisions and/or business markets. Looking at the larger dataset,
with the exception of a few individuals, J&J job titles included both
a function and a specific product division within the company. For
example, rather than "VP of Marketing" at Abbott, the title would
be "VP of Marketing, J&J Cardiovascular Division" at J&J. This
was true for both VP positions and director positions listed at J&J.
None of the other three firms exhibited the same pattern.

These "matrixed" positions, with job titles that reflected both a function as well as a division, lend additional insight into J&J career paths. Unlike at Merck or Abbott, where people entered into a specific function or area (typical examples include molecular biology at Merck or sales at Abbott), at J&J, individuals entered sales or marketing positions within a product division and then, over time, could become strongly affiliated with that division. Or, as mentioned before, people entered the company through acquisitions.

Consequently, the capabilities developed at J&J were *functional* (since people entered a function within a division at J&J); *technical* (since, over the course of time, individuals developed knowledge about their division's product); and also, but to a lesser extent than at Baxter, oriented toward general management. As two long-time J&J employees of pharmaceutical businesses explained:

> There wasn't an interest in having *everybody* understand how the enterprise made money. You had general concepts: there was sales and there was R&D and there was operations. And how it all came together was a little bit of mystery.

> You were not encouraged to have an understanding of everything else that was going on . . . At J&J, it was like, "Well, I'm in sales" or, "I do manufacturing." There was no general feeling of "We're all moving this ball forward." . . . J&J was so big, and so disconnected, that nobody actually believed that they made a big difference.

The second quote suggests that J&J's size stood in the way of some individuals feeling that they could have an impact on the company's bottom line. On the other hand, this more-focused perspective enabled people to develop significant expertise over time within J&J. As one J&J alumnus described:

> As senior executives rose in J&J, there was a natural reliance on what they already understood. So if you get somebody who's a

finance officer, all they're going to want to talk about is numbers. If you get somebody who came up through sales, what they're going to want to do is drill the sales plan.

J&J's functional start to the managerial career path matched what I heard from informants familiar with other pharmaceutical companies during this timeframe said:

The nature of the pharma industry is simply—and especially back then—an industry where everything gets integrated only at the very top. It was like the automobile industry in the sense that the pharma industry was enormously capital intensive. Below the top of the company, you had many fewer opportunities to hive off the business and have somebody have all responsibilities for that business [because of] the capital intensity of that pharma industry. You had people who came up on the sales side, who were leading multihundreds-of-million-dollar sales organizations, or even billion-dollar sales organizations, but had had nothing to do with manufacturing, had nothing to do with development. And then you had people on the marketing side coming up here, and then you had science people coming up. But really, integration only took place at the top.

J&J careers, like those at Merck, cultivated functional knowledge. However, at J&J, whereas people did develop functional expertise before advancing to management positions, they did remain within a single operating company for several years, giving them the opportunity to develop some product-based expertise as well.[17] As one J&J consultant explained, "People would stay long enough to know their markets since they had the hierarchy where they could challenge people." Consequently, like Merck managers, but unlike Baxter managers, J&J managers did develop confidence due to expertise—here, product-based expertise—that stemmed from the deep product and business knowledge they developed.

J&J's matrixed and highly decentralized jobs also cultivated diverse intraorganizational networks. In this respect, J&J's career imprint was much like Baxter's career imprint but for different reasons. At Baxter, these kinds of ties were developed as a result of multiple career moves across subsidiary boundaries. At J&J, the matrixed nature of managers' jobs required connecting with both corporate headquarters, at the functional level, and one's subsidiary regarding the business and product line. As a result, diverse intraorganizational networks were developed within J&J, as at Baxter.

Even though J&J was highly decentralized, with many autonomous business units, it had very centralized control systems; it employed what management professor Bob Simons termed "interactive control systems." For example, senior managers were highly involved in meetings in which short- and long-term goals were set. These meetings also included operating managers from all levels of the organization. At these sessions, managers made presentations and were challenged by superiors, subordinates, and peers.[18] Thus, J&J managers needed to be able to work across functional, hierarchical, and often divisional boundaries at J&J in order to appease the concerns and requirements posed by Corporate and still deliver for one's own relatively autonomous business unit. In this respect, J&J careers also cultivated learning-based efficacy since, in order to negotiate for resources, people had to learn how to "work your way through the company," as one alumnus put it. In that way, they developed confidence in their ability to find answers to their resource needs.

Working through these organizational control systems and matrixed bureaucracy required a different mindset or cognition— one that is more process-oriented than was the case at Baxter. Managers were expected to come to meetings with fully prepared presentations, often having floated their ideas by multiple members of senior management in advance of meetings. As one J&J alumnus described, prework was extremely important and reflected J&J's dedication to process as well as hierarchy. Responsibility for pre-selling remained with managers, as J&J's president James Burke described (in 1985):

> J&J is extremely decentralized, but that does not mean that managers are free from challenge. . . . If a manager insists on a course of action and we [the Executive Committee] have misgivings, nine times out of ten we will let him go ahead. If we say, "No," and the answer should have been, "Yes," we say [to the manager], "Don't blame us; it was your job to sell us on the idea, and you didn't do that."[19]

This contrasts with the stories told about Graham's hands-on management style and the kind of responsibility Baxter managers were given—to make their numbers and "sink or swim." It also contrasts sharply with the surprise visits from Baxter corporate and the "project teams" that kept Baxter subsidiary managers on their toes. J&J management's emphasis on process also led to a very different atmosphere for getting work done at J&J. As this quote from a former J&J manager who later worked for a Baxter alumnus at a biotech firm describes:

> J&J was polite. You just got used to it. [In contrast], if you go up in front of [Baxter manager] and you don't have your act together, you're going to take a public beating. Just get prepared. But I think the message is, "Don't let it happen." Whereas at J&J, you'd get talked to privately later . . . or you'd just disappear. . . . There would never be a debate though. It's just a different environment.

J&J's decentralized structure and sophisticated planning and control systems also led to managerial careers that stressed different capabilities than at Baxter. At J&J, managers learned how to negotiate across and within firm boundaries and how to make strategic and long-term decisions regarding the allocation of capital. Whereas Baxter managers had their *20/20* mantra, J&J managers used a very different phrase—"manage for the long term"—to describe their own focus and cognitive orientation.[20] As one person who has worked with J&J managers for years explained:

> General managers [at J&J] were asked how to make trade-offs. . . . If you invest more in R&D, then what's the trade-off? Their [planning and control] systems were very interactive: face-to-face discussions, very aggressive, very innovative. . . . They are good at figuring out how to allocate capital.

Additionally, J&J alumni reported that these kinds of managerial control systems taught them a great deal about finance and cost accounting. Taking this point to the extreme, one longtime J&J manager claimed that "J&J was basically a bank."

Clearly, with so much attention to financial detail and accounting controls at J&J, people developed sophisticated skills in financial management. Yet these skills were quite different from the kinds of financial capabilities that were cultivated at Baxter. At Baxter, people were building and entering new or emerging markets and dealing with many financial variables that remained uncertain or difficult to determine. At J&J, the emphasis was on designing and developing new products within businesses that already had a stake in a particular market; the financial analyses hinged on engaging efficiently and effectively in new product introduction and innovation. At J&J, then, there was much greater emphasis on making strategic and financial decisions that would allow an established business to flourish.

In terms of connections, since J&J VPs and below were not running entire subsidiaries or business units (and if they were, these were usually established businesses that had been acquired), the career paths at J&J did not provide exposure to working with external constituencies, such as regulatory agencies, as did the career paths at Baxter. In several instances, J&J alumni recalled instances in which this lack of an external network was surprising to them:

> Physicians—the big shots—want to talk to the boss; that's the way it is. But [J&J senior management] didn't have any idea of how to

To understand how this aspect of Baxter's career imprint emerged as important, let's return to the scientific developments and the first scientific products in biotechnology. The late 1970s, when the first wave began to move out of Baxter and into biotechnology, was just around the time in which genetic engineering began to explode. Recall that the early 1970s were the years in which the splicing of DNA took place along with the production, by Cohen and Boyer, of the first recombinant DNA organism.[19] Soon thereafter came the first generation of monoclonal antibodies.[20] In 1976, Herb Boyer and Bob Swanson founded Genentech, what has been widely considered the first biotech firm.

Cohen and Boyer's patent on the recombinant production of proteins was a significant scientific milestone for the industry. This was a method for splicing and replacing gene code so that a certain protein could be produced "recombinantly." Before this new recombinant technology, firms, such as Baxter, relied primarily upon extraction techniques to derive needed proteins. For example, Factor VIII was a known protein that, if given to hemophiliacs, would enable blood to clot. It was originally extracted from blood plasma, as Schmergel described from his Baxter days. Later, it was produced recombinantly and became the first major product of Schmergel's company, Genetics Institute.

In addition to Factor VIII, there were several other major products in the early days of biotechnology that were based on recombinant DNA technology and that were, in essence, focused on treating known diseases with new science. Insulin, for example, was originally extracted from the islet cells of pigs and used to treat diabetes. Genentech developed a product called Humulin, a recombinant form of insulin, which Lilly then sold. Similarly, Genzyme's product Cerazyme, which is used to treat Gaucher disease, is a recombinantly engineered protein. This protein replaced Ceradase, which was originally extracted from human placenta.

Erythropoietin (EPO), one of Amgen's blockbuster products, and Tissue Plasminogen Activator (tPA), which is marketed by Genentech as Activase, are also examples of early biotech products based upon this same basic process of producing proteins recombinantly. However, as opposed to the other early products that were, essentially, "replacement proteins," these two were "novel proteins" in which the precise application or market was not as clear at the outset.

Most of the first wave out of Baxter entered companies that were working on this early recombinant technology. Further, although some companies, such as Genetics Institute, did eventually try their hand at the novel proteins, most of the early products of this group were replacement proteins.[21] This early research and development was focused on known diseases, and the central issue was production—process research and development and the production of proteins. In several respects, this focus on production turned out to fit nicely with certain aspects of Baxter's career imprint. Still, VCs initially were neither aware of nor focused on these particular aspects of Baxter's career imprint when wooing the first wave.

In what unforeseen ways was Baxter's entrepreneurial career imprint a relatively good match for the ways in which these scientific products evolved? First, the underlying challenges associated with the early biotech products hinged on the capabilities associated with process development and manufacturing. In biotechnology, this entails the production of proteins and the scaling up of such processes in a safe and efficient manner; this was also a core aspect of Baxter's career imprint.

Second, as previously described, the science of that time period was geared toward developing biotech products for known markets. This shifts the emphasis toward tactics rather than strategy. Markets are known; process development is the key. In line with this, Baxter career imprint consisted of capabilities that centered around implementation and not strategy. Baxter managers clearly developed a dogged focus on what they called the "pragmatics" of the business—as the phrase "just do it" suggested.

Graham was the one pulling the strings on strategy. Thus, their focus and experience on the implementation side of the business could prove quite useful, given the direction of the early stage science in this industry.

Of course, it is important not to overstate this evolving match between Baxter's career imprint and the ways in which the early science played out in biotechnology. It wasn't perfect. As one alumnus explained, "It was a good enough match—a 75 percent match and the rest, well, you could learn once you got there." Here, Baxter's "just do it" emphasis on implementation in which managers were "learning by doing" turned out to be useful as well.[22] At a minimum, it appears that the gaps in Baxter's career imprint— that is, the general lack of experience developing strategy along with scientific expertise—were not particularly detrimental at *this early time* in the industry's history and given how these early firms got started.

These ancillary benefits, however, were unforeseen by VCs at the end of the 1970s. What was recognizable and primarily appealing was Baxter managers' "P&L driven" perspective and general management capabilities. Over time, biotechnology products did indeed turn out to require many more millions of dollars to produce than anticipated. As Bill Holodnak, one of the top headhunters in the biotech industry, summarized:

> Baxter recruited great people, gave them an honest deal, beat the shit out of them . . . vigorous Darwinianism . . . and paid them well, but never so much as to let them to get soft. . . . [Later, once they were in biotech], that discipline and awareness allowed them to envision how to stretch $10 million over three years.

Over time, as the development of biotechnology products and the industry evolved, it is likely that these capabilities and confidence and other unrecognized aspects of Baxter's career imprint contributed to the kinds of success they had, at least initially, in the IPO marketplace.

From the First Wave to the Second Wave:
Factors that Facilitated Spawning

The evidence presented so far suggests that the VC view of the requirements for running a small biotech matched relatively well with Baxter's career imprint. But, of course, neither the first nor the second wave might have left Baxter had they not felt dissatisfied in some way—that either (a) internal opportunities were decreasing for them within Baxter and/or that (b) external opportunities were rising out in biotechnology. Both of these things happened: organizational changes within Baxter, including Graham stepping aside, contributed to growing dissatisfaction within Baxter. Further, as the first wave proved successful, people began to experience their success collectively and so were enticed to make similar moves.

There were also facilitating factors that accelerated the rate of change out of Baxter. Specifically, the peer networks between the first wave and those still remaining at Baxter made it easier for a second wave to enter firms in biotechnology, through obvious mechanisms such as referrals to headhunters. In addition, Baxter's "ecosystem perspective," which encompassed a positive long-term orientation to departures, helped propel people outward.

We will explore each of these facilitating conditions— dissatisfaction within Baxter, a collective experience of success, social networks, and Baxter's ecosystem perspective—in turn.

Dissatisfaction Within Baxter, a Precondition for Career Change

A lot of these people wouldn't have left if Baxter hadn't changed. They weren't even leaving because they got fired or because they were bad people. They were the stars, the fast rising stars, who started bumping up against a lot of division presidents that'd been there a long time and weren't moving, . . . and the structure had gotten much more rigid.

Unless there is a reason to change jobs, individuals—particularly stars—don't tend to move. As decades of management research on turnover shows, one of the greatest predictors of turnover is (dis)satisfaction.[23] Therefore, no matter how convinced VCs might be that one company is a better recruiting ground than another, it is unlikely that people will actually change careers if they don't have any reason to do so.[24]

In the present case, three factors led people to greater and greater dissatisfaction at Baxter at the turn of the decade (from the 1970s to the 1980s). This dissatisfaction opened up a window of opportunity for VCs who were attracted to Baxter's career imprint to try and convince Baxter managers to make a move into biotechnology.

First, as Schmergel's story described, there was the "inevitable narrowing of the Baxter pyramid." Baxter managers had held general management positions and had become accustomed to feeling like they were "mini-CEOs." And yet, there was minimal opportunity to continue in that fashion since, as they often reminded, "There was only one CEO job at Baxter."[25]

Second, compounding this dissonance between what they had been brought up to appreciate at Baxter and where their careers were heading was the fact that Bill Graham, who had hired many of these now-managers at Baxter, was stepping aside. According to people who left Baxter, who stayed with Baxter, and who never worked at Baxter, there was a marked change in the way Baxter ran its operations when Graham stepped down as CEO in 1981, leaving a position he had held for twenty-seven years. These changes reduced many managers' commitment to Baxter.[26] Some people simply disagreed with the direction in which Vern Loucks, Graham's successor, and others were taking the company:

> One of the reasons I left the company [was that] Mr. Graham was backing off and Vern had organized his own internal group . . . and they were doing stuff I thought was nuts, like [creating] Baxter consulting hospital services. They were selling their services to hospitals as consultants in order to help hospitals save money . . . at the

very same time we're over here trying to sell parenterals to these
people at higher and higher prices.

Other Baxter managers felt that these organizational changes
reduced their autonomy, which they had come to enjoy as general
managers under Graham's leadership. In many respects, Baxter's
career imprint—the cultivation of entrepreneurial capabilities,
connections, confidence, and cognition—was shifting. People who
had been hired under Graham felt their original psychological
contract had been breeched.[27] The following account sums up this
sentiment well:

> In the early eighties . . . [Loucks] put in internal boards of directors
> for every business unit, every division. . . . And once a quarter, you
> had a board meeting. . . . Our joke was that it took several weeks to
> get ready for it; it took a week to do it with fine-tuning the presen-
> tation; it took several weeks to recover and answer all the questions
> that they asked you; and then, for a few weeks, you could run the
> business before you started the cycle again.
>
> So you had a combination of a group of animals that they had
> hired, and then trained to be entrepreneurs, and then they said,
> "But now we're changing the rules and it's not entrepreneurial
> around here any more. You don't have time for that; you've got
> to do all this bullshit." And I think [that] pissed off a lot of people
> who had had a good time up until then, thought it was fun, and now
> this wasn't fun. And so you had this exodus just at a time that the
> biotech industry was, in the early eighties, . . . looking for people
> who had an entrepreneurial bent, who had solved a lot of prob-
> lems, who had been in a very fast-growing environment.

Additionally, as Baxter managers began to read about the
advancements in genetic engineering, several were surprised and
disappointed that Baxter did not appear to be interested in investing in this new science themselves. Why the skepticism within
Baxter about biotechnology? Interviews with people inside and

outside of Baxter suggest three kinds of explanations: wrong business, poor advice, and missed opportunities. Regarding the first, the
vast majority of Baxter's products were device related. However,
the Hyland Division had entered the biological products area, and
yet, even at Hyland, it was outsiders who articulated the connection between Baxter and biotech. As Castaldi recalls:

> A professor up at the University of Washington was telling me,
> "Dave, this is a major revolution that is going on right now. And
> you're in the biological products business; you ought to be getting
> involved in this!" So, based on his scientific mentorship, I started
> visiting companies and learning what this technology was, and then
> bringing that back in [to Baxter] and educating. . . . [But] by this
> time we were starting into the DRGs [diagnosis-related groups], and
> money was scarce, and you couldn't do everything you wanted
> to do, and so while we did ultimately realize the recombinant Fac-
> tor VIII drug opportunity, we missed a major multibillion-dollar
> recombinant-erythropoietin drug opportunity that I had strongly
> recommended.

As Castaldi's account suggests, clearly Baxter was not ignoring
this new field entirely; they just weren't directly in the business
themselves. Largely due to people like Castaldi and his boss, Bill
Gantz, external opportunities for Baxter were becoming apparent.
Still, in many instances, such as Greene's pitch for monoclonal
antibodies, the perception was that Baxter's senior research people
were not interested.[28]

In a related fashion, Baxter managers such as Henri Termeer
became concerned that the advice that Baxter's new leaders were
receiving was causing them to miss out on significant opportunities:

> Consultants concluded that it was too late for Baxter to compete
> in the biotechnology field because the accumulated experience in
> genetics and other earlier-started firms was so large that you couldn't
> catch up anymore. . . . I was enormously frustrated that none of

these great things [got done] . . . like we proposed EPO before Amgen really got into it. Because we knew about EPO! Baxter knew more about blood and blood products and components of blood than almost anybody else!

In sum, the perception of these first-wave managers was that senior management at Baxter was not encouraging them to pursue possibilities in biotechnology that they found intriguing.

Overall, this welling dissatisfaction within Baxter opened up an opportunity for VCs who were attracted to Baxter's entrepreneurial career imprint to make their pitch to young Baxter managers. Importantly, this was not the case at other companies, such as J&J and Merck, where people were often described as "comfortable." Returning to the comments of one prominent VC, it was virtually impossible to lure people away from Merck at that time: "Hire out of Merck?! Forget it! People didn't leave Merck." Similarly, as an alumnus who spent decades in J&J during this same time period described:

> J&J has a lot of hangers-on. . . . They invest a lot of money in having you feel good about the corporation. So they do a masterful job of selling the image that is J&J. And they thrive on that—they support that whole imagery.

In contrast, biotechnology was not only an opportunity that appeared to match much of what managers at Baxter had cultivated, it also filled a void, as Baxter jobs became less entrepreneurial during the early 1980s. As one Baxter manager put it:

> Baxter had this very ambitious, competitive, well-educated, bright, energetic core of young people growing up who started to see that the same kind of growth opportunity isn't present that used to be present. . . . The biotechnology revolution was beginning to unfold in the same time period—the very end of the seventies and into the early eighties when DRGs hit. So here was the environmental

impetus that kind of drew this group of people . . . out into that opportunity, where you could try to recreate Baxter, the old Baxter environment.

A Collective Experience of Success

During the early 1980s, as the first wave took their companies public, their business success became highly visible—both to VCs as well as to managers who were still at Baxter. These visible accomplishments signaled that Baxter's career imprint "worked out," which led to positive perceptions and behaviors that accelerated the movement out of Baxter.[29] These early and visible wins inspired others to make similar career moves, as this quote by a second-wave Baxter manager suggests:

> Remember that there wasn't an obvious life after Baxter. We were young; the company was young. Over time, it became more permissible and possible to leave [and do well]. As people left, others saw that they could manage scientists, bring products to market, raise money. You could do great things! Create great products! Like Graham did! So, the great track records of those who were the first to leave Baxter really inspired those who came behind.

As people left for biotech, and as they developed "great track records," three things happened: first, people who were still working for Baxter began to believe that they *could* leave and second, people began to believe that there were financially attractive career opportunities beyond Baxter. These perceptions affected the behavior of a second wave of managers to leave Baxter for biotechnology firms. Third, VCs' early choices were confirmed, affecting their priorities for selecting people the next go-round.

Prior to biotech, the worldview revolved around Baxter. Post the first wave, the worldview shifted toward the "permissible" and "possible"—the notion that "maybe I can leave Baxter and be successful too." Not only was this larger collective of Baxter managers a "band of brothers with something to prove," as one interviewee put it, this was also a group of people who felt connected, whether they had actually worked directly together or not.[30] They had endured similar crucible experiences; they had a common set of "wars" and so, when one person "made it," others felt they could as well[31]:

> Gabe had left—Gabe had just left! Carpenter had left. Ted Greene and . . . I looked at all the prospectuses coming out. . . . In late 1982 and 1983, these guys were worth $5 million; by my calculations, I'd be worth one, $1.5 million if I stayed thirty years with Baxter. . . . I said, "Jeez, look at this!"

Second, as this quote also suggests, as people saw the successes of the first wave, they became convinced not only that it was permissible and possible to leave Baxter for biotech, it was also lucrative to do so.[32] Indeed, as recent research on stars has shown, high-performing employees are more likely to turn over when they feel they can no longer appropriate the wealth or "rents" they deserve.[33] The first wave's success made this discrepancy quite apparent.

Third and perhaps most important, the favorable track records of the first wave generated momentum among intermediaries, such as VCs, who similarly associated themselves with these early successes, confirming for them the merits of Baxter's career imprint. Referring back to an earlier quote, as one VC recalled, "I have the impression and was told . . . [that Baxter managers] catapulted ahead of the normal organizational structure, . . . and those were the people who left to run biotech companies." This general impression that Baxter managers were "ahead" coupled with the success of the first wave, as they took their firms public, led VCs to go back to Baxter and recruit again, which launched a second wave from Baxter into biotech.

The Power of Peer Networks

> It's sort of like being thrown into the freshman dorms when you're first going to college, and you're all a little scared and you have a shared experience in getting to know how to deal with being away

from home. Going to Baxter and getting thrown together with all of the challenges . . . [gave] this group of people a real sort of bonding experience within Baxter that made their interpersonal working relationships very close, . . . friends as well as just people that worked together. And those friendships have endured over several decades.

This account is from someone who never worked for Baxter but who worked for several ex-Baxter managers during his career in biotechnology. As this quote describes, Baxter managers cultivated strong peer relationships while at Baxter that later developed into strong social networks post Baxter. These external networks affected the second wave's movement into biotechnology in several respects: by introducing Baxter managers to headhunters, by directly hiring former colleagues, and by providing advice and information to Baxter managers to entice them to leave Baxter for biotechnology. In each instance, the credibility of these social network behaviors was enhanced due to the early and visible accomplishments of the first wave.

In the first instance, the first wave served as referrals for those still at Baxter, who had developed similar capabilities, connections, confidence, and cognition as they had. Indeed, as prior research has shown, referrals tend to improve the success rate of job seekers by improving the match between individuals and the positions available.[34] Still, it is also fair to conclude that the "great track records" of the first wave would have made their referrals even more credible and valuable to the second wave. Indeed, these referrals might have had limited value had it not been for the visible and early wins of Baxter's first wave.

In the second instance, the first wave simply hired people to join their own companies. As one alumnus described, Bob Carpenter had been calling him and calling him to "come out" East to join a biotech company. As he recalls:

I can remember that he had his IPO party, and he was opening bottles of champagne, and he called me [on the telephone]! He had been calling me and calling me and saying "come out!" and so, finally [after this phone call], I came out.

Similarly, Gabe Schmergel called on Tuan Ha Ngoc to join Genetics Institute, and Ted Greene called on Tim Wollaeger to join Hybritech. Such offers were all the more enticing when they came from the first wave, due to their promising track records. Additionally, the strength of Baxter's career imprint made going back to Baxter for new recruits easy. As Leon Schor, long-time consultant in the industry described, they spoke a similar language:

> Henri Termeer basically surrounded himself with Baxter guys. There was a common shared language that nobody had to learn.

Third, the success of the first wave and what had been learned at Baxter enabled others, like Gabe Schmergel, to offer credible advice to people still remaining at Baxter who were contemplating the move into this new industry. As Jim Tobin of Boston Scientific recalls:

> Gabe came to Boston as head of GI when GI was like five employees. He had been head of Europe; we had all worked for him when he was running Europe. . . . He would just make it a point to pose names to headhunters. And, he'd talk to the [Baxter] guys and say, "This is pretty good; you get to do x, y, and z in biotech" . . . and little by little, a number of this crew ended up going into biotech. So I think it was the raw material in the first place, the experience that you got in the process, and then Gabe acting like a little siren song, bringing everybody to Boston.

Finally, in addition to the actions of Baxter alumni, intermediaries also used the momentum of the first wave to convince others to join up with young biotech firms. VCs depend upon those they have already placed for information about people to tap for the next top management job. Additionally, finding people who can serve as "role models" can make all the difference in convincing someone to join a young biotechnology company—particularly during the early years of the industry. As Brook Byers, an early investor in Genentech and many other pioneering biotech firms, put it:

> Role-modeling is extremely important in recruiting. Sure, we always use a search firm and our large network of professional friends, but role-modeling is always essential. It was required back when biotech was a young industry because the idea of leaving a large company for a young one with few resources was frightening and seemed full of risks. So, we would fly to Chicago and meet with a candidate and be greeted with a stone face. We would tell the executive or scientist about the great idea, the cool science, the wonderful scientific advisory board, the founders, and the candidate would begin to warm up. But, there was still a "prove to me that leaving what I have is a good idea." To break through that objection based on fear, I would have people we had already recruited out of large companies call the candidate and tell their stories of transition and [how they were] finding joy in working in an entrepreneurial environment. . . . That worked better than anything else.

The strong peer networks that were part of Baxter's career imprint similarly affected the mobility of a second wave into biotechnology. Importantly, however, these ties would have been relatively useless had it not been for the perceived success of the first wave. The VCs were more likely to believe the advice of the referrals and to use those people as referrals, as were the managers who remained at Baxter. Thus, we find that both the ways in which Baxter's career imprint led to a first wave that had a "great track record" as well as Baxter's peer network were critical to a second wave leaving Baxter for biotechnology.

An Ecosystem Perspective

A final factor that facilitated the many career moves out of Baxter and into biotechnology was Baxter's ecosystem perspective.[35] When formal employment relationships ended, Baxter left open the possibility for future business interactions. Thus, Baxter had what could be called an "ecosystem perspective"—that is, the orientation that relationships should remain intact since, eventually, departures may benefit the firm. As one Baxter alumnus described, "When you left Baxter, there might be a little bit of grumbling, but basically the attitude of [Baxter senior managers] was 'OK, that's life; now what can we do together?'"

Baxter's ecosystem perspective was especially apparent after the acquisition of American Hospital Supply (AHS) in 1985 when several reorganizations followed. These reorganizations resulted in fewer general management jobs, and so, even greater possibility of departures. Yet even prior to the AHS acquisition, once their alumni began to gain recognition and visibility in the industry, Baxter had begun to develop its ecosystem perspective. Senior managers such as Gantz and Castaldi recognized that working with alumni could provide a perfect entrée for Baxter, as a firm, into biotechnology. The deal made between Baxter and Genetics Institute in 1982 is one good example of this mutual interest and of the benefits of Baxter's ecosystem perspective.

Additionally, Baxter's ecosystem perspective derived from the kind of psychological contract that Mr. Graham developed with prospective managers, as described in Chapter Three. Given the small number of senior management jobs available, people expected there would be turnover among the middle management ranks and learned, from their experiences at Baxter, how to maintain extraorganizational ties:

> Everyone knew that when they hired fourteen MBAs, that at the end of year one, there would be eight, and at the end of year two, there would six. Everybody knew it. Those facts and figures were well known. . . . It was the way the system was set up from the beginning. So rather than fight it, Baxter just expected people to leave and then kept the connections. It was almost like a fraternity or a sorority; you kept [those] close college ties.

Baxter's ecosystem perspective revealed itself in a number of ways, including the "alumni reunions" that Baxter held. The first alumni reunion, a Sunday brunch, was held around the winter holidays of 1981 at Bob Carpenter's house; about twenty people attended. Over the next four years, other Baxter alumni took turns hosting such gatherings, including Pete Phildius, Gene Zurlo, and later, Gabe Schmergel. Rumor has it that there is even a Baxter flag that traveled from house to house, which I was jokingly asked to trace during my interviews.

Later, in the mid- to late-1980s, these alumni gatherings were sponsored by Mike Kenyon and Doug Scott's consulting firm, which they formed after leaving Baxter. By the end of the 1980s, as many as one hundred people were attending these formal gatherings. As one alumnus commented, "A fair amount of what Baxter biotech is now came out of those [alumni] relationships."

Even during the 1990s, after the early alumni reunions had tapered off, people still found opportunities to gather. Nearly every ex-Baxter manager interviewed mentioned the gala event they attended for Bill Graham's eightieth birthday in 1999. As pictures attest, it was a black-tie affair, and Graham had his picture taken with every Baxter alumnus who attended. During this event, Graham expressed his pride in the accomplishments of Baxter alumni. Graham told them all:

> You know, I have been very proud of what Baxter has become and accomplished. . . . I'm most proud of the fact that there are, I think, forty-three CEOs in this room.

Vern Loucks attended alumni gatherings as well and made similar kinds of statements commending Baxter alumni. These appearances and speeches legitimated, in many respects, Baxter managers' decisions to leave Baxter for biotech and so fueled the aforementioned collective experience of success and referral networks that were percolating amongst the first and second waves.

In Contrast

None of the other healthcare firms that VCs most often mentioned as potential breeding grounds for top managers in biotech—Merck, J&J, and Abbott—had as early a first wave as did Baxter. Figure 7.1 shows the timeframe of when people left for top positions in biotechnology from the four different firms studied.

As previously described, VCs generally viewed the managers working at these other firms as less "entrepreneurial" and so were less inclined to recruit from them for top management positions at the very start of the industry. The only company that comes close to generating such a visible group of CEOs in biotechnology is Abbott, with CEO/entrepreneurs such as George Rathman, Jim Vincent, and, more recently, Paul Clark. Abbott, recall, was Baxter's fiercest competitor. However, as Figure 7.1 shows, top management spawning from Abbott occurred later and in a much slower fashion than was the case with Baxter. Overall, as we will explore again in Chapter Nine, spawning out of Abbott was more often into lower-level management positions rather than top management positions such as the CEO or president.

Further, Abbott's spawning did not yield the same scale in terms of numbers of executives in biotechnology as did Baxter. One reason for this may be traced to Abbott's relatively insular, as opposed to ecosystem, perspective on departures. Consider the following personal observation from a Baxter alumnus who hired several people away from Abbott:

> It was totally different with Abbott [than with Baxter]: when you left, it was like you didn't exist; you were the scum of the earth. It was just a totally different attitude. And I hired three people away from Abbott! The day they left, Abbott didn't want to know that they had ever existed. I just sat back and said, "That's real strange." I saw that as being very odd, given the Baxter philosophy.

And, consider the following quote from an Abbott manager who made similar comparisons between Baxter and Abbott regarding departures:

Figure 7.1 Waves of People Who Left Healthcare Firms to Become CEOs and Presidents in Biotechnology (1979–1996)

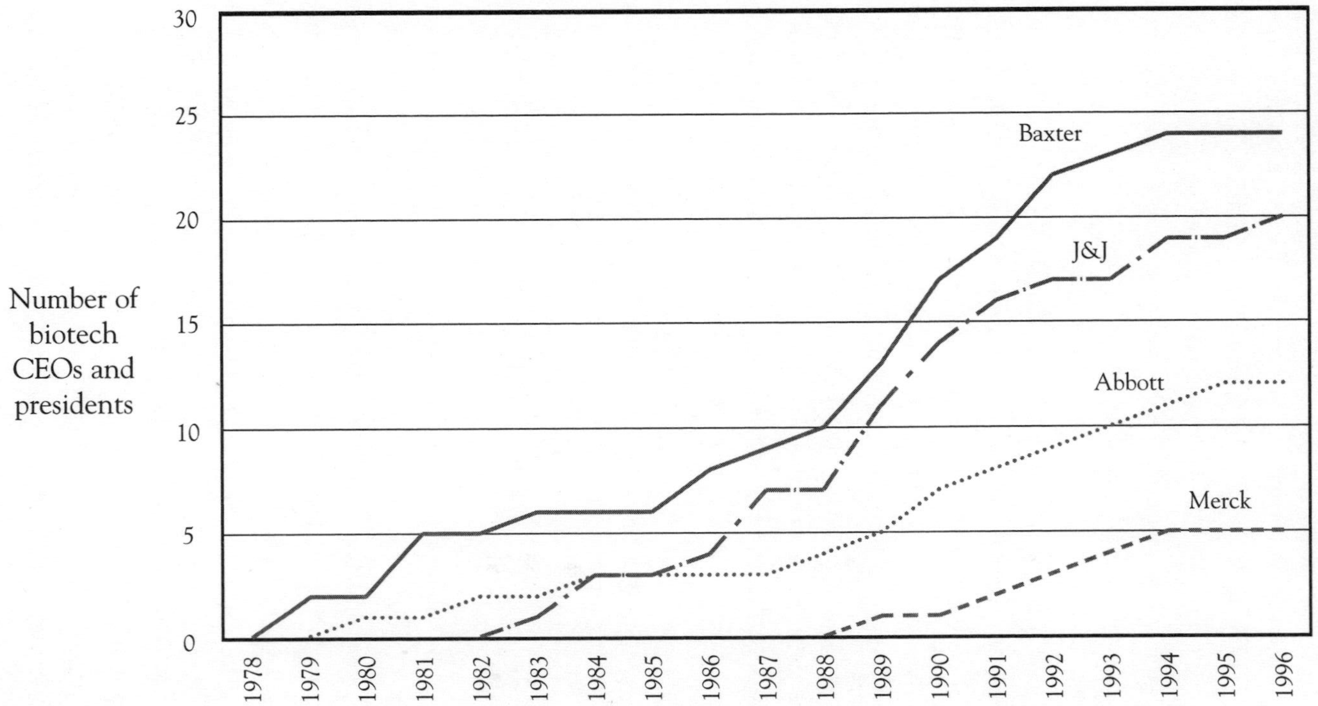

[Abbott management would say], "When are you leaving? You're never going to be happy again. . . . Do you realize what's *out there?* I mean, look at what we have! . . . My God, I mean you'll never be happy again. . . . But, by the way, if you do choose to leave, don't let the door hit you on the way out. And you have fifteen minutes to clean out your office—because we don't really like stupid people around here who don't get it."

In contrast to this defensive stance, Baxter senior managers like Graham were disappointed, of course, but later made individuals feel proud by publicly recognizing their successes—at the alumni reunions, for example. One Abbott alumnus who had witnessed the Baxter alumni gatherings and the business that was being done both between Baxter and its alumni and between the alumni themselves tried to create the same kind of helping behavior among Abbott alumni. Unfortunately, his efforts were not successful, at least not in the way that he had intended. As he recalled:

So [Baxter] would have all of these . . . old studs—previously young studs—who had left [Baxter], come together, grab a beer and chitchat, connect, laugh, make contacts too, pick up the tab too—unheard of at Abbott. . . . So my point was, let me go to Abbott guys who left, and see if we can establish the same thing. . . . I tried to establish an Abbott alumni association. . . . [But] what it became was an arena for Abbott guys who had left to become headhunters—to find candidates—or for people without assignments to come and beg for jobs. And it was not what I had intended it to be. I had intended it as an opportunity for a bunch of my colleagues to network, to come together, to do the same thing [as Baxter alumni had done].

We can also get a sense for the lasting impact of Baxter's ecosystem perspective and what this Abbott alumnus thought was useful beyond "job hunting" if we look at the alliances formed between these two firms and their alumni in biotechnology over the years. Here, we find that Baxter's one deal with GI surpassed all of the deals put together between 1980 and 2002 between Abbott and biotech firms led by Abbott alumni. Overall, during this time period, Baxter has done over four times the dollar volume in deals with Baxter alumni-led public biotech firms, compared to Abbott.[36] Thus, this ecosystem perspective may have benefits not just for providing managerial talent to young biotech firms but for helping them establish financial footing.

Summary

Career imprints affect the evolution of industries, particularly when powerful intermediaries—such as VCs—find them appealing. VCs and headhunters have worldviews that can shape the decisions that people make about joining new ventures, and those perspectives are influenced by the kinds of career imprints they observe at different firms. In this instance, VCs were looking for businesspeople to partner with scientists who had been working in academic laboratories who could build, grow, and run "genetic engineering" businesses. They also had their own pressing needs not only to "get in on" but also prove themselves by producing returns for their investors in this emerging industry. Among the many healthcare firms that VCs could have turned to for top managers in young biotechnology firms—including Merck, J&J, Abbott, and Baxter—VCs found Baxter relatively more appealing, as the data suggest, due to the kinds of entrepreneurial capabilities, connections, confidence, and cognition that managers had cultivated while there.

In addition to the perceptions of VCs, the perceptions of those making these career moves are important to consider. Career imprints shape the kinds of perceptions people have about what they *could* do and so, can influence the perceived opportunities for career change as well. Here, Baxter managers perceived that their general management capabilities and confidence were well-suited to the emerging biotechnology industry, relative to those at other firms, and so were drawn to consider the kinds of opportunities to which VCs were exposing them.

In the longer run, career imprints can have an impact on an industry's evolution, particularly once a first wave has left and has shown signs of success—in this instance by raising money and by taking their companies public. As Schmergel, Carpenter, Termeer, Chubb, and Greene began to build "great track records," the match between Baxter's career imprint and the requirements of the industry not only became more clear, the strategy of recruiting out of Baxter was, in a sense, confirmed. VCs became even more convinced that Baxter was a place to return to for managerial talent, propelling subsequent mobility into biotech.

Beyond this collective experience of success associated with the first wave, three other factors facilitated this spawning process: growing dissatisfaction within Baxter, as the company underwent significant change, external networks among Baxter alumni that served as referrals for others still remaining at Baxter, and Baxter's ecosystem perspective and behaviors that legitimated these career moves. Each of these factors, both separately and together, facilitated the movement of a second wave out of Baxter and into biotechnology. Even Baxter's fiercest competitor, Abbott, could not benefit from a lasting spin into biotechnology, since it did not have the final component—an ecosystem perspective.

Chapter Eight

The Legacy of Career Imprints for Organizations

> That was the signature: seeing how delegated
> responsibility along with accountability can allow
> even young inexperienced managers to grow and
> develop. . . . That's the big lesson that I think just
> about everybody in that organization took away,
> how powerful that is. And I think that's reflected
> in the organizations these guys have built.
>
> —*Baxter alumnus Christopher Bartlett*

We've considered the broad, industry-level consequences of career imprints; in this chapter we'll turn the prism slightly to examine the effects of career imprints on organizational design and focus. Career imprints travel as people move from employer to employer and so can have a lasting effect on organizations beyond the ones in which they were cast. Particularly during critical times in an organization's life, the career imprint a leader brings to a new organization can have a profound impact on how that firm evolves.

One way to think about the effect of career imprints on organizations is in terms of what management scholars call "logics of action." When faced with tough organizational decisions, managers try and simplify their political and organizational landscapes; they look to rules and frameworks that they trust to help them navigate through various uncertainties.[1] In the prior chapter, in which we focused on VC decision making, we saw how VC criteria such as a "general manager . . . with a P&L view of the world" was a logic of action that VCs used to make hiring decisions. In that case,

Baxter's organizational career imprint helped VCs simplify their decision making such that, as one VC said, "When you see Baxter on a résumé, it means something." Following this example, knowing that Baxter produced people who were "P&L driven" matched VCs' logics of action regarding the requirements for running a young biotech firm and so helped VCs decide where to recruit. Over time, as one Abbott alumnus described VC behavior, "Baxter became the darling of the biotech industry."

In this chapter, we will explore how organizational career imprints include logics of action that individuals take with them regarding how to lead and design a young firm. Here, "logics of action" could be thought of as an aspect of the "cognition" component of an organizational career imprint. People take with them from an employer capabilities, connections, confidence, and ways of thinking about the world that include, but are not limited to, how one should lead and design an organization.[2]

Put differently, leaders with strong career imprints often try to re-create aspects of where they "grew up" in their careers by employing logics of action from a previous employer; they try to re-create their old breeding grounds. Since organizational strategy, structure, and culture are key design factors that affect the opportunity structures and, hence, career experiences of individuals, we would expect to see reflections of these design features in the firms these leaders built.

Starting Points for Understanding
the Legacy of Career Imprints

Throughout the data gathering for this study, outsiders, such as VCs and consultants, described Genzyme as a "mini-Baxter." Phrases such as "Genzyme could be the next Baxter" came from multiple sources, suggesting that this would be a logical starting point for understanding the legacy of career imprints. However, examining only Genzyme and how Henri Termeer's organizational design choices reflect the breeding ground Termeer experienced at

Baxter could be misleading. That's why this chapter compares the organizational decisions of two leaders, Henri Termeer from Baxter and Jim Vincent from Abbott, who moved to Genzyme and Biogen, respectively.

These two leaders' design choices are useful as points of comparison in several ways. Vincent worked at Abbott for the same length of time and at approximately the same time that Termeer worked at Baxter (from 1972 to 1982, approximately). Vincent headed up Abbott's Diagnostics Division, whereas Termeer headed up Baxter's Hyland Division. Both had MBA degrees from prestigious business schools (Harvard and Wharton). Vincent joined Biogen at approximately the same time that Termeer joined Genzyme (1985 versus 1983). Both companies are located in the Northeast in Cambridge, Massachusetts—indeed, right across the street from one another. This is important since firms located in the same regions could, arguably, benefit from similar kinds of regional advantages (e.g., being equally close to major research institutions such as MIT).

To the extent that Baxter and Abbott had different career imprints, we'd expect to see these differences play out in the kinds of design choices Termeer and Vincent made as leaders of the biotech firms they joined. But in addition, to be fair in this comparison, we will also consider similarities in the design choices of these leaders.

It is also important not to overstate the comparison. First, whereas Termeer came directly from Baxter and had limited experience prior to working at Baxter, Vincent spent eight years prior to Abbott at Texas Instruments (TI). This is why, as appropriate, we need to be careful to attribute the imprint to TI and/or to Abbott, as necessary. As Vincent himself explained, "My approach to the Abbott responsibilities was a refinement of what I learned at TI."

Second, there are certainly many factors, in addition to a leader's prior career imprint, that affect the implementation of design choices such as corporate strategy and structure. For example, there are times in a firm's life that may make it more or less ripe for the cultivation of a new career imprint. In the case of Biogen, for example, Vincent faced a turnaround situation and one in which a company already had a good deal of history including, perhaps, the organizational career imprint inspired by Wally Gilbert, Biogen's CEO prior to Vincent. In contrast, Termeer arguably had far more latitude, in many respects, to effect change, given the limited history associated with the company when he joined Genzyme. That is why, at the end of this chapter, we will also explore some of the potential barriers to exporting an organizational career imprint by taking a look at one more case—Gabe Schmergel's early decisions at Genetics Institute.

A brief historical overview of the early years of Genzyme and Biogen will provide a sense for the context in which Termeer and Vincent made organizational design choices. These two firms evolved differently; here, the idea is that at least one contributing factor to such differences lies in the logics of action or cognition that leaders exported from their respective experiences at Baxter and Abbott. A summary of the similarities and differences in the organizational design choices of Termeer and Vincent discussed in this chapter is shown in Table 8.1.

Genzyme, The Early Years

Genzyme Corporation was founded by Henry Blair, an enzymologist, in 1981. Blair had been working to supply the National Institutes of Health (NIH) with the enzyme glucocerebrosidase for use in the NIH's experiments on enzyme replacement therapy for the rare genetic disorder Gaucher disease. In 1981, Blair received venture capital backing, along with his NIH contacts, and began to grow the company, Genzyme, through acquisition. Some of these initial acquisitions were international; Genzyme's early offices were in the U.K., and so the company had an international presence from its inception.

Henri Termeer joined as president of Genzyme in October 1983, was made CEO in 1985, and remains CEO as this book goes to press; Blair is a Genzyme director. When Termeer joined, the firm

Table 8.1 Comparing Core Organizational Design Features:
Genzyme versus Biogen

| | Differences | | Similarities |
	Genzyme	Biogen	
Strategy ↓	• Niche focus, narrow markets[*] • Independent from big pharma	• Product breadth, big markets[**] • Collaborative with big pharma	• Focus business on generating $ through biotechnology • FIPCO† model • Global strategy
Structure ↓	• Decentralized, business units[*] • Overseas GM positions, operations[*]	• Centralized, functional[**] • Overseas marketing and sales positions[**]	• International positions
Culture	• Process development and manufacturing driven[*]	• Research intensive	• Tough, not cruel management style
	[*]Similar to Baxter	[**]Similar to Abbott	

Organizational Design Dimensions

†Fully integrated pharmaceutical company.

had an office building on the top floor in an old loft building in Boston's "Combat Zone" (a rough area in the city). Genzyme was an operating company, based upon its enzyme business; however, it was losing money. At that time, the company had approximately twenty employees; by 2004, it had grown to over 5,500 employees worldwide. As described earlier, before joining Genzyme, Termeer had been working in Baxter's Hyland Therapeutics Division, which produced products derived from blood for people with hemophilia and surgical patients. Genzyme's twenty-year anniversary book—published in 2002—describes Termeer's joining up as follows:

> With his business education, healthcare experience, and interest in biotechnology as a means of avoiding safety issues with human-blood-based products, Henri was just the sort of person the

biotechnology industry was looking for. At Baxter, he had seen the powerful human impact and the business value a niche product could have, and he liked [that] practical, product-based start. . . . Henri Termeer brought to Genzyme important elements of what would become its ongoing business strategy and culture. In part because of his experience at Baxter, Henri helped establish individual responsibility and drive, empowerment, risk-taking, and teamwork as essential values. As other Baxter alumni joined Genzyme, they reinforced this groundwork.[3]

In November 1983, Blair, Termeer, Genzyme's scientific advisory board, Genzyme's senior management team, and some venture capitalists began to formulate strategy for the young biotechnology firm. Genzyme's first patient was treated in 1983 with a Genzyme-supplied enzyme, glucocerebrosidase, at the NIH. This enzyme was used to treat Gaucher disease, a very rare genetic disorder that is caused by an enzyme deficiency. In 1984, Genzyme began work on a recombinant form of that enzyme, which eventually led to the approval and production of Ceredase in 1991, Genzyme's first significant therapeutic product. In 1994, a genetically engineered version of this enzyme, called Cerezyme, was approved; this product has been employed to treat approximately 3,300 people worldwide who have Gaucher disease. Since Ceredase, Genzyme has pursued enzyme replacement therapies for other rare genetic disorders such as Fabry disease, Mucopolysaccharidosis (MPS) I, Pompe disease, and Niemann-Pick Type B.

In addition to these developments in therapeutic enzymes, in the early days of Genzyme, the firm also marketed diagnostic raw materials (enzymes and substrates) to manufacturers of diagnostic kits, manufactured fine chemicals and the difficult-to-produce antibiotic clindamycin phosphate, and developed surgical biomaterials. Genzyme sought to retain the value of these products through vertical integration and so in the 1980s quickly set up manufacturing, marketing, sales, and distribution capabilities, all in-house.

During this same timeframe of the 1980s, two other biotechnology firms were also founded that have since joined Genzyme.
Integrated Genetics (IG) is one such firm, which was founded by
Bob Carpenter, also a Baxter alumnus, in 1981. IG focused on
producing therapeutic proteins through mammalian cell culture
and on using DNA probes for genetic and diagnostic testing. IG
went public in 1983, Genzyme went public in 1986, and the two
companies merged in 1989. In 1990, IG Labs, one of the only
DNA labs outside a hospital or university context, was spun out
as a separate operating company; Genzyme maintained majority
interest and IG was later bought back in 1995 to become part
of Genzyme General Division. IG Labs, with the acquisition of
approximately fifty labs, has remained among the largest
providers of genetic testing in the United States. IG's expertise
in the area of therapeutic proteins was instrumental in Genzyme's
preparation for the production of the recombinant version of
Ceradase.

Biomatrix was also founded in 1981 and focused on extending
the uses of hyaluronic acid (HA), a product that Genzyme had
been manufacturing during this same timeframe. Biomatrix went
public in 1991 and was combined with Genzyme Tissue Repair
and Genzyme Surgical Products in 2000 to create Genzyme
Biosurgery. Much of Genzyme's early success came from the production of HA as a medical-grade bulk product. Over time and
with the acquisition of Biomatrix, Genzyme expanded its purview
of the application of this product and usage to many other surgical
procedures.

The 1980s, after Termeer joined, were the formative years for
Genzyme. Both the business and scientific foci were solidified, and
Termeer dedicated himself to putting the firm on sound financial
footing. At the end of the 1980s and through the beginning of the
1990s, Genzyme underwent tremendous expansion, particularly
overseas. Whereas Genzyme was an international organization
when Termeer joined in 1983, much of the overseas operations had
been in sales and marketing. In the later 1980s and early 1990s, the

firm's strategy of vertical integration expanded overseas, as Genzyme set up multiple international manufacturing facilities. Additionally, during the 1990s, Genzyme expanded into oncology.

Biogen, The Early Years

Biogen was founded three years earlier than Genzyme, in 1978. At the time of founding, the firm was a collection of approximately a dozen prominent scientists, including Phillip Sharp, Charles Weissmann, Walter Fliers, Ken Murray, and Wally Gilbert, among others. Several, including Wally Gilbert, would go on to earn Nobel Prizes in their areas of expertise. Two venture capitalists, Dan Adams and Ray Schafer, helped bring this collective together to create a transatlantic company dedicated to a wide range of commercial, biologically based products.[4] Most of the original employees of Biogen were post-docs of the founding scientists and many were based in Geneva.

The late 1970s and early 1980s were an exciting time to be a scientist in a research-based organization such as Biogen. The NIH had funded an extraordinary amount of research in biology, and this was leading to some intriguing possibilities for biologically based products. It was also a time of fierce competition among early players in the industry such as Amgen, Cetus, and Genentech. As Joe Rosa, director of Development Interface at Biogen Idec, explained:

> In those days, the whole industry was working on many of the same things . . . tPA, EPO, . . . things for which there was already a lot of biology understood. Consequently, there was good reason to believe that, if you could just make these things, you'd have a drug. And so the name of the game was to clone them, get the patent, and then make them. Make a lot of them.

Biogen was one of the original biotech companies competing in these early races—for example, against Amgen, for the development of EPO, which eventually became one of Amgen's blockbuster products.

Despite Biogen's early losses in these areas, Wally Gilbert, Biogen's scientific founder, was eager to continue to explore path-breaking scientific work in biology and so turned to research contracts to support these efforts. In 1983, Biogen completed its initial public offering. Over time, Gilbert, who was then CEO of Biogen, became intrigued with the idea of building the company around its own product. To do this, Gilbert decided to gamble on a cancer-fighting drug called Gamma Interferon. Unfortunately, Gamma Interferon met some unanticipated difficulties during clinical trials, which, given the amount of resources dedicated to this initiative, ultimately led the company into a precarious financial situation.

In 1985, Gilbert stepped aside as CEO (though he remained on Biogen's board), and Jim Vincent joined Biogen. Vincent had graduated from Wharton's School of Business in 1963. His first post-MBA job was at Texas Instruments (TI), where he launched TI's Germany and Tokyo businesses. Vincent considers the first "major gear shift" in his career to be when he moved from semiconductors at TI to medical devices at Abbott. Vincent spent ten years at Abbott, from 1972 to 1982. At Abbott, he developed the Diagnostics Division into a formidable competitor, and, as one Baxter alumnus described, completely "muscled Baxter out of their diagnostics business." This division, along with Roche, has retained leading market share in the diagnostics business worldwide.[5] At Allied Signal, where Vincent spent three years post Abbott, he launched Allied's healthcare business. From there, Vincent joined Biogen, where he remained as CEO and/or chair of Biogen from 1985 until July 2002.

Vincent is credited with turning Biogen around and, indeed, with its survival. As Vincent recalled, when he first considered Biogen, it looked about "ready for the casket!" Preceding Vincent's arrival, Biogen had been viewed by the investment community as "wasteful," and in many instances, Biogen's "inefficiency was interpreted as symptomatic of a company run by scientists."[6] When Vincent joined Biogen, expectations were high for Vincent to "make the tough decisions." As one investment report glowed:

> Mr. Vincent is no stranger to the healthcare industry nor to steering a business through its growth phase. At Abbott, he established and built the diagnostics operation, as he did at the healthcare business of Allied-Signal. Known for his strong-willed, no-nonsense approach to running an operation, Mr. Vincent is already focusing on cost control and the development of an optimal strategy for product development, licensing, and marketing.[7]

The 1980s for Biogen, like Genzyme, was a period of dramatic growth and renewal. After Vincent sold off Biogen's mirror operations in Geneva, investors reported that the company was "emerging wiser and more focused."[8] One area of focus was Alpha Interferon. In 1986, Schering-Plough, which had obtained worldwide manufacturing and marketing rights, began commercial sales of Intron A (Interferon alfa-2b), the first Biogen-developed product for the treatment of hairy cell leukemia. And in 1989, SmithKline Beecham, Biogen's licensee for its hepatitis B technology, launched Engerix-B (hepatitis B vaccine) in the United States. By 1988, Biogen had recovered financially, with $50 million in cash in the bank and with many promising scientific milestones well within its grasp.

During the 1990s, both Biogen's scientists and products increasingly gained worldwide recognition and acceptance. In 1993, Biogen founder Phillip Sharp received a Nobel Prize in Medicine for his discovery of split genes. That same year, another Biogen founder, Kenneth Murray of the University of Edinburgh, was knighted for his discovery of hepatitis B antigens. In 1996, the FDA approved Biogen's Avonex (Interferon beta-1a) for the treatment of relapsing forms of multiple sclerosis

(MS), and a year later, the European Medical Evaluation Agency (EMEA) approved Avonex for European marketing and sales. Then, in 2000, Biogen and Elan Corporation announced their collaboration and commercialization of the drug candidate Antegren (natalizumab) in MS and Crohn's disease indications.

Comparing the Legacies of Career Imprints at Genzyme and Biogen

With this background information on the early years of Genzyme and Biogen, let's turn to the kinds of organizational decisions Termeer and Vincent made when they came to these firms. Here, we'll consider three kinds of organizational design choices these leaders made in the 1980s—organizational strategy, structure, and culture. These three elements were identified in Chapter Three as important for understanding the developmental context in which individuals' careers unfold and in which career imprints emerge. Organizational strategy and structure affect the types of stretch opportunities people are given, whereas organizational culture affects the social reinforcement of what is learned at an employer.

We begin by examining leader decisions regarding organizational strategy. Organizational strategy is often considered a driver of many other kinds of design choices, including organizational structure and culture.[9] These leaders' early choices regarding strategy narrowed the degrees of freedom regarding the organizational structures and culture that would fit with their chosen strategy. Still, the data here suggest the choice of strategy did not *necessitate* other choices; the influence of early career imprints had an effect on design choices beyond strategy, such as organizational structure and culture. Over time, of course, organizational strategy, structure, and culture become intricately interrelated, making this, necessarily, a simplified account of what is a highly complex and dynamic process.

Organizational Strategy

Similarities in Strategy between Genzyme and Biogen. One of the first strategic moves Termeer and Vincent each made was to restructure and consolidate their respective organization's activities. Like Termeer, Vincent began at a biotech company that was in dire straights financially. And although the two situations are quite different, given the stage of the science at these firms, there are some interesting parallels to consider.

First, in response to the financial crises, both Termeer and Vincent took immediate steps to restructure overseas operations. At Genzyme, Termeer eliminated unrelated wasteful spending such as the company racehorse and cottage; Termeer kept the U.K. operations open because they had already started generating revenues from diagnostics and fine chemicals.

At Biogen, the situation was quite different in that the company was not generating revenues; rather, Biogen Geneva was a research location that many felt was duplicating efforts that were going on in the United States. Closing down Biogen's Geneva offices was painful for many, given the company's historical roots. Still, as scientists who lived through Vincent's decision described, "It was inevitable," given the dire situation the company was in. For Genzyme, Termeer's elimination decisions were similarly coded as inevitable by investors, since the company had swayed from its original mission in biotechnology.[10]

Second, both leaders focused maniacally on the commercial viability of their companies' biotechnology activities. Termeer immediately sold off noncore assets, and several reports suggest that Vincent eliminated 85 percent of Biogen's scientific projects. As Joe Rosa of Biogen recalls, Vincent used to sit in board meetings and ask the most simple and yet compelling questions, such as "Why would a company like Biogen want to do this?" Thus, both leaders took steps to turn their companies into viable business entities focused exclusively on biotechnology.

Third, both leaders wanted to build global organizations. And yet, their reasons for doing so varied. Vincent chose to compete in

Organizational Design Dimensions (label on left, with downward arrow)

large markets, which, from his perspective, meant that he had to compete globally:

> In order for a long-term pharmaceutical strategy to succeed financially, it must be global. The high cost of R&D must be amortized over the global market.

Termeer envisioned Genzyme as a global organization from the early years as well, but this emanated from a very different strategy—his focus on orphan drugs and so the need to build close relationships with the international communities in order to both abide by and influence their laws governing such markets. As we will see, these similarities and differences in globalization strategies dictated some aspects of organizational structure at the two firms as well.

Finally, both leaders had a similar long-term vision or end goal for their firms—to become a fully integrated biotechnology firm, one that could market and sell its own products. This was the fully integrated pharmaceutical company (FIPCO) model, and it was attractive to many early biotech firms, including Genentech and Amgen. Yet, again, there were many different ways to achieve this long-term goal, as we will examine next.

Differences in Strategy between Genzyme and Biogen. Genzyme's strategy, under Termeer, can be summed up simply as niche focus and independence. One interviewee described a conversation he had had with Termeer in which Termeer described Genzyme's niche strategy as follows:

> We find these orphan-drug situations where there is huge value for the patient, and we deliver something that they can't get otherwise.

Gaucher disease was one such market, a place where there were unmet needs for a rare genetic disorder. Pursuing this very rare disease appeared at first to be a huge bet for Genzyme since tackling this disease required extraordinarily expensive R&D and manufacturing operations. Termeer's decision to go after Gaucher disease was extremely unpopular at the time; it went against the advice of Genzyme's scientific advisory council and other senior managers, who were concerned the move might bankrupt the company. It did fit within the government's "orphan disease" category, which raised barriers to entry for the following seven years.[11] Still, recalling the uncertainties of the mid-1980s, one NIH member was quoted as saying, "I would like to ask Henri how he had the guts to make that decision."[12]

One reason that Henri had the "guts" stemmed from the second core pillar to his strategy—maintaining independence as a company by internally generating the funds it needed to finance "risky" projects. Rather than overextending itself, Genzyme minimized risk by using nonequity investments as well as internally generated sources of revenue. In 1987, one year after Genzyme's IPO, Termeer was quoted as stating:

> Genzyme's operations continue to grow at a formidable pace. . . . We are operating on a cash positive basis so that we now have more cash available to fund our expansion than we did a year ago. Genzyme's strategy continues to be to build a highly profitable, human therapeutics company on the sound foundation of a profitable business. Our resources are sufficient to support our continued growth and expansion without reliance on the capital markets.[13]

In line with this philosophy, Termeer engaged in a wide variety of equity financing tools, all of which were designed to allow Genzyme to maintain as much control as possible over its products.[14]

Analyst reports echoed this vision. The following quote from a Prudential Securities report in 1988 is typical of the coverage Genzyme received during the 1980s: "The company will focus on niche markets of drugs that are technically difficult to produce, not merely commodity products that any other generic drug maker could easily produce."[15] As Kidder Peabody reported that same year:

These current businesses and niche drugs are plenty to justify the current valuation and to support Genzyme's evolution into a small growth company with predictable expansion of sales and earnings and steady appreciation. The positive investment case is one of high probability with little downside risk.[16]

In many respects, then, what appeared to be a "risky" bet to go after niche markets such as Gaucher disease was actually quite conservatively managed. Termeer was determined to fund this and other projects from within—to continue to generate cash internally and thus build the company "on the sound foundation of a profitable business." During the early years, it is clear that Genzyme's production of HA was one such source of revenue. In 1988, the investment community remarked on the unusual nature of this strategy:

> The opportunity for Genzyme [is] to participate in the success of a number of potentially interesting therapeutics, without incurring the same degree of risk associated with innovative drug development. . . . Genzyme has already established a presence in the diagnostic enzymes and fine chemicals markets with an extensive line of products currently being sold to the research market and corporate customers. Revenue derived from the sales of these products has served to offset the costs associated with the company's longer-term therapeutic projects.[17]

Finally, significant margins for Genzyme's products, once those niche markets were served, enabled the firm to generate internally the resources it needed to explore new opportunities. In a 1988 analyst report, Termeer was quoted as saying:

> The current average margin for the company is around 45 percent, which is made up of a mix of high-cost production of new products and low-cost production and higher-margin sales of products like diagnostic enzymes and research biologicals. . . . In products that we will market directly ourselves, [the margins] will be relatively high

(in the 75 percent range). . . . When we negotiate with companies (I don't think this is a reflection of greed, but more of a reflection of contribution), it is very important for us to have an interest that gives us 50 percent or more of the sales dollar of the product.[18]

In several respects, Genzyme's niche strategy and independence reflect key elements of Baxter's career imprint. First, Termeer's focus on orphan drug development and, more generally, targeting niche markets is remarkably similar to Graham's Willie Keeler "hit 'em where they ain't" strategy, in which Baxter targeted niche opportunities that had been neglected by other companies. Genzyme's niche market strategy was to focus on hard-to-produce products for a very small targeted market. Thus, the entrepreneurial career imprint Termeer picked up at Baxter seems to have carried over in a very direct fashion to Genzyme—in particular, in the types of "new market" opportunities Termeer sought.

Second, Genzyme's focus on being "independent" and Termeer's determination to become and then remain a profitable business also reflect Baxter's entrepreneurial career imprint. One of the core capabilities of the Baxter career imprint is the ability to manage the top and bottom line, as reflected in Baxter's *20/20* mantra. Baxter managers developed a sort of "scrappiness," as a VC described it, which was unusual for healthcare managers and highly valuable in the biotech start-up environment. At Genzyme, like at Baxter, managers were and remain still "maniacally focused on the P&L." As one Genzyme employee, unprompted and unaware of Baxter's *20/20* mantra, told me that Termeer often told investors that he expected "20 percent growth," as a benchmark. "It was 20 percent or greater. Always. No matter what!" Indeed, in January 2005 a story appeared in *The Boston Globe* quoting Henri Termeer, who told reporters that he wanted "Genzyme to achieve sustainable earnings growth of 20 percent a year."[19]

Termeer's steadfast determination to generate cash to fund new business endeavors echoes lessons learned about managing multiple businesses at Baxter. As one biotech executive who spent many years at Baxter reflected:

> None of us was particularly good in finance, . . . but we did all learn about how to capitalize companies [and] how to manage that capital to give you more flexibility to do what you wanted and what needed to be done.

Finally, Genzyme's niche strategy and the pricing strategy that went hand in hand with operating in low-competition market spaces were highly reminiscent of Baxter's pricing. Baxter's strategy was to corner as much of the market as possible and to price high—either because it had the superior product or because it had the only viable product. So too was the case at Genzyme, in particular for their product Ceradase. As one Baxter alumnus, again unprompted, remarked:

> Henri Termeer's the one that learned the lesson the best of all of us [from Baxter]. . . . Termeer's pricing of that product that he sells for $250,000 a year?! I think he got the niche thing straight!

In Contrast, Biogen's Strategy: Big Market Focus and Collaboration. Many biotech companies during the 1980s engaged in early partnerships with pharmaceutical giants just to stay afloat. As of 2004, only a handful of mature biotechnology firms had been able to generate sustainable profits. In those cases, earnings have derived from the rare opportunity to retain rights on a biotech company's own products. In contrast, most young biotech companies engage in licensing agreements with big pharmaceutical companies, particularly during their early years. This more traditional strategy was the one followed at Biogen during the 1980s.

When Vincent joined Biogen in 1985, he refocused Biogen's strategy. Gilbert, Vincent's predecessor, had envisioned Biogen as a fully diversified biotechnology company, whereas Vincent wanted to build a "biopharmaceutical" company that focused on human therapeutics. Still, even with this new focus on human therapeutics, compared to other biotechnology companies, including Genzyme, Biogen maintained a relatively broad product pipeline and big market focus throughout Vincent's tenure at Biogen.[20] As Vincent described his mission back in 1987 in the annual letter to Biogen's shareholders:

> Our mission is quite simple. We intend to be a fully integrated pharmaceutical company focused on human therapeutics. . . in just three fields—AIDS therapy, inflammation, and selected cancers. . . . We have and will continue to establish licenses with leading pharmaceutical companies to provide a financial base and enhance our revenue growth.[21]

The investment community responded favorably to this broad focus in therapeutics. It saw Biogen as "emerging from an extended period of . . . serious financial distress" and was bullish on Biogen's prospects in the late 1980s:

> Biogen has one of the broadest product development programs to be found anywhere in the industry. Its portfolio includes products at various stages of development and in most of the major product areas available for development in biotechnology today. . . . An investor in Biogen gets broad participation in biotechnology without risking the investment on any single product candidate.[22]

Biogen's strategy was the relatively more popular strategic approach to building a biotechnology company at that time. Unlike a niche strategy, it did offer investors the opportunity to spread their risk across a variety of potential markets. The logic was that if a company such as Biogen could spend the same amount of resources to develop a product that could serve millions as opposed to thousands of patients, then, priced appropriately, this could make a company quite profitable. As Vicki Sato, then head of R&D for Biogen, recalled:

> Jim always said, "Whatever you do, do it right. And, think big! It can't be too small, in terms of revenue capture. Think big—big enough to break out."

Many firms, including Genentech and Biogen, preferred this latter approach and so aimed for the large and more traditional markets, such as inflammatory diseases, immune disorders, and cancer.

The only catch to this approach is that Biogen, like other biotechnology firms at the time, did not have the internal resources it would need to actually service such large markets, even if it came up with a viable product. For example, a product, such as Humulin, the recombinant form of insulin for diabetics, is marketed to general practitioners and, because of this, requires a massive sales force. Furthermore, a sales force would need to be up and ready just as soon as such a drug is approved. Most young biotechnology companies couldn't make such enormous bets. If, however, a company such as Biogen could partner with a pharmaceutical company and license out its drugs during Phase I or II clinical trials, then the biotech firm would benefit from receiving cash as the product hit certain milestones, earn royalties when the product was on the market, and then apply those funds to its own research endeavors.[23] Indeed, this is the tack that Vincent ultimately took with Biogen.

Before Vincent arrived, as one investment report described, Biogen's "opportunity to reap a substantial return from the future commercialization of products derived from its research efforts was essentially lost to the corporate benefactors."[24] Vincent worked diligently to redefine these contracts into much more collaborative and longer-term relationships with big pharma. This way, Biogen could more easily benefit from royalties on the products it had licensed out. During the early 1980s, Biogen had two major innovations that fit this structure—Alpha Interferon, which became an anticancer and antihepatitis drug, and the sequencing of the hepatitis B genome. This collaborative approach was quite different from that taken at Genzyme, where Termeer refused to engage in partnerships with big pharma. Again, however, it is important to emphasize that Vincent was in a position in which he had inherited partnerships along with a company that was in dire straights; as Vincent remarked, "We had to do these partnerships just to keep the lights on!" Additionally, this collaborative approach fit well with Vincent's business strategy to go after "big markets," as he described it.

In many respects, the strategy that Vincent put in place at Biogen is reflective of Abbott's strategy during the 1970s and 1980s. Further, we see the same kinds of differences between Genzyme and Biogen as we do between Baxter and Abbott. First, like Biogen, Abbott did service a broad range of markets, including pharmaceuticals. Abbott's products ranged from diagnostics, consumer products, animal health products, and chemical products to pharmaceuticals.[25] Unlike Baxter, Abbott did not follow a niche market strategy.

Additionally, Biogen's focus on cultivating its own expertise (which, in this case, was in research) and then transitioning the product to other firms with different expertise (such as pharmaceutical firms, which were expert marketers) is reflective of Abbott's functional career imprint, in which business positions were relatively narrowly defined by function or area of expertise. As one long-time Biogen employee described, when talking about Biogen's use of contract research organizations (CROs) to do their clinical trials:

> That's something [that] has become a bit of Jim's legacy. . . . We try to spend our resources, intellectual and financial, on things that matter. The things that you need *one* of are not worth building in-house.

Vincent's "legacy"—focus on what you can do and outsource the rest—contrasted quite a bit with Termeer's more independent and entrepreneurial approach. As stated in Genzyme company documents:

> As an entrepreneurial organization, Genzyme is committed to maintaining its independence. This commitment led us to adapt financing mechanisms from other industries that would enable Genzyme to keep the rights to its technologies and products. As the biotechnology industry developed, many young companies raised money by selling such rights to large pharmaceutical companies, but Genzyme would not follow that path. Instead, the company relied on product revenues and novel financing.[26]

Organizational Structure

In many respects, the differences in Genzyme's and Biogen's organizational strategies affected the kinds of leadership choices Termeer and Vincent made with respect to organizational structure.

Similarities in Structure between Genzyme and Biogen. The major similarity between the organizational structures of Genzyme and Biogen is the international reach of these two organizations. Having a global organizational structure was a direct result of pursuing a global organizational strategy. As described, Genzyme had operations overseas in the U.K. when Termeer joined Genzyme, and Biogen had research offices in Geneva when Vincent joined Biogen. And even after Vincent closed down the Geneva facility, he maintained the European side of the Scientific Advisory Board to maintain the company's international connection to the scientific community. Termeer did not shut down Genzyme's diagnostics and fine chemicals operations in the U.K. upon his arrival, and he expanded upon Genzyme's international presence substantially, particularly in the 1990s. These leaders had different rationales for pursuing a global strategy, and these differences are reflected in the two firms' organizational structures.

Differences in Structure between Genzyme and Biogen. As part of Termeer's strategic efforts to remain "independent," he organized Genzyme as a vertically integrated firm with multiple functional areas all under Genzyme's roof. From the start, Termeer's divisions were organized by product line.

When Genzyme went public in 1986, Termeer promised investors that he would not rely upon corporate partnerships to fund research projects. In order to achieve such autonomy at the division level, Termeer employed innovative financing arrangements at Genzyme. In many respects, these arrangements enabled Genzyme to maintain a highly decentralized organizational structure.

Eventually, in 1994, still determined to remain an independent company, Termeer pioneered the use of tracking stocks in biotechnology. Tracking stocks (also known as "targeted" or "lettered" stocks) are traded independently from the corporation's stock, which created very autonomous business units. In the 1990s, Genzyme set up four such tracking stocks: Genzyme General, Genzyme Tissue Repair, Genzyme Molecular Oncology, and Genzyme Surgical Products. The rationale was as follows:

> This "company-within-a-company" approach allows each business unit to act entrepreneurially, with its own focus and own access to capital. It also enables investors to choose areas of special interest. And it allows the divisions to draw on the resources of the overall company in such areas as R&D, regulatory affairs, and manufacturing.[27]

In recent years, this organizational structure has come under increasing scrutiny, eventually culminating with the consolidation of these entities in 2003. Still, the evolution toward a more and more decentralized organizational structure, under Termeer's leadership, does appear to reflect more than just the niche strategy that Termeer chose. Businesses were very much regarded as separate entities, with division heads who were ultimately responsible for every aspect of making their particular business profitable. The head of the

Pharmaceutical Division at Genzyme, which did *not* have a tracking stock, described the relative advantages of that structure:

> For me, tracking stocks are a motivation story. Without them, there is very little I can show illustrating our achievement. . . . I can be proud of our P&L, but because of our size [only one hundred employees], it disappears in Genzyme General's annual report.[28]

Termeer also changed the structure of Genzyme to become an even more global organization during the 1980s and, in particular, during the 1990s. By 2003, Genzyme was marketing and selling its own products in eighty different countries and had substantial operations in the United States and beyond, including the U.K., Switzerland, Ireland, France, Germany, Italy, the Netherlands, Brazil, and Japan.

In several respects, Termeer's decision to make Genzyme both highly decentralized and global reflects Baxter's entrepreneurial career imprint. First, both Graham and Termeer adopted decentralized organizational structures as a tool to motivate and develop its employees. At Baxter, the organization was decentralized geographically, whereas at Genzyme, the organization was decentralized based upon both product lines and geography. Genzyme's division heads and country managers, like Baxter's country managers, were held accountable and so were developing skills and capabilities at managing many aspects of an entire business. At Baxter, running a division or country was a "sink-or-swim" opportunity and results were highly visible. Similarly, results were highly visible at Genzyme, particularly in the era of tracking stocks.

Additionally, and more generally, Termeer's progression toward a division-oriented structure fits with Genzyme's "entrepreneurial ethic" and so with Baxter's entrepreneurial career imprint. Particularly in Baxter's International Division, where Termeer spent many years, Baxter's decentralized organizational structure allowed for a great sense of autonomy among the employees and required a "just do it" action-oriented approach—a "nothing is impossible" orientation. So too was the case at Genzyme. As Termeer describes:

> I look for people with a passion to tackle things that seem impossible to solve. Practical dreamers who have a sense of compassion but believe they can change things. . . . And we attract people who see what we are doing as a worthwhile fight.[29]

In Contrast, Biogen's Structure: Matrixed with Global Marketing and Sales Structure. In contrast to Genzyme's decentralized divisional structure, Biogen was organized around scientific and business areas of expertise in a more centralized and matrixed fashion. Unlike Genzyme, Biogen had no product or country divisions until 2000, when Biogen opened a single division in Canada. In that instance, it was a marketing and sales division. Further, unlike Genzyme, prior to 2000 and since the closing of Geneva and its small operations in Zurich, Biogen did not build any operations overseas. Rather, in 1995, Biogen built its own centralized manufacturing operations in North Carolina's Research Triangle.

To understand how Biogen's organizational structure emerged, we need to return to the context in which Vincent joined Biogen. The original structure of the company was scientifically based. Members of the firm's large and impressive scientific board were charged with acting as sponsors of their own particular projects and were promised shares in proportion to their projects' impact over time. In effect, although Biogen also had a business board of directors with members from top pharmas such as Schering and Monsanto, the scientific board was functioning as Biogen's operating committee. This was unusual for a biotechnology company— to have scientists essentially running the business of the firm—and this went on for seven years before Vincent joined Biogen. When Vincent, a businessman, came on board, he was initially viewed with much skepticism. As Vincent recalled:

> They saw me as a suit, not a scientist, . . . who's "trying to bring large-corporation lessons to us!" They expected me to bring down

the tablets, to have the answers [and they] were shocked when I
said, "No, we're going to figure out the answers together."

In order to put the firm back on sound financial footing,
Vincent hired in many "suits"; depending upon who is asked, anywhere from eight to ten to fifteen people were on Vincent's senior
management team. As several Biogen managers commented,
"Biogen was *very* centralized . . . even micromanaged, by Vincent."
This created a certain amount of tension within the firm. Although
many scientists understood that these changes were inevitable, it
did dramatically shift the informal sources of power within Biogen
as well as Biogen's formal reporting structure.

On the "business side," Vincent filled in traditional functional areas such as human resources, finance, and business
development. However, in addition, and reflecting the kind of
organizational structure he had experienced at TI, and to some
extent the Diagnostics Division of Abbott, Vincent decided to
put in place project managers who were each responsible for specific projects that the company was working on. This led to a relatively flat and yet matrixed organizational structure. As Vincent
described:

> If I had my druthers, I would have kept the organizations separate,
> but I couldn't afford that. They needed close-haul coordination
> from the CEO so that the company could move at flank speed with-
> out having to create line management for everything . . . without
> having to further decentralize.

Genzyme, in contrast, was further down on the continuum toward
decentralization, as it had divisions with full P&L responsibility
and, during the era of tracking stocks, even had external
constituencies to cater to, such as Wall Street.

Regarding geographical structure, there were clear differences
between the design choices of Termeer and Vincent as well.
Whereas Termeer consciously built a presence for Genzyme overseas both in manufacturing and marketing, Biogen licensed out

those activities during the 1980s. Biogen did benefit tremendously from international sales, however. As Joe Rosa, longtime scientist at Biogen recalls, "Jim is quite rightly proud of . . . the fact that . . . we're the first company ever to register a drug in the U.S. and Europe with fewer than a thousand employees."

In several respects, Biogen's more centralized and matrixed organizational structure does reflect aspects of Abbott's functional career imprint. And, as before, the differences between Genzyme and Biogen mirror differences between Baxter and Abbott. First, like Abbott, Biogen has had a much less decentralized organizational structure than Baxter or Genzyme. Although, clearly, Biogen's project management structure that Vincent says he took from his days at TI moved the pendulum further toward decentralization than was the case at Abbott, it is also quite clear that Vincent saw limits to decentralization that were not perceived by Termeer.

Further, Biogen, like Abbott, did not have many general management jobs (whether as country heads or division heads). Also like Abbott, Biogen had an international presence, but primarily with respect to the sales of its products, as opposed to operations. This contrasts with Baxter's and Genzyme's organizational structures, which did have significant operations overseas. More generally, Genzyme's organizational structure, like its strategy, was more business-oriented and highly entrepreneurial. This was also reflected in its culture.

Organizational Culture

Organizational cultures derive from shared assumptions about how one should behave and feel in an organization. Behaviors are manifestations of organizational culture and so can provide important clues as to what an organization's culture is.[30] In particular, leaders' behaviors can lend insight into the kinds of assumptions that organizations reinforce.

Similarities in Culture between Genzyme and Biogen. In the case of Genzyme and Biogen, we find that both Termeer and Vincent had a tough-but-not-cruel management style and an achievement orientation that pushed people to work very hard. The following account is from Richard Douglas, a senior vice president at Genzyme who has worked for five Baxter managers, including Termeer:

> One of my first introductions to Henri was going to a senior management meeting where [a senior manager] was reporting stuff about his business, and he hadn't done his numbers [and Henri got mad]. I couldn't believe that [the senior manager] didn't quit! The next day, [the senior manager] was there and everybody seemed happy. I had never experienced personally anything like that in my life! . . . But to some extent I just realized that that was part of the give and take that this group of people [from Baxter] had.

In a similar fashion, Joe Rosa of Biogen described Vincent's penetrating style as follows:

> At the board meetings, . . . Jim would always sit here [in the middle]. There'd be a stage and there'd be tables set [with] lots of seating in the back for everybody else. All the board would sit around the table and Jim would be right in the middle with Phil Sharp on his right [along with] Jeremy Knowles, Wally Gilbert, [and] Charles Weissmann; it was pretty amazing! But Jim would sit in the middle of the room and . . . inevitably, Jim would ask the most penetrating question.

Vincent, like Termeer, paid careful attention to the details and was no stranger to giving people tough feedback:

> [Jim Vincent] could be intimidating. But on the other hand, he wasn't aristocratic. You didn't feel uncomfortable in his presence, but . . . if you talked nonsense to him, he's gonna not be pleased.

As another employee recalled:

> If you had an idea, you *had* to make your case to Jim. And, it was tough—like running into a wall, again and again and again!

As these accounts suggest, Termeer and Vincent were direct in providing feedback and in asking tough questions of their managers. Still, neither leader created the same kind of "sink-or-swim" culture that characterized Baxter during Graham's era.

Differences in Culture between Genzyme and Biogen. A company's values can also lend insight into an organization's culture.[31] At Genzyme, Termeer instilled a set of values that centered mainly around process development and manufacturing. As one Genzyme alumnus described:

> Henri loves producing stuff. Manufacturing is Genzyme's strategic competitive advantage, not research, . . . which may rub some people the wrong way—but not Henri. Manufacturing has always given Genzyme the upper hand in negotiations because they know how to produce stuff and that's unusual. It's a business. Not a research institution.

This quote is from a long-time Genzyme employee who never worked at Baxter. The investment community also had the same impression of the culture at Genzyme. In 1988, in its "summary and recommendation" section, Prudential Securities tagged Genzyme as a "manufacturing-driven biotech company." Further, it highlighted this as unique among biotech firms:

> Unlike most of the other biotechnology companies we follow, the driving force behind Genzyme is manufacturing rather than research. As such, the company's biotechnology R&D effort relies primarily on leveraging its core technology through joint ventures and collaborative agreements—not contract research.[32]

One good example of this manufacturing orientation concerns Genzyme's core product, Cerazyme. Even prior to receiving FDA approval for Cerazyme, Termeer partnered with local community colleges and vocational schools to retrain its own engineers, technicians, and manufacturers so that he could get an operation facility up and running as quickly as possible. Termeer identified a site in Allston, Massachusetts, for the new plant, and Genzyme was already in the process of building the plant and had secured financing prior to the product's approval. It was clear to Termeer that there was a tremendous opportunity cost associated with not being fully operational when the FDA gave Genzyme the green light on manufacturing. Consequently, there was "an incredible sense of urgency"[33]—an urgency that revolved around Genzyme's manufacturing capabilities.

Genzyme's manufacturing-driven approach to the marketplace is reflective of Baxter's entrepreneurial career imprint in several respects. Most directly, this emphasis on operations reflects one of the core capabilities Baxter managers developed under the Graham regime—how to produce products efficiently and effectively and to the highest safety and quality standards possible. This was the reason Baxter won out over Abbott in the 1970s and was a central concern for many young general managers during that time in Baxter's history.

Of course, just as organizational strategy and structure are closely interrelated, so too are organizational strategy and culture. At Genzyme, the intense focus on operations and manufacturing is associated with the strategy Termeer put in place for Genzyme, as was the case for Graham and his strategy for Baxter. In the same way that Baxter identified a significant and existing healthcare market need as well as its own competitive advantage at filling that need more quickly and more efficiently than others, Genzyme did so, particularly in the case of its enzyme replacement therapies. Termeer knew the need was there and thus focused efforts on doing it better, less expensively, and more quickly than other technology allowed. Termeer's efforts are similar to the way Baxter used its fundamental expertise in plastics to revolutionize the blood-container market by replacing glass bottles with plastic bags, eventually revolutionizing not just the manufacture of containers but also the distribution of all kinds of surgical fluids and blood. In these respects, Genzyme's manufacturing-driven culture was closely tied to Termeer's strategy and reflected key aspects of Baxter's career imprint.

In Contrast, Biogen's Research-Intensive Culture. Biogen began as a research-intensive organization and retained that culture under Vincent's leadership. Even after Vincent sold off Geneva, he maintained formal linkages with the European scientists. As one Biogen scientist recalled, "Vincent knew the importance of research and . . . articulated it more than anyone else actually." To maintain Biogen's "research-centric" focus, Vincent actively encouraged Biogen scientists to look outside the firm to academia to build a broad base of academic collaborations. Scientists remarked that this was surprising, given that Biogen had been founded by not one or two scientists, as is often the case in biotechnology, but by about a dozen scientists who were themselves quite prominent.

Over time, as Biogen's products moved further along in the product development pipeline, one might expect this emphasis to change. Yet, reports suggest that Biogen's emphasis on research over manufacturing remained. Even much later, after the introduction of Avonex and after Biogen had built an immense and expensive manufacturing facility in North Carolina, research positions were still accorded greater status within the firm. As one employee described:

> For a long time we were a research-centric organization. . . . They [manufacturing] are usually [viewed as] second-class because they're pictured as not being good enough to be in the research group. . . . They really were not given the same recognition that people in research got. . . . But I would have thought that as the company got bigger and as [manufacturing] became more important, that that would have changed, but it hasn't really.

Although this intense focus on research is not reflective of Abbott's culture, the lack of a focus on manufacturing is something that managers at Biogen have sought to change. As one manager described the problem:

> People were put in charge [of the North Carolina manufacturing facility] who knew very little about manufacturing. They were managers, and they were being brought up through the organization [without training or background in manufacturing].

In some ways, these varying degrees of emphasis on manufacturing can be encapsulated in the well-known clash that existed between Jim Vincent and Jim Tobin, when they were both working at Biogen. Jim Tobin spent twenty-two years with Baxter, beginning in 1972 as a financial analyst and culminating, from 1992 to 1994, as Baxter's president and chief operating officer (COO). In 1994, Tobin left Baxter to join Biogen as COO, just as Biogen was transitioning to an operating company. Vincent was CEO. In 1997, Tobin became CEO of Biogen, while Vincent remained on board as chairman. Analysts credited Tobin with improving the sales of Biogen's only product, Avonex, its multiple sclerosis drug. Yet, after only two years, Tobin resigned abruptly and moved on to head up Boston Scientific. This was both a visible hire and a visible departure.[34]

According to both Baxter and Abbott alumni, the two leaders were "like oil and water." They simply didn't see eye to eye on how to run Biogen. As one long-time Biogen employee explained, Tobin's strength was "in the nuts and bolts of building a sales force, making sure manufacturing is in place, distribution, all those kinds of operational things" whereas Vincent's strengths were in "developing strategy." From some perspectives, Tobin wanted to "do more things more quickly [than Vincent]"; according to others, Vincent did not want to relinquish control to Tobin. Either way, Tobin's manufacturing capabilities and orientation, which reflect Baxter's career imprint, did not, it seems, jibe well with the kind of culture Vincent had built at Biogen.

In sum, although we do see similarities between the two cultures of Genzyme and Biogen in terms of the values that these strong leaders tried to instill in their firms—values such as hard work, focus, and paying attention to the business markets for biotech products— we also find some major differences between the cultures of the two companies. During the early years, when Termeer and Vincent were at their respective helms, Genzyme had much more of a manufac- turing than a research orientation, whereas the reverse was true at Biogen. Indeed, when speaking to Biogen employees about their competition, the name Genzyme never came up—despite the fact that Genzyme is literally next door to Biogen's main offices in Cambridge. Rather, they mentioned Genentech, a company located across the country in California. Why? As one Biogen manager offered:

> Biogen was very different from Genzyme, and probably a little more like Genentech in its inception, in that it was started by academics. . . . But nonetheless my *sense* is Genzyme is not a research-driven company. . . . They have a gazillion divisions, . . . but they've managed to make it work, somehow—probably because of Termeer's expertise.

Genzyme employees confirm this difference and suggest that one of the biggest take-aways from their time working with Termeer is his operations focus. The following is a quote from an employee who spent seven years at Genzyme and then left to take on a leadership position in a young biotech company:

> I've learned a lot from my experience at Genzyme . . . I really like Henri's operations approach to biotech. It provides discipline. There's a lot of interesting science to be done, but you can't drift down the path of not being productive without discipline. You need to gener- ate cash and profit to be successful. . . . After all, it's a business.

Thus, Termeer's "operations approach" reflects one of the core capabilities of Baxter's career imprint—managing operations efficiently to contribute to the firm's profitability—and stands in contrast to the research-oriented culture Vincent maintained at

Biogen. Again, these differences in values and beliefs that character-
ize these firms' cultures are closely tied to the firms' strategies. As
Vincent himself explained:

> Genzyme is entrepreneurial and fast on their feet. . . . They followed
> an entrepreneurial technology model . . . not a deep, internal, scien-
> tific discovery drug model. At Biogen, we went for a deep, scientific-
> based drug strategy.

Summary and Considerations for the Future

One of the important aspects of career imprints is that they last
beyond the organizations in which they were originally cultivated. Leaders, such as Termeer and Vincent, export or carry over
aspects of the career imprints of their early career employers, such
as Baxter and Abbott, which affect the kinds of design choices
they make as leaders in other firms—at Genzyme and Biogen.
Here, examining the kinds of organizations that Vincent and
Termeer built, we find evidence for regarding the legacy of career
imprints. We find differences in the design choices Termeer and
Vincent made with respect to Genzyme and Biogen's strategy,
structure, and culture, despite the fact that both executives took
over their companies in the same approximate time and location.
Additionally, both leaders came from the rival healthcare organizations, Baxter and Abbott, which were themselves adjacent to
one another, and both leaders spent approximately the same
amount of time and worked during the same time period prior to
entering biotechnology. Still, as we saw in the kinds of organizations these individuals built, Genzyme and Biogen had very different organizational strategies, structures, and cultures that
reflected very different career imprints.

Counterpoint: What Doesn't Get Exported

In the prior cases, we emphasized aspects of early career imprints
that appear to have been exported into new firms. However, we
can also learn from examining negative cases—cases in which an

organizational career imprint of a previous employer does not affect the subsequent design choices of a leader. Indeed, one could say that some of the factors studied here were stacked in Termeer's favor—after all, he came on board at Genzyme when the company was relatively new (unlike Vincent) and when the company already had an operating business, which gave him more degrees of freedom with respect to implementing Baxter's career imprint. One can reasonably ask, therefore, "What are the potential barriers to implementing an organizational career imprint?"

Answering that question would require much more than two case studies. However, to take a step in this direction, let's briefly reconsider the case of Gabe Schmergel and the leadership choices he made during his early years at Genetics Institute (GI). By looking briefly at this case, we can begin to identify reasons that an organizational career imprint may be more or less easy to export or take to another company.

As introduced in Chapter Two, Genetics Institute was a company that was started by two scientific founders, before Gabe Schmergel joined the company as CEO in 1981. According to Schmergel, when he came onboard, there was already a strong culture in place: "It was a demanding culture, a no-excuses, get-it-done sort of culture!" This performance-oriented culture fit nicely with what Schmergel had grown up with at Baxter. Yet Schmergel also remembers having heated discussions with the scientists about the direction of the company, about GI's strategy.

Recall that the product that Schmergel helped finance through his deal with Baxter was a recombinant version of Factor VIII. This was a niche product, just as it had been at Baxter, whose ultimate success enabled Genetics Institute to stand on its own as one of the leading-edge biotechnology companies at the start of the industry. GI, like Baxter, did ultimately pursue other product lines. One of the products GI pursued was EPO, which turned out to be a billion-dollar product for Amgen (generating over $2 billion in the United States and $6 billion globally in 2001).[35] However, in the early years of biotechnology, Schmergel points out that EPO was considered a niche product, actually, with estimated sales of only

$100 million from Amgen pronouncements for the United States.[36] In this way, from Schmergel's perspective, it was not terribly unlike Genzyme's Ceradase, which was estimated to be only a $40 million product during early stage development in the 1980s—but which easily surpassed that mark with sales of $95 million in its first full year on the market (1992) and $530 million in 2000.[37]

Still, there were other projects that Schmergel encountered that had been started by the scientists that were clearly not in this niche category—that were considered "big" market products at that time (whether or not that ultimately turned out to be the case). For example, GI's founding scientists were eager to pursue research on Gamma Interferon, which was "very sexy" at the time. However, after doing a quick survey, Schmergel reports that he "had identified twenty-seven instances of Interferon projects at other companies that were more advanced" than GI's developments; so, without much hesitation Schmergel "said no" to the GI scientists. In some respects, then, we see evidence of Baxter's career imprint in the steps Schmergel took to focus GI's strategy during the early years.

Yet, despite the fact that Schmergel viewed his initial strategy as quite similar to that of Termeer, GI did end up with a very different culture than Genzyme's. In the case of Schmergel at GI, the organizational culture was not something that Schmergel wanted to change and, indeed, GI's culture did not reflect Baxter's career imprint. Most importantly, Schmergel felt that Genetics Institute was largely driven by science when he joined. Indeed, manufacturing was also deemed important, and unlike the Biogen accounts, Schmergel did talk quite a bit about the significance of manufacturing for biotechnology early on in the industry. And yet, when Schmergel compared Genzyme to Genetics Institute, he identified some important differences regarding the role of science and how it shaped the companies' strategies and cultures:

> After [Termeer] got control of [Genzyme's financial situation], he thought big and broadened the business through acquisitions; they made more smart business moves than other biotechs at that time.

Genetics Institute was based more on science; . . . not that Genzyme
didn't have good science, . . . but more of this was developed
in-house at Genetics Institute. We were more driven by science,
especially developed in-house.

Importantly, as Schmergel explained, the scientific founders at
Genetics Institute "played a large role in setting the culture."
Although Schmergel did not change that scientific focus, he did
constantly remind people that the "science means nothing unless
you have a product!"

Thus, as this brief "counterillustration" suggests, there are many
barriers to exporting an organizational career imprint in full,
including, importantly, the people who are already working at the
company that a new leader joins. Additionally, there are situations
in which one's organizational career imprint is not appropriate in a
new leadership situation. Recognizing when and when not to bring
the career imprint of a previous employer to a new company situation can make or break a senior executive's transition to a new
company. These and other lessons for individuals involved in a
variety of aspects of senior executive mobility will be explored in
the next chapter.

Chapter Nine

The Opportunities and Constraints of Career Imprints

Throughout this book, the concept of career imprints has been offered as a lens to understand senior executive mobility—in particular "entrepreneurial spawning," or the situation in which many executives from well-established firms transition to young firms at the start of an industry. In Part I, we explored the factors associated with people, place, and paths that cultivate strong organizational career imprints, such as the one at Baxter. We also explored career imprints at Merck, J&J, and Abbott, to understand how career imprints vary from company to company, even in the same general field.

With an understanding of the career imprinting process and of differences in organizational career imprints from Part I of the book, we turned, in Part II, to the consequences of career imprints. First, in Chapter Seven we explored the consequences for *industries*. As we saw, initially, the VC worldview of the requirements for running a small biotech company matched relatively well with what VCs saw as Baxter's entrepreneurial career imprint. In this way, Baxter's organizational career imprint and perceptions of this imprint facilitated the career transitions of a first wave of Baxter managers into biotechnology and thus provided the starting point or "seed" for other mechanisms, such as "networks," that have been highlighted in previous studies.

Turning the prism, in Chapter Eight, we explored some of the consequences of career imprints for *organizations*, as senior executives such as Termeer, Vincent, and Schmergel exported aspects of the organizational environments in which they grew up to new firms in biotechnology.

In the present chapter, we turn the prism once more, this time to examine the consequences for *individuals* engaged in this phenomenon of entrepreneurial spawning. Recall that all of the organizations studied here—Baxter, Abbott, J&J, and Merck—spawned people into young biotechnology firms. Baxter was overrepresented on IPO teams among these and other top healthcare and pharmaceutical firms and, as described in Chapter Seven, was preferred by many VCs. However, as a *collective*, all of these firms contributed to the evolution of the biotechnology industry.

In this chapter, we will explore the consequences of career imprints for the *many* individuals who were involved in making career transitions out of these four different firms and into biotechnology. As we will find, different organizational career imprints tended to be associated with different kinds of career moves. That is, people tended to take on certain types of positions in these young biotech firms, depending upon the organizational environments they came from.

Taken together, this collective of career transitions and the consequences associated with *not one* but *many* different organizational career imprints help us understand the phenomenon of spawning at a broader level—not just at the level of the story of the Baxter Boys, but also at the level of the evolution of an industry.

But considering these transitions in turn at the individual level is also important and has implications for those involved in senior-executive mobility. That is, from the observation that different career imprints are associated with different career paths, we can draw lessons for the myriad people involved in senior executive career moves—VCs, human resources professionals, headhunters, recruiters, and the senior executives themselves.

Finally, exploring the data one last time reveals lessons that apply not just to the type of spawning studied here, but to the notion of senior executive mobility more generally. This chapter thus departs somewhat from prior chapters because in looking at the implications for a variety of individuals' involvement in senior executive mobility, it reveals actionable "lessons" of career imprints as well.

Different Imprints, Different Paths

Examining the many career moves out of large healthcare firms and into young biotech companies uncovers career patterns that can be traced back to the notion of organizational career imprints. Specifically, different career imprints seem to yield different dominant paths or ways into an industry. This finding shifts the discussion from understanding how one company, such as Baxter, yielded a disproportionate number of top management positions in an industry to understanding the nature of the many roles that people from a variety of companies took on in biotech and how those roles relate to their previous employers' career imprints.

Returning to Baxter, Merck, J&J, and Abbott, let's first consider the facts about the kinds of career moves these people made after their time at these employers. Did people from these different companies follow different paths into biotechnology? Further, is there evidence to suggest that these differences are linked to these companies' different career imprints? The answer to both questions is yes.

As described in Chapters Five and Six, all four companies cultivated strong career imprints. They had key imprinting elements—including stretch assignments, social reinforcement (e.g., strong corporate cultures), and demonstrated success—during this same time period. However, the career imprints generated were different. The consequences of these different kinds of career imprints are evident in the kinds of roles these alumni took on in biotechnology after their early career employers.

Analyses of the quantitative data on the career histories of biotech IPO team members who came from these top healthcare firms show that there is a significant company effect on the distribution into different functions in biotech. Put differently, a person's previous employer can make a difference in terms of the kinds of roles he or she ends up taking on when joining a young firm. These differences are depicted in Figure 9.1 and are summarized below.[1]

Figure 9.1 Summary Comparison of Positions Held at Baxter, Abbott, J&J, and Merck; and Later, in Biotechnology Firms*

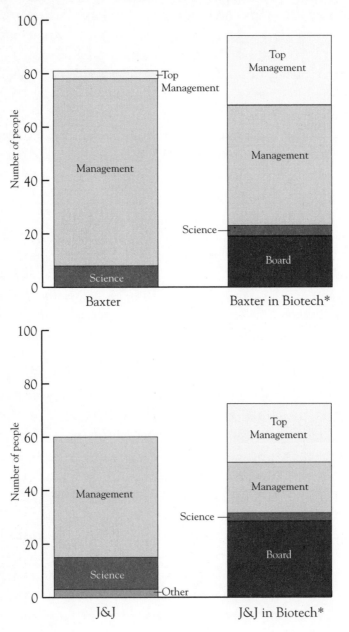

Figure 9.1 (*Continued*)

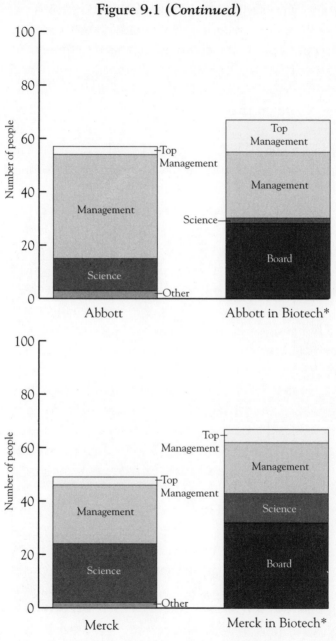

*Charts represent number of *positions* held. In some cases an individual simultaneously held more than one type of position in a firm, such as a top management position and a board seat.

Analyses of these data show that people who used to work at Baxter and who subsequently joined the IPO teams of biotech companies were significantly more likely to move into top management positions of biotech firms, compared to those who worked at the other three healthcare firms. Further, coming from Baxter significantly decreased the likelihood of taking on a board position at a biotech firm, relative to one's chances coming from one of the other firms.

Further, while Abbott, for example, did place people into management positions, Abbott didn't do so any more frequently than the other firms, whereas Baxter did. And, although Abbott incubated some individuals who became renowned leaders in biotechnology, such as Jim Vincent, the majority of individuals who left Abbott and eventually went on to run biotechnology companies took on middle-level types of management positions. Further, people left Abbott generally below the top management level. While this might suggest that people were younger when they entered biotechnology, the data do not support this. Abbott had the oldest IPO team members, with an average age of nearly fifty; Baxter's average age was forty-four. Together, these two pieces of data suggest that Abbott managers left but did not go directly into biotechnology companies. Indeed, the career history information from the larger data set support this conjecture. Whereas nearly 75 percent of the Baxter managers went directly from Baxter to biotechnology companies, only 54 percent went directly from Abbott to biotechnology.

Looking at the career history data differently, we can consider the number of steps it took people on average to move from Abbott (or Baxter) to enter a biotechnology company, whether private or public. These data suggest that many Abbott managers were simply not yet ready to take on general management jobs in biotechnology when they left Abbott: it took Abbott managers, on average, two steps to get to biotechnology; as mentioned, most Baxter managers transitioned directly.

In contrast to Baxter and Abbott, the majority of individuals who left J&J and Merck ended up playing a role in these IPO firms by sitting on their boards. A closer examination of these data show that of these board positions, 43 percent of those who came from J&J and were sitting on biotech boards did so as venture capitalists. J&J was the most likely to place people onto boards of biotech firms as members of VC firms, relative to the other four firms.

Those with Merck career experience, by contrast, tended to sit on biotech boards as scientists. That is, their board seats were held concurrently with a scientific position at another major pharmaceutical company (such as Merck). Thus, whereas J&J alumni played intermediary roles, Merck employees played the role of advisor—scientific advisor. Moreover, if we look at both board roles and management roles that are science related, we find that Merck was the only company that was significantly more likely to spawn people into science-related positions in biotech firms.

Considering these observations along with the career history data suggests that different career imprints are related to different dominant patterns in entrepreneurial roles and behavior. For example, whereas Baxter managers picked up general management capabilities, Merck managers picked up scientific capabilities, and these appear to be reflected in the types of leadership positions these individuals tended to take on beyond their early employers. Merck's scientific career imprint is reflected in the kinds of roles Merck employees took on in biotechnology—for example, as scientific advisors, sitting on the boards of young biotech firms. In contrast, the data suggest that Baxter's entrepreneurial career imprint is associated with CEO and top management positions in new biotech firms. Further, the boundary-spanning J&J career imprint appears to be associated with a pattern of VC roles held by J&J alumni. Finally, the functional career imprint indicative of Abbott career paths appears to be associated, most often, with middle-level management positions. In short, different careers (common to a particular employer) cultivate different imprints, which, in turn, correspond to different patterns in the dominant entrepreneurial roles people took on in biotech.

If we juxtapose this proposition—that organizational career imprints affect individual career mobility—with other plausible explanations, we might consider how prior functional experience could affect individuals' opportunities and, hence, role positions in a particular industry. Or, we could consider how other kinds of imprints, such as an educational imprint, might affect role positions in an industry. Looking at the qualitative data from the VC interviews in this study suggests that intermediaries were *not* selecting on educational or functional background, nor did they refer to "financial experience" or to "a Harvard Business School experience," for example. Rather, VCs referred to candidates as coming from Baxter, Abbott, J&J, or Merck, suggesting that employer reputations, which travel with particular career imprints, affect intermediary perceptions and decision making.

Considering the larger context of cognition and selective perception is useful here. While it may not seem surprising that the kinds of capabilities, connections, confidence, and cognition that an individual picks up from an employer, particularly an early career employer, affect opportunities and constraints later in his or her career, oftentimes it is difficult to recognize such connections. It is more common to think about lessons learned at a previous employer in terms of functional experience, rather than the company's overall career imprint. Reconsider this account provided by a longtime J&J alumnus:

> As senior executives rose in J&J, there was a natural reliance on what they already understood. So if you get somebody who's a finance officer, all they're going to want to talk about is numbers. If you get somebody who came up through sales, what they're going to want to do is drill the sales plan.

These kinds of function-based attributions are common. Yet, there is no scientific evidence that this is the way our minds actually work—for instance, in the prior case, that "finance guys" only "want to look at the numbers." Seminal management research by March and Simon back in the 1950s showed that people's minds are selective in how they attend to information.[2] Since we cannot attend to all the information we take in at once, we screen out what is important to us and attend primarily to that information.

Still, while there is general agreement that prior work experience does influence future cognition and attention,[3] scholars have yet to sort out just what "selective perception of managers" means. Most often, researchers, like the J&J manager quoted above, pin the perceptual screen on functional experience. In 1958, Dearborn and Simon did a study on managers in which they found that prior functional experience did selectively channel managers' perceptions. Thirty years later, however, Walsh did a study that showed that managers' belief systems were much *broader* than departmental function and so were not actually predictive of managerial decision making. Then, in 1997, in an attempt to resolve these differences, Beyer and colleagues redid these studies and found that functional background did not predict what managers did attend to but what managers *didn't* attend to.[4] More recently still, in 1999, research showed that senior executive decision making is less influenced by functional background than it is by social influence factors such as who one works with.[5]

The notion of career imprints and the research presented here suggest that senior executives do indeed engage in selective attention but that leader perceptions are not limited to prior functional experience; as Walsh suggested, perceptions are affected by career experiences that are broader than departmental function. As we saw in Chapter Eight, organizational career imprints are associated with cognition or worldviews that are tied to specific aspects of previous employers' organizational environments. Therefore, based upon the present research, we would *not* expect a person who worked in a sales position at Abbott to have the exact same perspective as a person who worked in a sales position at J&J, since these were very different organizational contexts. As we saw in

Chapter Six, these companies had very different organizational strategies, structures, and cultures, which affected the kinds of developmental opportunities people had, even within a single function, and yielded differences in the kinds of capabilities, connections, confidence, and cognition developed.

Further, even at a company with a functional career imprint such as Abbott, much more than a "sales perspective" was picked up from early career experiences. As described in Chapter Eight, people take with them logics of action that include perspectives regarding organizational design issues such as organizational strategy and culture. Thus, previous employers' career imprints, rather than simply previous functional positions, should affect leader decision making.

In addition to organizational design issues, the data presented in this chapter and earlier suggest that organizational career imprints may affect how people view their own career choices as well as those of others. As suggested in Chapter Seven, organizational career imprints can affect what people view as a possible next step in their careers. For example, having run a "mini-Baxter" as a country president, Baxter managers felt ready to take on the CEO position of a young company post Baxter. Further, as we saw, organizational career imprints affect the perceptions of powerful intermediaries, such as VCs, who are in the business of facilitating senior executive mobility. Together, these two factors—how career imprints affect managers' perceptions of their careers and how VCs view these managers' opportunities, given their career imprints—help explain why different career imprints may yield different paths, as the quantitative data show.

The implication here is that organizational career imprints influence both what employees perceive as opportunities and constraints as well as what are deemed opportunities and constraints by intermediaries such as VCs and headhunters. For VCs and headhunters, then, the present research suggests that organizational career imprints do play a significant role in selection processes and one should be aware that cognitive short cuts, such as choosing a company with a particular organizational career imprint, may strongly influence executive selection. Further, since *early* career appears to be a precious time for career imprinting, attending to early employer career imprints may be particularly informative. This stands in contrast to the temptation to talk about a candidate's current or latest job during a recruiting interview and illuminates a first lesson:

> Lesson 1: VCs, headhunters, and other intermediaries who are selecting senior executives should pay at least as much attention to early career experiences and employer career imprints as they do to later career or purely functional experiences, since early career is a precious time for organizational career imprinting.

Lessons also extend to the individual career decision maker. For individuals, it is important to understand that there are significant and longer-term implications of joining a company with elements such as a strong corporate culture that are likely to strengthen a company's career imprint. Again, this is particularly true for those in early career, since these are formative times during one's adult development, as described in Chapter Three. Out of this understanding comes a second lesson:

> Lesson 2: Individuals who are making early career choices should learn about a potential employer's career imprint from insiders, those who work at the firm, as well as outsiders, those who are well-positioned to compare organizational career imprints in a particular sector or industry.

During the job search, this means asking questions that move beyond job function and position level to collecting information about a potential employer regarding patterns in employee capabilities, connections, confidence, and cognition. For VCs, it means asking questions regarding career experiences and asking if and how these were *shared* at a previous employer in order to gain an understanding of that company's career imprint. How can one do this? Collecting data from outsiders is important and relatively easy to do, since external reports of companies—particularly public companies—are plentiful. However, collecting data from the employees themselves may be more difficult, given limitations of time and access. Asking for accounts of eventful learning experiences at a firm can lend insight into what is cultivated at that particular firm. Additionally, patterns in the kinds of language used to tell the story may prove useful, as we examined with the Baxter data. What is important is to look for aspects of career experiences that are shared, since organizational career imprints result from patterns *across* individuals' career experiences.

It is also important to gather information about people's career paths out of a particular company. Such information lends insight into the dominant kinds of patterns in career paths that are associated with this company and its career imprint. It also lends insight into the constraints associated with certain organizational career imprints. In this context, for example, headhunters told me that it was highly improbable that someone who spent many years at Baxter would be a good fit for a company like Abbott or Merck; these firms had completely different career imprints. The perception was that the requirements for jobs at these two companies were quite different. Indeed, only once did a Baxter alumnus mention that he had considered a move into another large healthcare firm (as opposed to a start-up in biotech) and that firm was J&J. Still, the hierarchy and time it took to get to a general management position at J&J, which this Baxter manager had already obtained, dissuaded him. And, as several interviewees noted, people "never went from Baxter to Abbott."[6] Therefore, while organizational career imprints offer the possibility for career choice and change, they can also limit future options, should that career imprint be a strong one. The recognition of those possibilities and limitations frames a third lesson that applies to intermediaries as well as individuals:

Lesson 3: Intermediaries and individual career decision makers should maintain relationships with external parties in their sector of interest, not only to develop an understanding about the evolving requirements for particular sectors but also to remain informed about the perceptions and opportunities associated with certain organizational career imprints.

Beyond implications for career choice and change, these findings regarding different career imprints and different paths have important implications for leader development. Indeed, one mistake both recruiters and job seekers often make is assuming that, simply put, "what worked well in one company should work in another". Senior executives are generally hired into a firm based upon their prior track records. But, beyond performance or identifiable results, a track record may reflect a certain kind of career imprint that person acquired. Therefore, if someone hired into a leadership position in an organization tries to cast a similar "old" career imprint on his or her new firm, there are no guarantees that that career imprint will work. Returning to the GE example, several articles have been written about the GE legacy and have expressed skepticism over the extent to which the "GE playbook" has been effectively "exported" to new firms:

> When the Jack Welch cult was at its peak, recruiters and corporate boards convinced themselves that GE-trained executives could work magic anywhere. Lack of industry expertise was shrugged off. Patience disappeared too. Mr. Welch needed a half-dozen years to hit his stride in the 1980s, yet a belief took hold that GE alumni could work magic almost instantly.[7]

This quote suggests one important constraint with respect to career imprints: they are content specific. Just as leadership scholar John Kotter concluded from his own research that there is nothing "general" about "general managers," so too can we claim that there is nothing general about organizational career imprints.[8] That is, career imprints are not simply bundles of capabilities, connections, and confidence devoid of context. As suggested in this quote, the business context matters. As we saw with the Baxter case, the types of extraorganizational relationships that were developed were not with *any* external body; they were with the FDA. Once these managers had left Baxter for biotech, they found that such ties were critical to a biotech firm's ability to bring a product to clinical trials, for example.

Similarly, the learning-based efficacy that was developed at Baxter was not content free. It had to do with learning how to learn from those who had requisite knowledge in science and healthcare in certain regions of the world. This orientation began during their first years on the job, when they were placed into assistant-to positions with more senior people in the firm and continued when they developed relationships with locals upon taking on a general management assignment, oftentimes overseas. Such confidence was helpful later on in biotech as well.

Additionally, in terms of capabilities, these were managerial transitions that were made from healthcare (Baxter) to healthcare (biotech) firms. Although one could argue that Baxter's business was "basically plastics," it was also a healthcare business. And, as Chapter Eight showed, the particular niches that these Baxter alumni went after, consistent with Baxter's Willie Keeler "hit 'em where they ain't" strategy, were in a particular domain with which they were at least somewhat familiar—or, as one interviewee recalled, in areas in which they knew where they had to go in order to figure out the potential for a business there.

Clearly, this has not always been the case with GE alumni, since several have been criticized for applying their "playbook" in fields they were unfamiliar with. For example, consider GE alumni Robert Nardelli and Larry Johnson, who joined Albertson's and Home Depot in 2001 and 2000, respectively. As Nardelli summarized in an article in *The Wall Street Journal,* "About 70 percent of the skills that you develop at GE are fully portable. . . . The challenge for Larry and for me is to step out of the industrial world and immerse ourselves in retailing."[9] Therefore, a strong organizational career imprint can indeed place constraints on an individual's potential, if one does not pay attention to the content that undergirds these core capabilities, connections, and confidence that make up a particular imprint.

As an example from another industry, consider General Mills alumnus Mark Willes, who was selected to run Times Mirror in 1995. Willes was criticized early on in his tenure at Times Mirror for comparing the publishing industry to the cereal business.[10] As reported, Willes told journalists:

> What we're trying to do is take the skills and experiences and, frankly, the attitude that exists in a consumer product company and apply them to our business. . . . Mass newspapers like the ones we print are basically consumer products. A lot of people in the newsroom don't like to think about it that way, but that's what it is.[11]

Willes also reorganized the flagship paper of Times Mirror, *The Los Angeles Times*, in the image of General Mills—with a product management organizational structure, in which each section had an editor in charge of content and a general manager whose role resembled a brand manager. This, like Willes's "consumer products" vision, received significant flack from the industry; industry experts harshly criticized the strategy as compromising the integrity of the journalists by so closely integrating the business and editorial sides of the newspaper. This intermingling eventually led to a scandal at the newspaper in which Willes agreed to publish a special of the magazine that focused on the new Staples center in Los Angeles and share the advertising revenue fifty-fifty with Staples. This blatant conflict of interest hit the front page of *The New York Times*, in which Willes was called a "cereal killer," and led to the departure of senior editors and reporters in protest over what they saw as Willes's inept handling of the public trust and the journalism profession.[12]

These examples and many others regarding the selection of outsiders for CEO positions do not suggest that organizational career imprints cannot ever be transplanted from one industry to the next; they do suggest, however, that paying close attention to the context in which an organizational career imprint was cultivated can help an executive calibrate the extent to which it would be useful elsewhere.

In addition, the example of Willes's career transition lends insight into a different, more subtle tripwire with respect to career imprints and leader development. Willes's first major job, prior to General Mills, was with the Federal Reserve Bank, where he eventually became the youngest person ever to be named president of a Federal Reserve Bank. At General Mills, Willes continued in his finance track by taking on roles such as CFO and, later, as vice chairman, where he was responsible for duties including corporate law and finance. The recruiter who selected Willes for the Times Mirror job described Willes as someone who was not a marketer, despite his time at General Mills; rather, his strength was finance, reflecting his first employment experience and training, which was in a finance organization. And yet, once at Times Mirror, Willes not only made some major decisions that financially restructured Times Mirror, he also began talking about marketing and focus groups. This was a surprise to those who had recruited him.

In this example, the tripwire hinges on recognizing which organizational career imprint one has actually cultivated, or which career imprint dominates one's own professional development. In Willes's case, it was more apparent to *outsiders* that the kind of financial career imprint he had cultivated at the Federal Reserve had dominated his leadership development, whereas it appears that Willes thought that he had cultivated General Mills' marketing career imprint. Generally, as discussed in Chapter Three, early career experiences trump those acquired later in life. These examples point to a fourth lesson, intended particularly for those who are in a position to advise individuals as they make career transitions:

Lesson 4: Intermediaries and human resources professionals involved in senior executive transitions should advise senior executives to actively reflect on how their design choices as leaders have been shaped by early and strong organizational career imprints, including the extent to which the context into which they are importing their former employer's career imprint is similar; such reflection may prevent the misapplication of prior career imprints.

Traditionally, strategic human resources literature and practice has tended to ignore the environmental context associated with a particular industry and how that larger context impacts senior executive mobility. Rather, person-job fit or person-organization fit has remained the central question for strategic human resources managers and, indeed, for studies of staffing.[13] The present findings regarding different imprints, different paths suggest that there may be particular roles and paths in certain sectors or industries that may be deemed more or less appropriate for certain kinds of organizational career imprints. This moves us beyond thinking only about the fit between an individual leader's personality traits and an organization or job to considering the fit between what an individual leader is likely to export from a previous employer and a particular role in a particular industry.

From a leader-development perspective, then, one important question to ask is about *future* fit and the extent to which a new job enables future development on the part of the leader. To the extent that what one "knows best" becomes a mental frame through which one views all organizational issues, this can be debilitating. Therefore, the risk is not that the context has changed, necessarily, but that the person holding the career imprint doesn't remain open to change, to reexamine his or her previous employer's career imprint and the extent to which that imprint applies.

Bill Gantz, former president of Baxter, described his process of active reflection as follows:

> I would never claim any of us were able to duplicate or replicate what Bill Graham was able to do. I think that was unique, but I

think each of us took pieces of it and assimilated that, and learned from it. . . . Each of us looks back and . . . will talk about it in terms of what Bill Graham did, or what we learned at Baxter. So when I sit down with Gabe, or I sit down with Henri, I'll zero back in on, "Well, here's what I'm doing that [Graham] did" or "that we did at Baxter." . . . So, people always use this as a reference point.

As this quote suggests, one way to engage in active reflection is with those who share a similar career imprint. Earlier, in Chapter Three, the importance of social reinforcement for the cultivation of a strong career imprint was emphasized. There, social reinforcement referred to what happened at the employing organization—in this case, at Baxter. Talking to people who share a prior employer's career imprint can provide a good sounding board or "reference point" for leaders as they take on new roles. One tripwire to this is overreliance on such resources, which could lead to tunnel vision or myopic behavior. On the other hand, without a "common language," it becomes difficult to compare new action to anything in particular.

Recently, research by Ibarra has suggested that a crucial aspect of professional development is "making sense" of what is "happening today [in one's worklife by] reinterpreting past events and [by] creating compelling stories that link the two."[14] By reconnecting with people who share a common career imprint, those connections and comparisons are easily drawn. One clear risk is not having any common basis for understanding certain aspects of "today" and the types of leadership choices one faces. Yet, in the case of the Baxter Boys, since many entered jobs in biotechnology, they had that common basis from which to learn from one another's experiences. This suggests a fifth lesson, targeted primarily at corporate leaders and the human resources professionals advising them:

Lesson 5: Corporate leaders and human resources professionals who are advising corporate leaders should encourage senior executives to benchmark their own exporting of a prior employer's career imprint with those who hold similar career imprints, particularly with those who have entered a similar sector or industry.

In sum, avoiding the pitfalls of misapplying an organizational career imprint requires an acute awareness of the similarities and differences between the organization and environment that contributed to a leader's early career experiences and the leadership challenges faced later in one's career, when organizational, cultural, social, and even market-based conditions may have drastically changed. Thus, while the idea of career imprints may prove a useful way to understand the origins of a leader's behavior and decision making, from a leader development perspective, an awareness of the contingent nature of the application and transference of prior career imprints is critical to consider. Building a set of developmental partnerships, including those with whom one has shared a strong organizational career imprint, can be a useful way to engage in this process.[15]

The Stickiness of Perceptions of Organizational Career Imprints

To close this chapter, we turn to opportunities and constraints associated with the perceptions of organizational career imprints. As we saw in the case of Baxter, it was the perceptions of Baxter's career imprint on the part of VCs and Baxter managers that served as the catalyst for many of these early career transitions into biotechnology. As Termeer recalled, "In the beginning, there was nothing there"; as Greene recalled, "The word [biotechnology] had not been invented yet"; and as Schmergel said, "There was tremendous uncertainty." Given all of this uncertainty, outsiders, such as VCs, turned to logics of action such as the need for a "general manager with a P&L view of the world" to make hiring decisions. Baxter's organizational career imprint helped VCs simplify their decision making, since overall, it appeared to match this logic. We also saw how, over time, this perception of Baxter as a "darling" recruiting ground was reinforced, as the first wave of CEOs from Baxter raised money and took their companies public in the early 1980s.

Yet, when thinking about this matching process, one of the most important things to remember about career imprints is that they are time specific. Recall the quotes by Baxter managers such as Tobin, who was hired by Graham and remained with Baxter long after the company's organizational transformation under Loucks. As his comments and others' indicate, organizational career imprints can change; individual leaders can make dramatically different organizational design choices that can affect the opportunity structures within their firms and so the kinds of career paths experienced at a particular firm. The implication is that if recruiters and headhunters do not update their perceptions of organizational career imprints, they could be surprised to find that the kinds of capabilities and so on that they thought they had hired for were indeed quite different.

To return for a moment to a quote from a venture capitalist, Bob Higgins, who was engaged in biotech deals during the 1970s and 1980s:

> Back in the 1980s, . . . whenever I bumped into a Baxter person, as opposed to someone from J&J or Abbott, I almost always saw them as more able to handle the entrepreneurial environment.

In this case, the VC qualified his comments by dating the time period in which he was evaluating different candidates. Yet, in many instances, people do not update their perceptions of a particular organization and the set of capabilities, connections, confidence, and cognition that one cultivates there. This lack of updating, this stickiness with respect to perceptions, can open up opportunities but it can also lead to tripwires—particularly for headhunters who are responsible for filling senior executive positions.

To borrow from a different context, hiring someone who held a management position at AT&T in the 1960s would yield a very different set of capabilities, connections, confidence, and cognition than hiring a manager from AT&T during the 1990s. In the 1960s, AT&T's career imprint would be one characterized by high levels of entrepreneurship, due to the autonomy associated with the Baby Bell organizations, whereas decades later the company had a much more bureaucratic and centralized structure and culture, affecting the kinds of capabilities, connections, confidence, and cognition one would acquire from working there. Similarly, hiring someone from IBM in the 1970s would yield a different kind of career imprint than it would in the 1990s. In the 1970s, IBM had a functional career imprint in which sales dominated, whereas during the 1990s, it has become much more technology driven, which has shifted the emphasis in terms of the kinds of capabilities, connections, confidence, and cognition shared among managers at the firm.[16] In short, we can't assume that what was cultivated at a company in one time period will necessarily "stick," or yield similar capabilities, connections, confidence, and cognition as if we hired from the same company in a different time period. This yields the sixth and final lesson:

> Lesson 6: Recruiters and headhunters should refresh or update their perceptions of organizational career imprints, since career imprints are not only specific to place, they are also specific to a particular period in time.

This final lesson brings us back to where the book began, to the question of senior executive mobility. In the present context, the Baxter story and resulting career imprint, including the comparisons to the practices and imprints of other organizations, demonstrates the power that a single organization can have on the evolution of an industry. And yet, as this industry changes, we, like the recruiters and headhunters for this industry, need to recalibrate what we see as relatively useful among organizational career imprints. Just as career imprints can create cognitive biases among those who worked at certain organizations and, hence, affect their design choices as leaders elsewhere, so too can they create biases in our own minds as observers and interested parties in their behavior.

I was reminded of this as I sat in a recent meeting next to a venture capitalist, who, as we were getting up to leave, said, "I'm looking for another biotech CEO—gotta get me one of those Baxter guys." Maybe. But maybe not. The entrepreneurial career imprint that was deemed appropriate at the start of the biotech industry may not be the preferred set of capabilities, connections, confidence, and cognition for today. Further, and this is another way we must remind ourselves of the stickiness of career imprints, those Baxter Boys have been living and working beyond their company alma mater now for decades. It is likely that they have made some adjustments over time in their own behavior—that they too have learned, reacting in ways that may alter what one might have expected from someone with a Baxter career imprint from the 1970s. In these ways, then, while organizational career imprints can provide a useful lens into phenomena as large in scope as the start of an industry to phenomena as small in scope as leader decision making, the ultimate risk we need to remind ourselves of is failing to recognize that individuals do have choices in how they will respond to the organizational career imprints they carry with them.

Chapter Ten

Career Imprints: New Answers, New Questions

The present research began with the observation of a phenomenon, the overrepresentation of Baxter alumni in young biotechnology firms, and has ended with an idea, that of career imprints.

This research has also suggested certain insights about senior executive mobility—namely, that certain conditions amplify the career imprinting process or make career imprints stronger and that certain conditions make career imprints more valuable. These insights are revealed, for example, when powerful intermediaries prefer one organizational career imprint over another, yielding an overrepresentation of one group of alumni in new ventures in an emerging industry.

This work has also allowed us to take a microlevel perspective, the study of careers, and apply it to macrolevel phenomena, such as the evolution of an industry. This micro- to macrolevel linkage is unusual, both from the perspective of the study of careers and from the perspective of the study of organizations.

This chapter summarizes these findings; it also sets forth a direction and possible agenda for future consideration. Each "answer" this research has uncovered has raised exciting and new avenues of pursuit.

New Answers

In general, scholarly work in the area of careers has tended to focus on understanding the factors that affect important career outcomes for individuals, such as professional advancement and work satisfaction. These studies have uncovered many interesting findings regarding the many ways that psychological, sociological, and organizational factors affect individuals' professional development. Rarely, however, have career studies looked at how the cumulative product of sequences of career experiences affect outcomes that extend *beyond* the individual—to an organization or industry.[1] This missing link can be filled by the study of organizational career imprints.

From a different perspective, organizational studies of industry evolution have examined how clusters of companies ebb and flow within the larger business environment. With respect to the particular phenomenon studied here, spawning, scholars often focus on macrolevel factors such as the collocation of institutional actors such as academic institutions, regulators, intermediaries, and professionals. Yet, the ebbs and flows of individuals' careers in a particular industry often remain unexplored. Questions such as "Why did so many people make these career transitions in the first place?" remain unanswered if we don't examine the microlevel foundations of this macrolevel phenomenon—if we don't examine individuals' career paths and experiences. Again, the study of organizational career imprints provides this missing link.

These kinds of macrolevel phenomena, such as the spawning of senior executives into new industries, are critical to the growth of our economy. These are important conversations to engage in and yet, ironically, with all of the insight that career scholars have gained about why and how people make career decisions and psychologists have gained about how certain life stages affect the course of professional development, we scholars trained in microlevel analysis have entered rarely, if at all, into these conversations—even though career transitions lie at the very heart of these macrolevel phenomena. The study of organizational career imprints provides an entrée into such conversations.

Over the past decade, a few organizational scholars who study populations of organizations have begun to examine relationships between individuals' career transitions and large-scale industry dynamics. These studies often focus on how phenomena such as the founding and dissolution of firms in an industry affect labor market conditions and so patterns in individuals' careers. In this respect, some industry studies have associated macro industry-level events with micro career-level events.[2] My research runs in the exact opposite direction and, with the career imprint concept, extrapolates up from patterns across individuals' careers within organizations to lend insight into industry-level outcomes. Thus, the concept of organizational career imprints lends insight into how careers create industries, rather than the reverse.

Another part of this macrolevel inquiry is understanding not just *that* patterns in career experiences cumulate to form patterns at an industry level, but that formative career experiences of leaders can have an effect on the course of the new ventures themselves, which are the building blocks of these emerging industries. Here, the notion of a career imprint suggests that individuals can export what they learned from a previous employer and bring aspects of that early career experience to subsequent organizational contexts. As we explored, one important aspect of an organizational career imprint are the logics of action regarding what are viable and useful ways to design and lead an organization.

Further, this research suggests that there may be precious times in the life of an organization, such as its beginning, during which leaders have a unique opportunity to import previous employers' career imprints and so, essentially, re-create aspects of the organizational environments that shaped their previous work lives. Although, as organizational scholars, we often note the many ways in which individuals' careers are shaped by powerful organizational factors such as organizational systems and culture, the notion of career imprints invites, as well, the possibility for a different perspective—that careers are not just embedded in organizations but that organizations are embedded in careers.

At a more practical level, using the career imprint lens to study a macrolevel phenomenon such as spawning allows us to draw implications for those who are engaged in this important kind of senior executive mobility. Indeed, without breaking the phenomenon down to understand how and why collections of individual career transitions occurred, it becomes difficult to cull lessons for VCs, headhunters, human resources professionals, or executives themselves—people who all are in various leadership positions in society and who can make a difference in our economy. In this study, by examining patterns in the career accounts of the individuals who moved from well-established firms to new ventures at the start of an industry, it was possible to move toward implications for practice—toward "lessons"—as we did in the prior chapter.

New Questions

The present research also suggests new areas of inquiry into understanding how organizational career imprints affect broader-level phenomena. These new questions center around three main topics: the dynamics of career imprints, the contingent value of career imprints, and the generalizability of career imprints.

The Dynamics of Career Imprints

The case studies in Chapter Eight, which explored the legacy of career imprints for organizations, raised some interesting questions regarding the dynamics of career imprints. For example, we can ask, "Under what conditions are organizational career imprints likely to last and have an effect on subsequent organizational design choices?" Understanding the answer to this question could help executive headhunters conduct more effective searches and could also help human resources professionals prepare their organizations for the transitions that might occur as a new CEO comes on board.

With respect to this first question, the evidence provided here suggests several conditions to consider: First, the extent to which the career imprint was strongly cast likely affects whether or not it is used as a starting point for making important organizational decisions. As discussed in Chapters Three and Four, the strength of an organization's career imprint depends upon a number of factors including (a) the extent to which that imprint was egosyntonic or value congruent with the individual who worked there; (b) the extent to which the individual believes that the types of capabilities, connections, and confidence picked up at an organization lead to positive results (i.e., that the imprint "works" to produce positive organizational outcomes); and (c) the extent to which the imprint was shared by people who worked with that individual at the same time (e.g., a cohort) can socially reinforce what is being learned and so the strength of an organization's career imprint.

Second, organizational career imprints are likely to have a lasting effect on subsequent design choices to the extent that these design choices happen de novo—as in the case of an individual taking charge of a new venture. Clearly, this was more so the case with Termeer than it was with either Vincent or Schmergel.

Third, career imprints are more likely to have a legacy if the leader is surrounded by people who also worked at the same early career employer and so have a "shared language." As one Genzyme employee described:

> When we came to Genzyme . . . especially the Baxter mafia that came in about that time, the thought process was, "We're going to bring what really worked, what we really liked at Baxter, but we're going to leave the rest behind."

A second question raised by this analysis concerns *how* career imprints are carried over from organization to organization. Here, evidence suggests that simply because Termeer has internalized a *20/20* mentality and has the capabilities himself to effectively manage cash does not ensure that his employees at Genzyme will be or do likewise. Rather, those core aspects of the career imprint manifest themselves in the ways in which a leader sets up the company—to reward the very things he or she has come to value. What appears to carry over from one organization to the next are logics of action regarding the organizational design choices that he or she perceived contributed to the demonstrated success of a previous employer. These logics of action are part of the fourth "C" of an organizational career imprint and range from design choices such as organizational strategy to choices regarding corporate culture.

The analyses also suggest a third important question: "How do organizational career imprints change?" A career imprint reflects patterns in the many careers of individuals within a single *organization* at a single point in time. It differs, then, from individual-level constructs, such as Schein's concept of a career anchor, which is based upon patterns in the career history of a single individual.[3] This is why we can talk about a "Baxter career imprint" but not a "Monica Higgins career imprint." Therefore, when individuals such as Gabe Schmergel leave Baxter, they take with them Baxter's career imprint and so cannot, ex post, change Baxter's career imprint.

However, new leaders do have the opportunity to make different organizational design choices over time—just as Loucks did after Graham stepped aside—that can alter people's career paths and so an organization's career imprint over time. Thus, just as Schein, a management expert on corporate culture, examined the extent to which Digital Equipment Corporation's (DEC's) leaders were and were not able to change DEC's corporate culture over the years, so too could we examine Baxter's leaders, the design choices they made, and thus how Baxter's career imprint has changed over time. From such analyses, we might conclude that Graham made decisions that led to Baxter's entrepreneurial career imprint during the 1970s, whereas Loucks made decisions that led to Baxter's more bureaucratic career imprint during the 1980s.

As the following quote from a longtime Baxter alumnus suggests, Loucks's organizational design choices fundamentally altered people's careers at Baxter and by extension, then, Baxter's career imprint:

> We lost all country management structure, and that was a real loss; that was the cost of the thing. But we drove sales growth through the roof. OK, now, the flip side is, back to the original, "bring these

guys in, train 'em for a year, and dump 'em into a country." That [change] blew up all those country jobs. So now there's no place to dump these guys. So they stopped coming. . . . I guess what I'm saying is, the good news is that a global organizational structure absolutely reunited growth and redirected R&D dollars to where they could be way more productive, and it really got things going. . . . Bad news is, it took away the farm team; it took away the place you could grow the new guys.

Unlike Loucks, however, Baxter alumni such as Termeer cannot change their prior employer's career imprint once they leave that firm; still, they can decide what they will do with that strong career imprint once they move on to lead other firms, such as Genzyme. Unlike the biological processes associated with filial imprinting, then, as discussed in the first chapter, people can reflect on the organizational career imprints they have experienced at previous employers and even challenge some of the worldviews they developed there. They can decide whether to react positively or negatively to that career imprint, which, over time, can affect their design choices as leaders. Termeer, for example, upon reflection, chose to reject certain aspects of Baxter's competitive culture that he had engaged in during his early career, rather than to recreate it at Genzyme. As he explained:

Baxter . . . did not have a very well-developed human culture. The human factor in Baxter in terms of the interaction between people, and how they worked with each other, was much more competitive than some environments, than this environment [at Genzyme]. . . . And I put enormous value on the human factor.

Finally, the present research suggests that career imprints carry both challenges and opportunities. One of the challenges, as this quotation suggests, is that leaders must be cognizant of the role-modeling that they engaged in early on in their careers and how that may affect how they, in turn, manage and lead others.

Leaders do have choices—both in what they decide to adopt in terms of design choices for their firms and, by extension, in terms of the career imprints they create for others through their own firms. Passing on a career imprint is not inevitable, then, but if it was a strong career imprint that was cultivated at a previous employer, as was the case at Baxter, then considerable effort may be necessary to "undo" even certain aspects of it. Reflection of this kind is not easy since, in many respects, it may involve uncovering assumptions that were developed very early on and perhaps during the formative years of one's adult development; however, as discussed in Chapter Nine, there are lessons to be learned that can facilitate this process. Thus, career imprints have implications for leader development beyond the firm in which they were originally cultivated.

The Contingent Value of Career Imprints

Was this spawning "good" for Baxter? Is it useful for an organization to cultivate an entrepreneurial career imprint? Although many different kinds of career imprints were examined in this research, clearly, the career imprint that received the greatest attention was Baxter's, which was an entrepreneurial career imprint. Let's turn first to the question of the contingent value of entrepreneurial career imprints, then, and later to the question of the contingent value of strong organizational career imprints more generally.

In the case of the entrepreneurial career imprint, the probability that people will leave and perhaps even join rival or competitor firms is especially high. This is the particular dilemma of cultivating an entrepreneurial career imprint: employees develop the capabilities, connections, confidence, and cognition that make them not only valuable to the parent company but, at the same time, well-positioned to leave and run their own firms—including firms that could compete in some way with the parent company.

As we saw with the case of Baxter, Mr. Graham created such a strong entrepreneurial career imprint that the imprint itself began to influence people's career desires. By creating entrepreneurial types of general management roles early on for these Baxter managers, managers developed the appetite for such roles to the point at which Baxter simply couldn't satisfy their hunger. Having run "mini-Baxters," the only way to advance was to run something bigger; eventually, for many, that meant leaving the firm.

Therefore, in the particular case of an entrepreneurial career imprint, the risk to the organization of creating such autonomy, responsibility, and empowerment that helped the company achieve favorable results in the first instance is that valued employees may choose to leave earlier than their firm would like. At Genzyme, where certain aspects of the Baxter entrepreneurial career imprint seem to have taken hold, senior managers have been engaged in thoughtful consideration of how to offer more jobs at higher levels that match that "entrepreneurial spirit" they so clearly prefer at Genzyme. As Elliott Hillback, who has led Genzyme's recruiting efforts for years, described:

> Henri and I had a little battle here, a friendly battle. We've had an MBA program for seven years here, hiring anywhere from three to five a year. And at one point, several years ago now, Henri said, "How come these people aren't in bigger jobs? These people are really highly paid. . . . And they have bigger résumés than what we had when we came out of business school." I said, "It's us, Henri; it's not them; we aren't pulling them forward to the edge."

Thus, in part due to the kind of entrepreneurial environment cultivated at Genzyme, as was the case at Baxter, Genzyme may indeed face challenges with respect to keeping the people it has developed over the years. The result? This is an ongoing challenge that Genzyme has attended very closely to and is acting on. Otherwise, "Genzyme may be the next Baxter," as one management consultant explained.

One solution to this problem, as we saw in the case of Baxter as well as Genzyme (but not Abbott), is for the firm to adopt an ecosystem perspective with respect to its employees. If a firm with an entrepreneurial career imprint can embrace the significant possibility that individuals who grow up in the company's own image or imprint may leave sooner than expected, then both the individual and the company have the possibility for mutual gain. This was the case with the deal done between Gabe Schmergel's company, Genetics Institute, and Baxter in 1982. Yet at Baxter, it is important to note that its ecosystem perspective was relatively passive. Not until the first-wave managers were successful did Baxter senior managers start attending alumni parties and celebrating their alumni's successes.

At Genzyme, Termeer has consistently maintained a proactive, not passive, approach to maintaining ties beyond Genzyme. As one consultant to the industry commented:

> The biggest difference [between Genzyme and Baxter is that] there are all these people who Henri has only partially let leave. And by that I mean, that he's either put them in another one of his investments, or he's maintained good relationships with people.

Moreover:

> Henri did a great job at the beginning setting up all these little companies and letting them go. . . . They all have their own companies; the yo-yo has come right back into his fist, hasn't it? He runs 'em.

Thus, whereas Baxter did a limited number of deals with its alumni—the deal with GI being the most significant—Termeer actively engages in cultivating relationships with Genzyme alumni and even, on occasion, has been able to pull such firms back under the Genzyme umbrella. Recent Genzyme alumni lists suggest that since Termeer has been CEO, thirty-four top managers have gone on to other biotechnology companies, all of whom are in senior management positions and nineteen of whom are either president and/or CEO. Further, since taking over as CEO, Termeer has done over $1 billion in deals with public Genzyme alumni-led biotech firms alone.[4]

Like Graham, Termeer is disappointed when people leave, but is explicit with employees about maintaining ties to the company—not to him, to Genzyme. Like Baxter, Genzyme alumni parties have become a tradition—usually taking place the night before one of the industry's two largest annual conferences (the BIO convention and the Hambrecht & Quist conference) begins. Each year, different alumni take turns hosting the preconference dinner in the town in which the conference is held. Oftentimes, Termeer makes an appearance—like Graham used to make—legitimating the kinds of entrepreneurial moves that his former employees have made into biotechnology. As one longtime Genzyme employee who recently left Genzyme to join a new venture in biotechnology remembers, prior to his departure, Termeer said:

> Let's stay in touch. . . . Good deals are based upon good relationships, and good relationships take time.

The lesson here is not that entrepreneurial career imprints are necessarily "good" for a company but rather, if one determines that this is the preferred career imprint for an organization, then complementing this with an ecosystem perspective can reap benefits for both the parent and child organization. Organizational benefits may come in the form of employee referrals for deals, for potential new-hires, for public policy or regulatory information, or, more generally, in the form of reputational benefits that could enhance the firm's status in an industry or sector.[5] The Baxter story illustrates the potential upside for firms of keeping their doors open rather than slamming them shut when people leave the firm.

In addition, one of the factors that made this approach possible and productive for Baxter was the constant source of new talent at Baxter. As Bill Holodnak, a senior executive at one of the top recruiting firms for biotechnology, advised:

> People should come up and go out . . . that's good parenting. You are loving, help them [learn to] do the right things, and you are tough

> to make them stronger and self reliant. . . . And this [letting people go] is OK as long as you continue to invent people to come in after them. . . . That's better than paternalism or socialism . . . it aerates the soil and creates an external population of loyal constituents.

This stance toward staffing and departures is exactly the one taken by Bill Graham, as described in Chapter Five and as contrasted with that of Abbott in Chapters Six and Seven. Many different companies put a great deal of time and effort into delivering the message that, simply put, "Even though you have left the company, you're still family." Consulting firms such as McKinsey and Bain have perfected this practice by setting up alumni associations for former employees, hosting events and social hours, and generally not only supporting but also celebrating the successes of former employees. Indeed, it makes good business sense for *them*, since alumni of consulting firms often take on roles at other companies that make them prime candidates as clients.

Yet downstream spawning is not the most difficult kind of "tough love parenting" that Holodnak calls our attention to. Upstream or horizontal spawning is much more difficult for companies since the "win-win" solution, such as becoming that spawning firm's client, is much less obvious. That is, supporting the departures of one's employees, particularly good employees, seems counterintuitive. Yet, as Holodnak's comments also suggest, for companies that have cultivated an entrepreneurial career imprint, adopting an ecosystem perspective is an easier stance to take if the company has a reliable source of talent to return to.

Indeed, one of the organizational design levers Graham used to "professionalize Baxter" was staffing. As that famous quote about Graham's response to the Chicago reporter who asked whether he was worried about losing people goes, Graham said "Well, yes, we do lose talent, but there always seems to be somebody right behind 'em to pick up the slack." Here, Graham relied upon one consistent source for talent—MBA programs. Although MBA programs are not necessarily the correct or only source for talent for companies that cultivate an entrepreneurial career imprint, having a consistent recruiting plan did help perpetuate the image of Baxter as an excellent training ground; it kept people coming. Thus, a constant source of talent is an important factor in sustaining an entrepreneurial career imprint.

Considering the contingent value of career imprints in the context of industry-level dynamics opens up additional areas of inquiry as well. For example, we can ask whether certain kinds of organizational career imprints, such as an entrepreneurial career imprint, offer incumbent organizations the opportunity to investigate more easily business opportunities associated with an emerging industry.

For many years, management scholars have examined the trade-offs between organizational efforts aimed at "exploiting" a firm's distinctive competencies and "exploring" new opportunities in an emerging customer and/or technological space.[6] Research by Christensen suggests that well-established firms are often less likely to engage in new areas of innovation—particularly if the new technology is "disruptive" or first enters a lower-cost segment of the customer market.[7] Here, although it is not evident that biotechnology was a disruptive technology for Baxter, it is evident that well-established firms, including Baxter, were not actively encouraging employees to explore this new industry at the start of the industry. Recent work by Tushman and colleagues has suggested that certain organizational structures and strategies can enable even well-established organizations to be "ambidextrous" and so both exploit and explore opportunities simultaneously.[8]

The present research raises the question of whether well-established firms can "explore" new industries with their offspring.[9] The data presented here suggest that exploration need not be formal, such as through alliances; rather, channels for exploration may be quite informal, as was the case with Baxter alumni gatherings that senior executives from Baxter attended. Thus, organizations such as Baxter that have both an entrepreneurial career imprint and an ecosystem perspective may open up opportunities for organizations to learn—through their alumni—and also to explore an emerging technological arena.

Pursuing this new line of inquiry and investigating informal alumni-based channels of "exploration" would be difficult; as illustrated in the opening pages of the book with the story of Stan Erck asking a fellow Baxter alumnus if he could borrow a couple of hundred thousand dollars for his privately held firm, informal helping behavior is often difficult to track. Still, if the alumni of firms with entrepreneurial career imprints who end up taking on leadership positions in new firms and new industries also remain connected to their former employers, through informal alumni gatherings and the like, then the parent employer may benefit as well—through the passing along of information, access, and even resources that eventually enable the company to explore a new arena. Indeed, although not studied here, it would be interesting to pursue the ways in which some of these companies, including Baxter, did eventually build their own biotechnology division and the genesis of that effort, as compared to other firms with other kinds of career imprints and with or without an ecosystem perspective.

Exploring the contingent value of career imprints raises questions at an even broader level, as we consider the evolution of an industry. As discussed, leaders carry career imprints with them as they move from organization to organization, particularly if those career imprints were strongly cultivated. To the extent a whole group of people, such as the Baxter Boys, leave a particular organization at a particular point in time to take on leadership positions in young firms in an emerging industry, it is possible that there will be commonalities among the ways in which they decide to organize their firms that are recognizable and that serve as a blueprint for other firms to follow.

In Chapter Eight, we explored the legacy of organizational career imprints with the examples of Termeer at Genzyme, Vincent at Biogen, and Schmergel at Genetics Institute. If we push this exploration one step further to test the proposition that career imprints affect organizational design choices in predictable ways, one could examine whether groups of people from different organizations who all start firms in the same industry in the same location at the same time adopt similar strategies. Given our understanding of the lasting effect of strong career imprints, we would expect to find greater differences between firms with leaders who came from different firms than between firms with leaders who all came from the same firm.

However, more interesting still would be to examine the extent to which hallmarks of a particular career imprint become the dominant organizational structure (or strategy or culture) within a particular industry. As mentioned in the first chapter, organizational research by Stinchcombe suggests that certain kinds of organizational structures vary systematically according to their environmental context and time period in which firms are founded in an industry.[10] Over time, as certain forms prove more effective, these forms become institutionalized and adopted by others. Here, the notion of organizational career imprints opens up the possibility that dominant organizational forms may emerge from the previous employment experiences of a dominant group of alumni in an industry.

In particular, if, as we saw with the case of the Baxter Boys, this group is viewed as successful in some way early on (e.g., raising money), then, this group's strategies and structures may be essentially "copied" by others as well and so come to dominate within an industry. Furthermore, if leaders, such as Henri Termeer, are active and visible spokespeople in professional associations, we might find even greater potential for such dominant forms based upon a dominant career imprint to emerge. Thus, the present research suggests an important role for organizational career imprints in driving what management scholars call "institutional isomorphism"—the tendency for organizations to imitate one another over time.[11]

In these ways, not only might organizational career imprints influence the very beginning stages of an industry's evolution, but dominant career imprints might also affect some ways in which an industry evolves over time. For example, if VCs had chosen Merck's career imprint over Baxter's, yielding a disproportionate number of CEOs from Merck, then we could imagine a scenario in which the biotechnology industry could, arguably, look quite different over time. Thus, the notion of organizational career imprints and, importantly, the ways in which they are perceived by outsiders may yield even greater insights into industry evolution than suggested by this particular study.

Generalizability of the Consequences of Career Imprints

Future research may also test the generalizability of the conclusions drawn here with respect to the linkages between organizational career imprints and industry evolution. Specifically, the question raised is, "Have we seen this before?" And second, "Where and when might we see this happen again?"

In other industries, we have seen similar sorts of spawning phenomena occur, such as when Fairchild spun off "Fairchildren" into the semiconductor sector and, specifically, into Silicon Valley.[12] In that instance, of the original thirty-one semiconductor firms that began in Silicon Valley, the vast majority of these were started by people who had come from Fairchild.[13] Research that compares the career experiences of people who worked at Fairchild, and so Fairchild's career imprint, with that of other potential spawning organizations during that time period may lend insight into what kinds of capabilities, connections, confidence, and cognition were seen as particularly relevant to the perceived requirements of this emerging industry. Here, as was the case in the present research, one would want to consider the perspectives of individuals who came from Fairchild, such as Andy Grove, as well as individuals such as Eugene Kleiner, who eventually became a prominent venture capitalist in Silicon Valley. Then perhaps, by comparing the present research with such analyses, we could offer conclusions regarding the role of career imprints during the early stages of industry formation more generally.

Additionally, one could revisit Saxenian's comparison of Silicon Valley and Route 128, but study as well the microlevel foundations of these regions and how they evolved into leading locations for electronics innovation and production. For example, by looking at the differences between the organizational career imprints of companies such as Fairchild, which spawned people into Silicon Valley, and Digital Equipment Corporation, which spawned people into Route 128, along with more macrolevel and systemic factors such as university and military spending, we might gain a more complete (or perhaps even different) understanding of why and how these two regions evolved so differently.

A second line of inquiry raised regarding the generalizability of the present study concerns the nature of VC and intermediary decision making. When an industry is just beginning and perceptions about what is needed to run a new venture are just being formed, there is little tangible evidence to rely upon, as track records are just being formed. In these instances, intermediaries can play a huge role in shaping the inflow or outflow of managerial talent, and it is during these times that perceptions of an organization's career imprint can have a powerful effect on how that mobility unfolds. The Baxter story provided an illustration of the powerful role of VCs at the start of an industry.

As we consider different industries and different contexts and the role of VCs more broadly than considered here, we can ask, "What are the similarities and differences in selection criteria among powerful intermediaries, such as VCs, across industries? Do their logics of action regarding what is appropriate or required to run a business evolve substantially over time or do they, like aspects of the strong organizational career imprints in this story, become 'sticky' as well?"

Examining the early career experiences of VCs would lend insight into *their* organizational career imprints and so provide a better understanding as to how certain logics of action in the VC community have evolved. This would contribute as well to research on VC decision making, which has focused primarily on what specific aspects of a firm these evaluators attend to, but not why. Such an undertaking would also extend the present research; that is, if we understand the organizational career imprints of VCs, perhaps we would gain an even deeper understanding of why certain companies come out on top as the "preferred" recruiting grounds in emerging industries.

If we broaden our purview beyond the *early* stages of an industry's evolution, we could also consider *later* and yet still precious stages in an industry's evolution when spawning of a different sort could occur. For example, we could consider how recessionary times have hit certain industries and how the career imprints of leaders can help organizations respond. For example, in the case of houseware products, including plastic containers, Rubbermaid was deemed not ready for the recession and so GE alumnus Stanley Gault was called in to "awake the sleeping giant." Gault was credited with making some very aggressive steps, such as firing about 11 percent of the white-collar staff, restructuring and consolidating the company's core operations, and moving Rubbermaid into entirely new product markets. According to Gault, the credit goes to GE and "especially its emphasis on financial controls, strategic planning, quality products and management training."[14] Thus, certain firms, like GE, are known for breeding turnaround experts and, during certain times in an industry, this may be just the kind of career imprint that is preferred.

Bringing these macrolevel topics back to the issue of senior executive mobility, we can ask, "As industries evolve and firms must respond to external pressures, if organizational career imprints are resistant to change, how might such external pressures affect the mobility of senior executives who already hold leadership positions in an industry?" Further, "How 'successful' are firms and the people who lead them, who hold certain career imprints that seem relevant early on in an industry's life course?" And, "What makes some organizational career imprints more resilient than others?" Perhaps some career imprints include metacompetencies, such as "learning how to learn," that enable leaders to cope more effectively with change—much as Bennis observed that certain leaders were more skillful at hopping corporate cultures.[15] These questions also raise an interesting possibility in the present case: as Henri Termeer pondered, "Perhaps we [Baxter alumni] are all just good at starting companies." On this, the jury is still out. The longer-term consequences of career imprints for industries are interesting and open to further exploration.

Patterns of Inquiry for the Future

Organizational career imprints confirm for us what seem like givens in our careers, postulates such as the following: that we take with us aspects of our early career experience as we evolve and develop as leaders in society; that effecting change within an organization does not eradicate one's past but rather provides an opportunity to engage it—even to re-create aspects of one's past unwittingly.

Yet, the idea of organizational career imprints offers boundaries on this intuitive logic by suggesting that not everything is transferable. Rather, there are certain conditions, including social reinforcement and demonstrated success, that make some organizations more fertile than others as breeding grounds for career imprinting and so more likely to cultivate a particular logic of action that *can* then transfer to subsequent organizations. Likewise, not every career experience is likely to be formative—rather, there are certain times in one's adult development when people are more open to career imprinting. From an organizational perspective, then, there are special times when career imprinting is most likely to take hold. Likewise, as a leader of an organization, one can employ levers to create a strong environment for career imprinting—levers such as creating a strong organizational culture that can affect the career imprinting process. And finally, this book identifies several core dimensions of organizational career imprints—capabilities, connections, confidence, and cognition—that provide a more tangible sense of how career experiences can affect leader development.

The idea of career imprints requires us to consider much more than a single level of analysis, however, when we look at careers and the development of leaders. Individuals cultivate or pick up organizational career imprints; certain individual-level factors, such as educational background and career stage, can affect the extent to which an organization's career imprint is likely to have a lasting effect on that individual's leadership development. Yet, ultimately, organizational career imprints are housed at the organizational level, since they reflect patterns in sets of individuals' careers at a particular point in time. As a collective, then, once individuals leave organizations, they can, as a group, affect change at a much broader level—not just in terms of the design choices they make when they move to new firms, but as a collective, on the evolution of an industry.

These broader-level connections have been the focus of the present study. In addition, tracing these connections back to the people, place, and paths—to the career imprinting process itself—fosters a deeper appreciation for the origin and substance of macrolevel effects such as spawning that we observe at the start of industries. Thus, the notion of organizational career imprints, while placing boundaries on common phrases such as "you take what you learn with you," also inspires us to consider what happens at a much broader level, as collectives of individuals "take with them" common threads of an earlier experience. These patterns of career experiences create an organizational career imprint that can have a profound impact on the course of an industry—as the "Baxter Boys" had on biotechnology.

Appendix A

Research Design and Methods

The Preface and Chapter One of this book provide some information on the design of the present research. Rather than repeat that information here, this appendix offers additional details regarding research design as well as research process. Limitations are noted here, and implications for future research are discussed at length in Chapter Ten.

Research Design and Evolution

As described in the Preface, the design of the present research reflects a journey. I did not begin with specific hypotheses that I then set out to test; instead, I began with the observation of a phenomenon that triggered a research project that led to the development of an idea—the idea of organizational career imprints. Therefore, the research design reflects a process of exploring, probing, and analyzing patterns in the data collected. Both quantitative archival data and qualitative interview data were collected. Employing both kinds of data is especially helpful when the nature of the research is exploratory and phenomenologically oriented (Eisenhardt, 1989; Glaser & Strauss, 1967). Working inductively with the career history data along with literature on careers and leadership development led to the conceptual development of the idea of organizational career imprints, along with an understanding of its antecedents and consequences.

As described in the Preface, the phenomenon that began the present research project was the observation of help-giving and receiving between biotech executives who had all previously worked at Baxter. This helping behavior seemed useful to these executives with respect to their own career advancement and, based upon my observations, I conjectured, with respect to the performance of the young firms they were leading. In order to investigate this, I engaged in some initial interviews with the CEOs whose helping behavior I had witnessed. My goal in these early interviews was to begin to gain an understanding of these individuals' early career experiences at Baxter and also the extent to which they still relied on this Baxter network in their new posts in biotechnology.

As part of this early inquiry, I conducted five approximately two-hour interviews in the early 1990s with four Baxter alumni; all of the questions were open-ended and focused on their career histories and the extent to which they communicated with their Baxter colleagues. All of these interviews were transcribed. These early interviews confirmed that, at least from their perspective, the Baxter employment affiliation had helped them get their firms off to a good start. Still, I felt that it was important to investigate as well whether, from a more "objective" perspective, having an affiliation with Baxter was indeed helpful in some way—in particular, with respect to the performance of these young firms. Thus, in many respects, the objective in the first phase of this project was simply to confirm that there was indeed a "real phenomenon"— that having worked at Baxter was "helpful" to new venture performance in some fashion.

Quantitative Data Collection

To collect independent "objective" data, I turned to the final prospectuses of young biotech companies since the SEC requires young firms to record the five-year career histories of their managing officers and board members when they go public. In 1996, I began to collect information on the career histories of not just Baxter alumni but of all members of IPO teams (i.e., managing officers and board members) of biotech firms that had gone public in 1996 or earlier (dating back to 1979). As described in the Preface, the five-year career histories of over 3,200 executives from approximately three hundred public biotechnology firms were collected, classified, and coded by function, title, and employer(s), including board positions. These data were compiled in a relational "people" database.

In tandem, a relational "company" database was created that included firm-level factors also found in a final prospectus—information such as the amount of private financing raised, the stage of the firm's lead product, the venture capitalists who were on board, the firm's location, and so on, as described more fully in Appendix B. In this way, information could be pulled from both databases and then used in analyses predicting firm performance.

As described in the Preface, analyses of these data helped establish that having a Baxter alumnus on board an IPO team did indeed positively affect the IPO performance of a young biotech firm (detailed in Appendix B). Moreover, these data show that nearly one-quarter of the firms that went public between 1979 and 1996 had on their IPO team at least one person who had worked at Baxter. Further, chi-square analyses reveal that, compared to other potential spawners such as J&J, Merck, and Abbott, this overrepresentation of Baxter alumni in the biotech industry remained significant and positive even after accounting for firm size. Taken together, these analyses suggest that Baxter alumni did indeed have a positive influence on the evolution of young firms in the industry and, as a collective, on the growth of the biotechnology industry overall.

Qualitative Data Collection

Armed with this evidence, I turned my attention to the next logical question, a question that ultimately motivated the writing of this book: "Why was Baxter such a generative institution—such a good spawner of entrepreneurial activity at the start of the biotech industry?" To engage in this inquiry, I returned to the field and conducted additional interviews—primarily between 2003 and 2004. These were semistructured open-ended interviews. My starting assumption was that there were factors associated with the people, the place, and the paths of these individuals that would help account for the effects observed. During this phase, I focused on gathering data on the career transitions of the individuals who had made the move from Baxter and other prominent pharmaceutical and healthcare firms into biotechnology. This microlevel career perspective offers a novel lens on the phenomenon of spawning, as described in Chapters One and Ten.

My goals for this interview stage of the research were threefold: to better understand the phenomenon of spawning exhibited here; to uncover patterns in the career paths of the individuals whose career transitions were at the center of the phenomenon; and to begin to generate theory and propositions based upon these observations. Throughout, Baxter was used as the primary case and research base for the book. In addition, a comparative approach was employed. That is, in order to understand why Baxter was more representative than other firms in the upper echelons of young biotech companies and in order to understand more fully the ideas that were emerging regarding organizational career imprints, I investigated as well the people, place, and paths associated with other healthcare firms during the same timeframe. The Preface describes the rationale for choosing to conduct interviews with three other healthcare firms in particular, Merck, J&J, and Abbott; all of these firms could be similarly considered "at risk" for spawning managers into biotechnology and so serve as useful points of comparison, given the phenomenon that motivated this research.

To this end, I conducted interviews with people (a) who were hired into Baxter during approximately the same time (by Bill Graham; and worked at Baxter during the 1970s) and later left for biotechnology; (b) who were hired into Baxter during this same time period and did not go into biotechnology; (c) who were not hired into Baxter (i.e., those from a comparable company such as Abbott) but moved into biotechnology; and (d) who were in neither category—that is, people who did not work at Baxter and did not end up working directly in a biotech firm *but* who were involved in some way with healthcare and/or biotechnology at the time and so could provide a useful perspective as well. The vast majority of people in this latter category were intermediaries such as venture capitalists.

In total, seventy-eight interviews of approximately 1.5 to 2 hours in length were conducted for this research. The total number of people interviewed was sixty-one (since several were interviewed on more than one occasion), and the breakdown, according to the aforementioned categories, is shown in Table A.1.

Among those who had not worked at Baxter but who had been employed at a major healthcare firm, I strove to find at least two people from each of the three comparison companies who could serve as expert informants. These were people I could go back to for follow-up questions; they had also worked for these firms during the same time period in question. In the Not Baxter/Not Biotech quadrant, I primarily interviewed intermediaries—that is, people who had been venture capitalists, consultants, lawyers, and headhunters during the early years of the biotech industry. In the Baxter/Not Biotech quadrant, I interviewed people who had gone into different industries after Baxter (e.g., consulting). Some of these individuals were let go from Baxter; some who were interviewed from the Baxter/Biotech quadrant were let go as well. In many of those cases, the departures were mutual, given Baxter's steep organizational pyramid (as described in Chapter Three). In

Table A.1 Employment Affiliations of Interviewees

	Biotech	Not Biotech	Totals
Baxter	24	12	36
Not Baxter	12	13	25
Totals	36	25	61

the Baxter/Biotech quadrant, all of those interviewed were hired during the same time period—mid-1960s and 1970s; thus, the cohort was restricted to hiring during the "Graham era" and to having worked at Baxter primarily during the 1970s. Five of the thirty-six former Baxter managers were "journeymen"; that is, they were hired without an MBA or advanced degree; two of the thirty-six were still working at Baxter at the time I interviewed them.

Focal Interviews. Following is the interview protocol for the core career history interviews of individuals who worked at Baxter, Merck, J&J, and Abbott. Three aspects of this design are important to highlight: first, this interview protocol follows an individual's career history from the perspective of the interviewee. Although additional data were always collected on the individual from secondary sources prior to the interview, this information was not used to prompt the individual during the interview. This interviewee event-centered approach is consistent with other scholarly work in the area of careers, such as the interview protocol used in Schein's Career Anchors Self-assessment Instrument (Schein, 1993). From this perspective, individuals are not primed beforehand nor reminded of jobs or positions by the interviewer; rather, key events are named by the interviewee so as to gather a sense for their own construction of the major events in their careers. From the data collected, it is then possible to back into the objective or résumé-like aspects of the career history while capturing the experienced-based or subjective side of the career as well (the importance of both aspects of a career, the objective and subjective, is described in Chapter Five).

Second, I did not ask interviewees for their interpretations of the "finding" that Baxter was overrepresented on the IPO teams of biotech companies at the start of the interviews. Indeed, such an approach would have been problematic for two reasons: first, it would have primed the participants as to that particular juncture in their careers and so, perhaps, prompt retrospective sense-making as they engaged in recalling their own career experiences before and when they were transitioning into biotech (if they did). Second, that level of abstraction is much higher than is useful for culling patterns from career history data. Instead, in the present research I sought the most grounded-level data I could retrieve; I asked questions that prompted interviewees to give examples of career experiences *they* named by using phrases such as "How did this come about?" and, "Describe how X happened." This approach encouraged interviewees to recall events, stories, and episodes, all of which reflect behaviors, cognition, and attitudes rather than the interviewee's own interpretation of those same things. If the interviewee stepped up the ladder of abstraction, I tried to return to grounded data with phrases such as, "Can you give me an example of what you are saying?" This kind of probing is useful in inductive research, since such follow-up comments can generate new and unexpected insights (Glesne, 1997, ch. 4).

At the very end of the interviews, I did engage in a more open conversation regarding their personal learning from all of these experiences (see Part III of the interview protocol), which lifted the conversation up a level and allowed for a more general discussion. And, oftentimes at the very end, I invited their reactions to the "finding" of Baxter's overrepresentation on biotech IPO firms.

Finally, this interview protocol was designed to get at two levels of analysis—first, the individual-level career histories and, second, the organizational context in which these career experiences unfolded. Oftentimes, in career research, researchers account very little for the social context in which career experiences unfold. These latter kinds of questions occurred during the second part of the interview. At this point, interviewees were encouraged to comment on the broader healthcare environment and specific aspects, such as the introduction of diagnosis-related groups (DRGs) and good manufacturing practices (GMPs), that may have affected the kinds of career assignments and challenges they faced. Again, I did not prompt individuals to comment on these kinds of exogenous factors; rather, if such factors emerged, I probed further, as necessary, to understand their specific career situations.

Focal Interview Protocol

I. Personal Career History
    1. Please describe how you came to work at [Baxter (or Merck, J&J, or Abbott)]. What career decisions, coincidences, people led to your working at [Baxter]?
    2. What (and when) was your first major job at [Baxter]?
        a. Describe your experience joining up with [Baxter].
        b. What were the most important relationships you had at that time (mentors, friends, advisors)?
        c. What were your first memories of [Baxter]?
        d. What was it like to start there?
    3. What was the next major event in your career at [Baxter]?
        a. How did this come about? Who initiated the change? What were the reasons for the change?
        b. How did you feel about the change?
        c. What were your important relationships at that time— perhaps these were of two types: people who were instrumental in making the change possible for you and people who were important to you in your own development and adjustment to your new role (i.e., helped you learn the ropes). . . . Anybody else?
    4. What was the next major event in your career at [Baxter]?
        a. How did this come about? Who initiated the change? What were the reasons for the change?
        b. How did you feel about the change?
        c. What were your important relationships at that time— perhaps these were of two types: people who were instrumental in making the change possible for you and people who were important to you in your own

development and adjustment to your new role (i.e., helped you learn the ropes). . . . Anybody else?

. . . . . . [repeat as necessary]

5. Why did you leave [Baxter]? (or Why didn't you leave? When did you see [key colleagues] leaving, and how did you feel at the time?)

   a. How did this change come about? Who initiated the change? What were the reasons for the change?

   b. How did you feel about the change?

   c. What were your important relationships at that time— perhaps these were of two types: people who were instrumental in making the change possible for you and people who were important to you in your own development and adjustment to your new role (i.e., helped you learn the ropes). . . . Anybody else?

II. Institutional Context Questions: Organizational Perceptions

6. How would you describe the culture of [Baxter] when you were working there? Did it change while you were there; if so, how/why?

   a. What were the norms? How did people act in meetings? In informal (unplanned) interactions?

   b. What were the expectations senior management had of folks like you starting out? How/did this affect your own development? Can you give me some examples?

7. How would you describe [Baxter's] organizational structure?

   a. Formal?

   b. Informal?

8. What's your perception of [Baxter's] strategy during this time period?

   a. How was this similar to another company at the time?

9. What were some of the formal practices/systems in place?

   a. Was there formal training? Did you partake in this; if so, what was it like?

   b. Did/does [Baxter] have systems in place to keep in touch with those who left?

10. Can you recall a friend at another company in the industry at that same time? What do you think they would have said about their company's culture/systems?

   a. How were the practices at that company similar/different from those at [Baxter]?

   b. Could I talk to that person?

11. How would you describe the dominant managerial style at [Baxter]?

   a. How do you feel you fit with that?

III. Impact on Professional Development

12. How do you think you developed personally and professionally from your career at [Baxter]?

   a. What did you gain the most, in terms of your professional development at [Baxter]?

   b. In what ways did [Baxter] let you down, if at all?

13. Who are you still in contact with who also worked at [Baxter]?

   a. Did you work directly with these people while at [Baxter]?

   b. How do you stay in touch?

   c. What's the nature of the relationship (personal/ professional)?

   d. Do you think that there still is some sort of [Baxter] network alive and well in the industry? Why (or why not)?

Intermediary Interviews. For those who were in intermediary roles—that is, they fell into the Not Baxter/Not Biotech box— I asked different questions. Generally, I began with similar questions about their entry into their current field. In some cases, I retrieved full career history accounts. In other cases, I skipped directly to their involvement in the senior executive transitions of people from Baxter and other firms into biotechnology. These interviews varied to a greater degree than the focal interviews since individuals had had different kinds of positions vis à vis the biotech industry. However, across the interviews, I did maintain similar goals.

First, I was interested in understanding both sides to the matching problems they engaged in: (a) what the requirements were for running a biotech firm, as they saw them during the end of the 1970s and early 1980s (at the start of the biotech industry), and (b) what kinds of people they thought could match those requirements, and where these people tended to come from. Again, the most productive interviews were those in which individuals gave me specific examples, and I pressed for these grounded data whenever possible.

Second, I was interested in their specific perspectives on those who came from Baxter; I asked about the extent to which they had recruited out of Baxter versus elsewhere and why. Here, I was interested in specifics about Baxter as a breeding ground for the kind of entrepreneurial talent they sought, and I was interested in their perspectives on how Baxter compared to other healthcare firms at the time.

Third, I asked many questions about "what it was like back then" at the start of the biotechnology industry to get a sense for the kind of uncertainty that they and others faced.

Transcription of Interviews. Focal and intermediary interviews were generally taped. Interviewees were asked before taping and assured that they could ask me to turn off the tape recorder if and as they wished. For those interviews that were not taped, I took extensive notes and then wrote these notes up as close to verbatim as possible directly after the interview ended. The taped interviews were all transcribed by individuals who were not involved in the interviews.

Participant Observation, Records, and Other Sources

Interviewees often invited me to formal and informal gatherings. During these gatherings, I learned through open dialogue and listening. At one dinner gathering, in particular, there were a number of speeches made about a focal participant; I was given a videotape of this event, which supplemented my own observations.

At the tail end of the project, the role of participant observer switched, as I had the opportunity to receive feedback from several Baxter alumni on the ideas that I was generating from the data collection. Two individuals came to one of my presentations on my research findings and provided feedback on the present research, and several other Baxter alumni (people I had previously interviewed) made themselves available for follow-up conversations. At that point, the data gathering became an iterative process, as I heard their reactions and found areas in which I felt I needed to probe further. Indeed, during the final months of the writing of the book, I returned yet again to the field to conduct four more extensive interviews to further triangulate what I was hearing and, in one instance, to consider a counterpoint example (as described at the end of Chapter Eight).

In addition to these opportunities for reflection, observation, and feedback from the field, I drew upon three types of documentation to develop the ideas presented in this book. First, many Baxter and non-Baxter interviewees dug through their own records to produce old magazine articles, newspaper clippings, lists from alumni gatherings, photographs, letters and memos, and write-ups of previous speeches. These secondary sources provided a first-hand look into these individuals' work lives decades ago and allowed me to cross-verify the interview data as well as better understand the historical context in which their careers had unfolded.

Second, I drew upon internal company records and memoranda, including anniversary books, company publications such as newsletters, and annual reports that were relevant to understanding these companies' strategies, structures, cultures, and practices. Third, I drew upon third-party documents and records such as analyst and investment reports to gain insight into how these companies and the leaders who built them were viewed in the investment community.

Data Analysis

Career Experiences and Paths

Analyses of the career history data entailed using both the quantitative and qualitative data and, reflecting the process of the present research, encompassed two stages. Early on, analyses of the quantitative data enabled me to develop an understanding of the significance of having worked at Baxter versus another healthcare firm—in particular, with respect to the performance of the biotech companies that many went on to lead and manage. Then, in order to explore the mechanisms that might account for the overrepresentation of Baxter alumni in biotech, I worked inductively with the career history data; these analyses enabled me to develop the ideas regarding career imprinting that form the basis of this book.

In the first instance, the quantitative data allowed for analyses of how career history patterns and, in particular, employment affiliations affect firm performance. These analyses are detailed in Appendix B. In the second instance, the qualitative data allowed for an exploration of patterns in people's career experiences within particular firms; these latter analyses eventually led to the ideas regarding the origins and consequences of career imprints presented in this book.

The first step in analyzing the qualitative data was to take apart the transcripts (which were event centered, as previously described) and reconfigure the data into tables consisting of dates and associated positions, as described in Chapter Five (and as shown in Table 5.1, with the example of Gabe Schmergel). To fill in missing data for individuals' career histories, I relied upon secondary sources, including information gleaned from the final prospectuses of their respective firms, along with other publicly available information (e.g., newspaper articles) as well as résumés, when available. These career history summaries were then compared to arrive at general patterns across these individuals' "objective" career paths, as described primarily in Chapter Five.

It was also important to find individuals from the comparison firms who had worked at their healthcare firms during the exact same time period as those hired during the "Graham era" at Baxter and to gather their career histories. The limitation here is that I had far more data to rely upon from those who had worked at Baxter versus elsewhere. Therefore, in addition to these expert informants' career histories, I relied as well upon secondary sources regarding the human-resources practices at these comparison firms to understand the general patterns or steps people's careers followed during the same time period as those followed at Baxter.

In addition to looking for objective patterns in individuals' careers, I sought out patterns in the subjective aspects of individuals' careers—that is, the ways people experienced their careers while at Baxter, in particular. To do this, I looked through the transcripts for reoccurring word-event patterns (e.g., stories about Abbott's 1971 recall), metaphors (e.g., references to "war"), phrases (e.g., "sink or swim"), and methods of address (e.g., "Mr. Graham"). This process enabled me to uncover the extent to which individuals had a "common language" for describing their career experiences—both within and across the interviews. I was particularly interested in the latter since it provides insight into the ways in which people engaged in *similar* sense-making in a particular company and at a particular point in time.

As described in Chapter Five, this approach has been employed in the study of managerial action and culture, but not in the area of careers. Here, this idea and method is applied to gain further insight into what was shared across career experiences—to analyze more fully the capabilities, connections, confidence, and cognition (and, in particular, the latter) that individuals cultivated at a particular organization. This approach is consistent with recent career research and, in general, with the Chicago School perspective that careers are at least, in part, in the eye of the beholder (e.g., Barley, 1989).

The four Cs of organizational career imprints emerged after culling through the transcripts and categorized portions of the transcripts based upon what these individuals were learning. Existing literature often provided a useful place to start and then, to develop theory, I relied upon my interview data (Strauss & Corbin, 1998). The first two main categories that surfaced were human capital and social capital, two theoretical pillars in organizational theory—here, termed "capabilities" and "connections." Upon further analyses, it became apparent both through the participants' own descriptions and use of the term *confidence* (and given recent research on leader development) that the category of "confidence" was also important to include as well (see Bennis & Thomas, 2002b, for a discussion of hardiness and Kanter, 2004, for a discussion of confidence in leaders and organizations).

The final category, "cognition," was the last to emerge. As I heard stories not just about what people learned but also about what people took with them to new companies, it became apparent that individuals had adopted a way of thinking about work and working, leadership and leading, management and managing that stemmed from their early career experiences. In social cognition literature, scholars refer to such "ways of thinking about the world" as scripts or schemas; here, the term *cognition* was used.

Armed with these categories, I went back through the transcripts again and again, to reclassify career experiences and stories, using these four general "C" category headings. Then, through a process of inductive iteration through these transcript data and through comparison across the interviews with people from different firms, it was possible to cull out differences *within* these categories (e.g., "learning-based efficacy" as opposed to "expertise-based efficacy"). Thus, although existing literature and the Baxter career history interviews served as the primary bases for the present research, in order to specify the exact nature of these four organizational career imprints, I had to compare within company experiences and then, as well, patterns in career experiences across the focal firms (Eisenhardt, 1989; Miles & Huberman, 1994).

Career Imprinting Processes: Analyses of People and Place

Two factors were used as starting points to examine the career imprinting process and, in particular, the factors that contribute to cultivating a particularly strong career imprint, as described in Chapters Three and Four: place and people. In order to gain insight into specific aspects of the social context—including firm strategy, structure, and culture (i.e., factors associated with "place")—I looked at the career history interviews in depth, as well as secondary sources such as company documents and investment reports.

With respect to the analyses of "people," I employed the career history data from the final prospectuses. Chi-square analyses were used to compare the educational backgrounds and age of individuals in the dataset with the six most-represented pharmaceutical employment affiliations. These analyses provide the *expected* count of different educational degrees, for example, within this population if the distribution were even across all companies, to the *actual* count of these degrees observed in the dataset. The six most-represented pharmaceutical companies on biotech IPO teams were Baxter, Abbott, J&J, Merck, Bristol-Myers Squibb, and Eli Lilly. These companies were used as the basis for the comparisons regarding people's backgrounds. The limitation here is that the data reflect those individuals who did ultimately end up taking firms public in biotechnology; therefore, there is some sample selection bias associated with these analyses, as mentioned in the notes to Chapter Four. In the main regression analyses reported in Appendix B regarding the impact of Baxter, sample selection methods were employed.

Legacy of Career Imprints: Case Comparisons

Chapter Eight explored the lasting influence of organizational career imprints—that is, how individuals take career imprints from previous employers with them as they change employers to lead other organizations. The primary case example was that of Henri Termeer and his exporting of the Baxter career imprint to Genzyme. This case was chosen first due to the preponderance of primary and secondary data available on Genzyme at the time of the study. In particular, since Termeer was still leading Genzyme at the time of the research, I was able to conduct substantial interviews with people who were current employees and recent alumni of Genzyme and so could comment on the kinds of leadership choices Termeer had made over the years.

The process that was used to explore the working proposition, that early career imprints shape the kinds of design choices a leader makes, included several steps. First, I gathered and analyzed data on Genzyme and the choices that Termeer made, as reported in analyst and investment reports, newspaper articles, and other public sources. Next, I developed a working model of Genzyme's core business strategy, structure, and culture. Then, as appropriate, I considered how such core design features did or did not reflect Baxter's strategy, structure, and culture.

After looking at these secondary sources, I turned to the primary interview data and to one expert informant to confirm that this depiction of Genzyme's strategy, structure, and culture was "accurate." I noted both similarities and differences between these aspects of Genzyme and Baxter and reviewed Termeer's transcript for information that directly addressed the issue of taking or not taking aspects of what he had learned at Baxter to Genzyme. Finally, I turned to the career history data of individuals who worked at Genzyme and looked for patterns in these data and then, backed into any reflections of the career experiences of Baxter alumni. These latter data are not reported extensively in Chapter Eight but were useful in the development of the ideas regarding the lasting impact of organizational career imprints.

In keeping with the comparison model, I next chose Jim Vincent's leadership of Biogen as a comparison case to that of Henri Termeer's leadership of Genzyme. As described in Chapter Eight,

Vincent worked at Abbott for approximately the same ten-year period as Termeer worked at Baxter (roughly 1972–1982). Further, they both left these firms to join biotech companies within only a couple of years of one another (1983 and 1985). Additionally, both Genzyme and Biogen are located within a block of one another in Cambridge, Massachusetts, allowing one to essentially control to some extent for other explanations such as regional advantage that have been set forth in the past.

Data on Biogen were compiled in a similar fashion as was the case for Genzyme and included interviews with both current and former employees of Biogen who worked with Vincent, along with an extensive career history interview with Vincent. After producing substantial notes on Biogen's strategy, structure, and culture, I then compared these aspects of Biogen with those of Abbott and, eventually, with those of Genzyme and noted similarities as well as differences.

As a final "check" on this comparison, I went back to the field to collect additional information on another firm—Genetics Institute (GI). Gabe Schmergel left Baxter to join GI at about the same time as Termeer and Vincent entered biotech firms. And, while Schmergel had more experience than either Vincent or Termeer prior to his career transition, GI seemed different than Genzyme in some respects, and so a potentially good "counterpoint" case. An analysis of this "counterpoint" example lends credence to the proposition that certain factors impede a leader's ability to fully export an organizational career imprint. The limitation here is that only these three firms' cases were examined in such detail. In the final chapter, the suggestion is made for future research to include a full analysis of biotechnology companies that were started by people from Baxter and from another firm, such as Abbott, and at the same time; then, one could compare the standard deviations between and within central aspects of these firms to test propositions regarding the legacy of organizational career imprints. The case analyses presented in Chapter Eight mark an entrée into such comparative research on organizational career imprints.

Different Imprints, Different Paths: Career Consequences of Career Imprints

In Chapter Nine, the evidence for the ideas presented stems primarily from the quantitative data once more. Here, the focus is on how different kinds of early career imprints might affect the career trajectories of individuals, as opposed to the course of firms or industries.

Specifically, the career history information from the final prospectuses allowed for an analysis of the likelihood of individuals following certain career paths, given the healthcare firms they had worked for previously. That is, I was able to examine the likelihood that an individual would end up in a particular role (e.g., in a top management role such as CEO) of a biotech firm, depending upon which firm—Baxter, Abbott, Merck, or J&J—he or she used to work for. These were chi-square analyses and are reported in Chapter Nine. Here, I compare expected counts to actual counts of numbers of individuals who end up in certain kinds of entrepreneurial roles, given where they used to work. These analyses show, for example, that Baxter alumni were significantly more likely to end up in top management positions, whereas J&J alumni were significantly more likely to end up in VC positions as board members on biotech firms. These analyses along with the interview data from the VCs lend insight into how and why different kinds of spawning activity may occur as well as the implications this may have for individuals and their career paths. The lessons included in Chapter Nine fall directly out of these analyses and the interview data that lent insight into the process of career imprinting (discussed in Chapters Three through Six) and the legacy and influences of career imprints (discussed in Chapters Seven and Eight).

Appendix B

Analyses of Baxter's Impact on IPO Success

This appendix provides additional detail on the analyses conducted to determine Baxter's impact on the biotechnology industry—as indexed by the performance benefits to young firms of having a Baxter alumnus on board the top management team when those firms go public. Here, the central proposition is that having a Baxter manager and/or board member onboard when a biotech firm goes public enhances that firm's performance in the IPO marketplace. This appendix focuses on this one aspect of Baxter's impact; other evidence is offered in the Preface.

The methods employed were similar to those employed in previous studies that also examine the performance implications of configurations of a firm's IPO team and so are reported elsewhere. (See Higgins, M. and Gulati, R. 2003. Getting Off to a Good Start: The Effects of Upper Echelon Affiliations on Underwriter Prestige, *Organization Science*, *14*(3), 244–263.)

Analyses

The primary data of interest are the five-year career histories of approximately 3,200 biotechnology executives who sat on boards and/or managed firms that went public between 1979 and 1996. As described in detail in the Preface, this dataset also includes information on firms that were founded in the same time period but did not go public. Heckman selection models were employed using these data to guard against the possibility of sample selection bias

(Heckman, 1979). In general, sample selection bias can arise when the criteria for selecting observations are not independent of the outcome variables. Here, I was investigating the effect of the prior employment experience of a biotechnology firm's managers and board members on various indicators of that firm's IPO success. Therefore, in order to conduct analyses on the core sample of *public* firms, it was important to first compare the sample of firms that did go public with a sample of private firms that were founded in the same time period but were not able to go public. Including these additional analyses (here, predicting whether or not a firm is able to go public) guards against the possibility that there is some other factor, in addition to those studied in the main analyses, that could account for the effects observed.

Heckman's procedure generates consistent, asymptotically efficient estimates that enable generalization to the larger population of biotechnology firms. The Heckman model is a two-stage procedure that uses the larger risk set of public and private firms, including firms that ceased to exist as of 1996 in both categories (n = 858). Probit regression was used to estimate the likelihood of completing an IPO during the first stage; estimates of parameters from that model were then incorporated into a second-stage regression model to predict the various success measures (Van de Ven & van Praag, 1981).

For the first-stage models, information was used that was available for both the public and private firms—geographical location, year of founding, and type of business—to predict likelihood of going public. (Two-stage models have been characterized as doing a particularly good job at estimation when there is at least one variable that may be considered an "instrument" that is a good predictor in the first stage but not in the second stage of the model. In this case, that "instrument" was business type; see Winship & Mare, 1992, for further discussion.) In the second stage, though the sample includes public and private firms, the standard errors reported reflect the smaller sample of firms (n = 244; there are 299 companies in the IPO dataset, but 55 of them have no underwriter prestige ranking and so are not used in these analyses. See discussion of the underwriter prestige measure below).

Measures

IPO Success. I employed both financial and nonfinancial indicators of the success of these young firms' IPOs. First, I chose to focus on the quantity and quality of investors who invest in an issuing firm as one important indicator of IPO success. Research in finance suggests that high-quality institutional investors can benefit new venture performance (Bushee, 1998). Unlike retail investors (e.g., high net worth individuals), institutional investors tend not to churn stock. Further, institutional investors tend to be more relationship-oriented and to have goals that are more likely to be aligned with young firms and thus are better positioned to help firms build long-term earning power (Porter, 1992). As finance research has shown, relative to individual investors, the sophistication of institutional investors enables them to more effectively monitor managerial behavior—for example, to ensure that managers choose R&D levels of spending that are in the long-term interests of the firm (Bushee, 1998). Given these findings, I evaluated IPO success as the amount and quality of investors the firm is able to attract as one primary measure of IPO success.

I obtained information on the institutional investors who endorsed the biotech firms from CDA/Spectrum Institutional Ownership Database from Thomson Financial Publishing. The SEC requires institutions to reveal all of their stock holdings on a quarterly basis by filing Form 13-F. The Spectrum database "reverse compiles" this information so that information may be obtained for companies being invested *in* rather than the company doing the investing. For these analyses, I looked at listings for the biotech companies for the first report post the IPO date. From Spectrum, it was possible to determine every institutional investor at that time and the percentage of available shares that each of those investors held. Using these data, I first determined the number of institutional investors that invested in the firm.

This information was further qualified by gauging the *quality* of the institutional investors that invested in the focal firm. Research by Bushee and Noe (2000) has shown that institutional investors may be classified into three different categories based upon the rate at which they turn over their portfolios and the extent to which the blocks of shares they purchase are diversified. The most savvy and relationship-oriented investors tend to have low portfolio turnover and low diversification strategies—what Bushee (1998) termed "dedicated" investors. Compared to other more "transient" institutional investors, "dedicated" institutional investors are most likely to be focused and interested in the company's longer-term growth prospects and so most likely to have the young firm's interests at heart (see also, Porter, 1992). I used Bushee's coding scheme, which classified institutional investors by year to categorize the institutional investors. The total number of *dedicated institutional investors* was used as another measure of IPO success.

In addition, the analyses employed a financial indicator of IPO success—cash raised at time of IPO. Specifically, I chose *proceeds to company* as one important indicator of IPO success; the more money a company raises through its offering, the more successful that IPO is generally considered. This information was obtained from the final prospectuses. Like the other financial information, these data were adjusted to constant 1996 dollars and logged.

Employment Affiliation Variables

Since the central proposition concerns having someone on the IPO team who previously worked at Baxter, it was important to code the 3,200 executives' career histories for this particular employment affiliation, along with those of other top spawners discussed in this book.

Here, seven dummy variables were included in the models that indicate the prior employment affiliations of the management team and board of directors; these were constructed from data found in the final prospectuses. In the "Management" section of any prospectus, all managers and board members listed must reveal at least their last five years of career history. If any member listed on the prospectus had a prior employment affiliation with a particular pharmaceutical company, the dummy variable for that company took a value of 1; if no member on the prospectus had a prior employment affiliation with that company, the dummy took a value of 0.

Here, employment affiliations were thus coded for the following companies: Baxter, Abbott, J&J, Merck, Eli Lilly, SmithKline, and Bristol-Myers Squibb.

Control Variables

Several control variables were included in these analyses to improve the robustness of the models. First, I controlled for uncertainty associated with the stock market for biotechnology companies at the time the firms went public. I employed a financial index developed by Lerner (1994) and cited extensively in research in the industry (e.g., Baum, Calabrese, & Silverman, 2000; Zucker, Darby, & Brewer, 1994), which gauges the receptivity of the equity markets to biotechnology offerings. Lerner's (1994) index was constructed based on an equal amount of dollar shares of thirteen publicly traded, dedicated biotechnology firms. The findings of Lerner's study suggest that an industry-specific index is the preferred method of capturing the favorability of the equity markets, as times of high valuations vary across industries and are not always in complete conjunction with the general market. I used the value of Lerner's *equity index* at the end of the month prior to the IPO date for each of the firms as an indicator of industry uncertainty at the time of the firm's IPO.

I also included controls for *firm size* and *firm age*, consistent with prior research on entrepreneurial firms and studies of IPOs. And, while not a direct indication of the size of the firm, the amount of *private financing* the firm received prior to the IPO does provide a reliable measure of the success the firm has had in the past in securing financial capital and so was considered an indicator of the firm's potential for growth as well. The measure of *private financing* was calculated by adding up the rounds of financing listed in the final prospectuses. This measure was adjusted to constant 1996 dollars and logged in the analyses.

Firms were also classified according to geographical *location*. Young firms located in areas that are rich with industry-related activity will likely have greater access to resources, including qualified personnel, suitable lab space, and technology, that can give them an advantage (Saxenian, 1994). Given the research and technology centers of the United States, locational advantage is likely to accrue to firms that choose to operate in central areas like San Francisco where the concentration of biotechnology firms is high (Deeds, DeCarolis, & Coombs, 1997). A dummy variable for *location* took a value of 1 if the main offices of a biotechnology company were located in one of the following areas that were consistently rated among the top biotechnology locations for the period of the study (Burrill & Lee, 1990, 1993; Lee & Burrill, 1995): San Francisco, Boston, or San Diego. *Location* took a value of 0 otherwise.

In addition, I controlled for the total *number of alliances* a firm has with business and/or research organizations at the time of the IPO, since prior research has demonstrated that strategic alliances have important implications for organizational performance. And, given prior research on the important role of venture capitalists during initial public offerings (e.g., Gompers, Lerner, Blair, & Hellman, 1998), I included a control for the *prominence of venture capital firms* at the time of the IPO. Prior research has shown that VC partnerships provide financial resources and expertise that serve as important signals of new venture quality that can positively affect IPO success (Megginson & Weiss, 1991). Partnerships with prominent VC firms help certify the present value of an issuing firm as well as a firm's future value, since VCs closely monitor their companies following their initial investment (Gorman & Sahlman, 1989; Sahlman, 1990). Therefore, a biotechnology company's partnership with a reputable VC firm should increase the biotechnology firm's legitimacy when it goes public.

To determine whether each of the biotechnology firms had partnered with a prominent VC firm, I created lists of prominent venture capital firms for each IPO year in the dataset. Specifically, I obtained rankings of venture capital firms from VentureXpert, a Securities Data Corporation database; rankings were based on total dollars invested by each venture capital firm in each of the eighteen years that comprise the timeframe of the dataset. Biotechnology firms were coded as 1 if any of the biotechnology firm's venture capital investors (with a minimum of a 5 percent stake) were listed as among the top thirty venture capital firms on the list of prominent venture capital firms for the year *prior* to the firm's IPO date and 0 otherwise.

In addition, I controlled for technological uncertainty associated with the *product stage* of the firm's lead product at the time of the IPO. These data came from the company sections of the prospectuses. I coded the product that was at the latest stage into one of the following categories: discovery stage, research and development, preclinical indication, phases I through III clinical trials, new drug approval (NDA) filing/FDA approval pending, final market approval, and revenue-generating, relatively speaking. I also examined the use-of-proceeds section of the prospectus to confirm that the lead product, as defined above, was also that which was designated to receive the most significant funding. Since biopharmaceutical research suggests that a relevant threshold for evaluation is the stage of clinical trials (Pisano, 1996), the measure of *product stage* was based upon a three-category classification: whether a company's lead product was in preclinical stages of development (coded as 1), clinical stages of development (coded as 2), or postclinical stages of development (coded as 3). Thus, those with lower numbers (i.e., earlier stages of development) were accorded higher uncertainty, while those that had higher numbers (i.e., later stages of development) were accorded lower uncertainty. In addition, information was obtained on the *number of patents* each firm had from the online database of the U.S. Patent and Trademark Office.

Investment bank prestige was measured using an index developed by Carter and Manaster (1990) and then updated by Carter, Dark, and Singh (1998). The measures are based on analyses of investment banks' positions in the tombstone announcements for IPOs and have been employed in recent organizational research on biotechnology firms that went public during the same time period as our study (e.g., Stuart, Hoang, & Hybels, 1999); this scale has been cited widely by finance and organizational scholars (Bae, Klein, & Bowyer, 1999; Podolny, 1994). Underwriter prestige information was available for all but twenty-five of the underwriters in the dataset. Mann-Whitney and Kolmogorov-Smirnov tests indicated that the firms for which this information was not available did not differ significantly from those that had this information along any of the main independent variables of interest.

The methods employed by Carter and colleagues to create the scale are similar to those used by Podolny (1993) to analyze debt markets. In brief, Carter and colleagues' indexes were created by looking at the hierarchy of investment banks as presented in the "tombstone announcements" for IPOs that appear in *Investment Dealer's Digest* or *The Wall Street Journal*. The authors assigned the highest integer rank (9) to the first-listed underwriter, the second highest integer rank (8) to the next-listed underwriter(s), and so on. Taking the second tombstone announcement, they then checked to see if any underwriter *not* listed on the first announcement was listed above any underwriter that *was* listed on the first annoucement; if this was the case, the new, more highly ranked underwriter was assigned the rank of the superseded underwriter, and the superseded underwriter and all lower-ranked underwriters were shifted one point down on the scale. This continued until all IPOs were exhausted. When more than ten categories became necessary to preserve the hierarchy presented on the tombstones, decimal increments were employed. Eventually, the scale as presented in Carter, Dark, and Singh (1998) is incremented in units of 0.125. Scores may assume a value ranging from 0, indicating lowest prestige, to 9, indicating highest prestige. In this dataset, the mean score was 7.63. Carter and Dark's (1992) analyses suggest that these measures provide a finer-grained evaluation than a simpler market share alternative (e.g., Megginson & Weiss, 1991). The name of the lead investment bank was obtained from the front page of the final prospectus.

Results

Correlational analyses revealed that the relationships between key variables of interest were in the directions predicted, and that there were no major issues regarding multicollinearity.

As Table B.1 shows, Baxter was the only company that had a significant effect on any of the IPO success measures, and it had a significant and positive effect on all three. That is, when compared to companies that had no affiliation with any of these major pharmaceutical or healthcare companies, Baxter was the only one of these companies that was associated with these success measures. These results held even when the dummy variables for these seven prominent companies were entered separately in seven different models, comparing only biotechnology firms with that one affiliation to the rest of the firms without that affiliation; Baxter was the only company with a significant effect.

These analyses show that the presence of a Baxter alumnus on the management or board of a biotech company had a definite positive impact on the performance of the young firm in the IPO marketplace—that is, on the number and quality of institutional investors who invested in the firm and on the amount of cash the young biotech firm raised.

Table B.1 Heckman Selection Models of Major Pharmaceutical Prior-Employment Affiliations on Biotechnology Firm IPO Success[a]

| | Dependent Variables | | | | | |
| | Number of Institutional Investors | | Number of Dedicated Institutional Investors | | Proceeds to Company[b] | |
Control Variables	Coefficient	Std. Error	Coefficient	Std. Error	Coefficient	Std. Error
Equity Index	1.20*	.51	-.01	.13	.08***	.16
Firm Age	.19	.18	.13**	.05	.00	.01
Firm Size	.01**	.00	.00	.00	.00*	.00
Location	.42	1.15	1.24**	.38	.03	.04
No. Alliances	-.07	.25	-.02	.06	.01	.01
VC Prominence	2.11*	1.07	.50†	.26	.06	.03
Private Financing[b]	2.04**	.72	.39*	.18	.10***	.02
Product Stage	.59	.65	.03	.15	.00	.02
Number of Patents	.14	.15	-.02	.04	.00	.00
Underwriter Prestige	.90**	.27	.21**	.07	.05***	.01

Healthcare Company Variables

	Coef.	S.E.	Coef.	S.E.	Coef.	S.E.
Abbott	−.14	1.25	−.02	.30	.03	.04
Baxter	**2.93***	**1.16**	**.86****	**.28**	**.11****	**.04**
Bristol-Myers Squibb	.73	1.13	.25	.27	.06	.04
Eli Lilly	1.89	1.23	.23	.30	.06	.04
Johnson & Johnson	−.07	1.25	−.09	.30	−.01	.04
Merck	1.16	1.21	−.13	.29	.06	.04
SmithKline	−.51	1.17	.15	.28	−.01	.04
Constant	−20.52	5.08	−6.10***	1.21	5.79***	.16
Selection Equation Variables						
Location	.55***	.11	.59***	.10	.55***	.11
Business Type	1.22***	.11	.73***	.17	1.23***	.11
Year Founded	−.06***	.01	−.06***	.01	−.06***	.01
Constant	122.87***	21.65	119.48***	20.57	116.73***	21.35
Wald Chi-Square	133.06***		96.11***		255.56***	
Rho	.16		.92		−.31	
N	244		244		244	

***p < .001 (two-tailed tests)

**p < .01

*p < .05

†p < .10

(a) Unstandardized regression coefficients reported.

(b) Adjusted to 1996 dollars and logged.

Appendix C

Baxter's Business and Product Timelines

Figure C.1 Baxter Product Highlights: 1930–1970

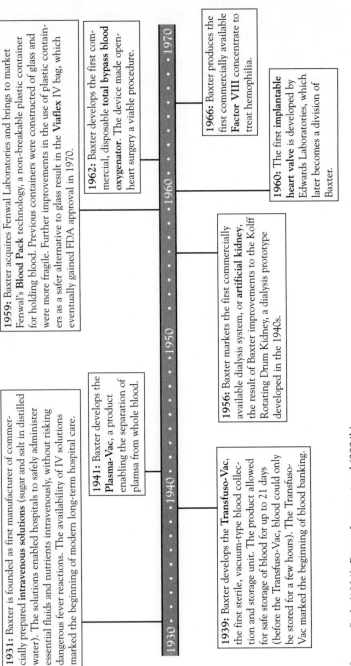

1931: Baxter is founded as first manufacturer of commercially prepared **intravenous solutions** (sugar and salt in distilled water). The solutions enabled hospitals to safely administer essential fluids and nutrients intravenously, without risking dangerous fever reactions. The availability of IV solutions marked the beginning of modern long-term hospital care.

1939: Baxter develops the **Transfuso-Vac**, the first sterile, vacuum-type blood collection and storage unit. The product allowed for safe storage of blood for up to 21 days (before the Transfuso-Vac, blood could only be stored for a few hours). The Transfuso-Vac marked the beginning of blood banking.

1941: Baxter develops the **Plasma-Vac**, a product enabling the separation of plasma from whole blood.

1956: Baxter markets the first commercially available dialysis system, or **artificial kidney**, the result of Baxter improvements to the Kolff Rotating Drum Kidney, a dialysis prototype developed in the 1940s.

1959: Baxter acquires Fenwal Laboratories and brings to market Fenwal's **Blood Pack** technology, a non-breakable plastic container for holding blood. Previous containers were constructed of glass and were more fragile. Further improvements in the use of plastic containers as a safer alternative to glass result in the **Viaflex** IV bag, which eventually gained FDA approval in 1970.

1962: Baxter develops the first commercial, disposable **total bypass blood oxygenator**. The device made open-heart surgery a viable procedure.

1960: The first **implantable heart valve** is developed by Edwards Laboratories, which later becomes a division of Baxter.

1966: Baxter produces the first commercially available **Factor VIII** concentrate to treat hemophilia.

Source: Cody (1994), Baxter International (2004b).

Figure C.2 Baxter Business Highlights: 1930–1970

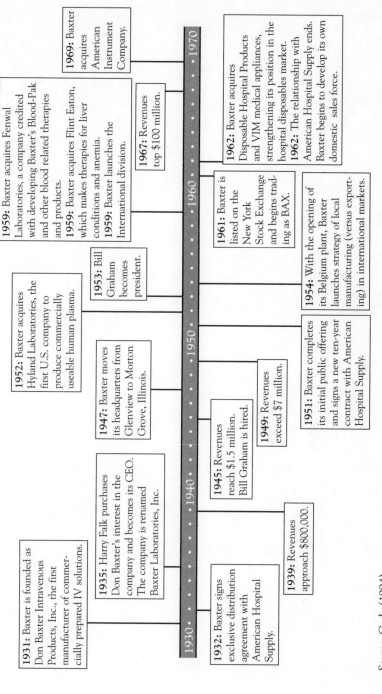

1931: Baxter is founded as Don Baxter Intravenous Products, Inc., the first manufacturer of commercially prepared IV solutions.

1932: Baxter signs exclusive distribution agreement with American Hospital Supply.

1935: Harry Falk purchases Don Baxter's interest in the company and becomes its CEO. The company is renamed Baxter Laboratories, Inc.

1939: Revenues approach $800,000.

1945: Revenues reach $1.5 million. Bill Graham is hired.

1947: Baxter moves its headquarters from Glenview to Morton Grove, Illinois.

1949: Revenues exceed $7 million.

1951: Baxter completes its initial public offering and signs a new ten-year contract with American Hospital Supply.

1952: Baxter acquires Hyland Laboratories, the first U.S. company to produce commercially useable human plasma.

1953: Bill Graham becomes president.

1954: With the opening of its Belgium plant, Baxter launches strategy of local manufacturing (versus exporting) in international markets.

1959: Baxter acquires Fenwal Laboratories, a company credited with developing Baxter's Blood-Pak and other blood related therapies and products.

1959: Baxter acquires Flint Eaton, which makes therapies for liver conditions and anemia.

1959: Baxter launches the International division.

1961: Baxter is listed on the New York Stock Exchange and begins trading as BAX.

1962: Baxter acquires Disposable Hospital Products and VIM medical appliances, strengthening its position in the hospital disposables market.

1962: The relationship with American Hospital Supply ends. Baxter begins to develop its own domestic sales force.

1967: Revenues top $100 million.

1969: Baxter acquires American Instrument Company.

Source: Cody (1994).

Notes

Preface

1. The notion of "institutional capital" differs from purely social structural views of social capital that focus on how firms or actors are tied to one another (e.g., Burt, 1992). In addition, it reflects a cognitive perspective—that is, the belief that people have some common affiliation with an institution, whether or not actual relationships exist (e.g., Podolny, 2001). See also recent research by Lawrence (2004) on organizational reference groups, for research on perceptions of work-group membership.
2. Additional details on the dataset and collection methods are provided in Appendices A and B.
3. See, for example, Barley, Freeman, and Hybels (1992).
4. See, for example, Powell, Koput, and Smith-Doerr (1996).
5. To do this, information was obtained from biotechnology research organizations including BIO, the North Carolina Center for Biotechnology Information, Recombinant Capital (ReCap), and the Institute for Biotechnology Information. Additionally, information was compared using three editions of *Biotechnology Guide U.S.A.* (Dibner, 1988, 1991, 1995). From these sources, an additional eighteen dedicated U.S. biotechnology firms were identified that went public but were not in existence in their original form in 1996. Such firms had experienced name changes, merged, or had been acquired. These firms were founded in the same time period and all had gone public by the end of 1996.
6. Dibner (1988, 1991, 1995).

Chapter 1

1. Helyar (1998).
2. Anders (2003).
3. Bossidy and Charan (2002). For a review of GE's human resources practices, see Bartlett and McLean (2004). Also, Nohria and Groysberg's (2003) research on the career transitions of GE stars shows that on the day GE stars' appointments were announced the share price of the hiring firm increased by an average of 10.4 percent; then, one and three years later, these GE alumni-led firms outperformed the market by 5 to 7 percent.
4. Rodgers (1986).
5. Schein (2003).
6. Indeed, such movement has become endemic, not just at the senior executive level. Individuals at many levels are increasingly facing what scholars have termed a "boundaryless career" environment in which job, organization, and career change are much more frequent than ever before (Arthur & Rousseau, 1996). In the context of high-technology, for example, scholars such as Todd Pittinsky (2001) suggest that individuals face an increasingly fluid career environment and barter with the knowledge they have acquired as they transition from organization to organization as "knowledge nomads."
7. Khurana (2002).
8. For example, research by Zucker and colleagues focuses on the regional location of biotech scientists and the founding of new ventures. See, for example, Zucker, Darby, and Brewer (1998).
9. Saxenian (1994, p. 161). See also, Eisenhardt and Schoonhoven's (1990) research on Silicon Valley as a region of innovation and Florida and Kenney's (1990, p. 9) depiction of Silicon Valley as a "social structure of innovation."
10. This approach is also consistent with recent calls for research that links the impact of regional variation with the roles of firms and

individuals in entrepreneurial firms (Thornton, 1999, pp. 31–32).

11. See Lorenz (1935) for the earliest detailed analysis of the imprinting phenomenon in animals.

 Imprinting in certain young birds and mammals, called filial imprinting, is a form of attachment typically directed toward the newborn's mother. Filial imprinting is an evolutionarily driven safety mechanism for animals that are physically independent (e.g., mobile) but not socially prepared to function without parental influence (e.g., they still need to learn hunting and mating behaviors from their own species). Imprinting resembles an involuntary instinct: a newborn chick will imprint on the first object it observes that exhibits a certain set of behaviors, such as moving or quacking. Filial imprinting produces genetically preprogrammed behaviors in the chick, such as "a following response that affects subsequent adult behavior" (Animal Learning, 2004). Importantly, imprinting has a lifelong influence on a chick's life (e.g., birds tend to seek mates that resemble the characteristics of the object of their imprinting—usually the mother).

 Thus, filial imprinting is an *attachment* mechanism that enables learning by focusing innate following behavior toward a caregiver. In contrast, career imprinting is a form of *learning* that encompasses the professional impression left on individuals by an organization. Filial imprinting is involuntary and permanent; in contrast, individuals can reflect on an organizational career imprint, recognize its influence on their behavior, and decide if and how to change their behavior.

 A current summary of filial-imprinting research can be found in the *Encyclopedia Britannica* (Animal Learning, 2004; Konrad Lorenz, 2004) and the *Dictionary of the History of Ideas* (Imprinting, 2004).

12. In organizational research, the more general notion of "imprinting" is often attributed to Arthur Stinchcombe (1965), who wrote a famous article called "Social Structure and

Organizations," which appeared in James G. March's *Handbook of Organizations*. In this piece, Stinchcombe showed that some very basic features of organizations (e.g., characteristics of the labor force, capital intensity, size of administrative bureaucracy, ratio of line to staff workers) vary systematically with the firm's time of founding in an industry. Thus, Stinchcombe asserted that "organizational forms tend to be founded during the period in which they become possible. Then, both because they can function effectively with those organizational forms and because the forms tend to become institutionalized, the basic structure of the organization tends to remain relatively stable" (p. 153). Note that this is also the article in which the term *liability of newness* was introduced and that a close review of this work reveals no explicit use of the term *imprinting*.

By comparison, I use the term *imprinting* in a related and yet somewhat different fashion. One key difference is that whereas Stinchcombe's work refers to environmental factors that imprint an organization, affecting organizational form and vice versa, I focus here on how organizations can cultivate a "career imprint" among their employees. Further, since people are the carriers of career imprints from one organization to another, career imprints can have a lasting impact on other organizations.

Career imprints can also be resistant to change (which is similar to Stinchcombe's concept of dominant organizational structures). As I will discuss at the end of the book, cultivating a strong career imprint, particularly early on in one's career, raises some very important issues for personal and professional development—not only with respect to choosing appropriate jobs but with respect to understanding when one's own career imprint may be standing in the way of what the "best" solution is in a given leadership situation.

Yet while career imprints may be resistant to change, they are not immutable to change. This raises a second difference worth noting between past conceptualizations of imprinting and the proposed concept of career imprinting. The second point is that, unlike prior imprinting theories, which are often functionalist arguments (i.e., things happen when they can happen), the concept of career imprinting is dynamic and unfolding. Therefore, although the argument I will make is that career imprints are likely to take hold when there is alignment among the people, place, and paths experienced in an organization, this is not to say that other kinds of alignment could not also take place, producing other imprints at this same time.

13. These categories echo recent research in career theory by Arthur, Claman, and DeFillippi (1995), which suggests that "knowing why," "knowing how," and "knowing whom" are core competencies that individuals develop in their careers.

14. One aspect that is not included as a separate category in the career imprint construct is *values*. Values derive, to a large extent, from experiences that stem from life experiences. Therefore, people enter organizations with values that are already molded and therefore comparatively less malleable. And, while values are not the same as beliefs, it seems reasonable that one's worldview is made up of beliefs that reflect values. Thus, organizations cultivate certain worldviews or cognitive schema that may themselves be value laden.

15. See, for example, McCall, Lombardo, and Morrison (1988) and Kotter (1988).

16. See, for example, Thomas and Gabarro (1999, p. 135).

17. McCall, Lombardo, and Morrison (1988, p. 175).

18. See, for example, Higgins and Thomas (2001) and Ibarra (1992).

19. See, for example, Kram (1985); Higgins and Kram (2001); and Thomas and Gabarro (1999).

20. Bennis and Thomas (2002b).

21. Kanter (2004).

22. See, for example, Lent and Brown (1996) and McLennan and Arthur (1999).

23. Schein's (1985a) notion of a "career anchor" differs from that of a "career imprint" in several respects. A career anchor is an

intraindividual construct that is based upon examination of the career experiences of one individual over the course of his or her career, whereas a career imprint is based upon examination of the career experiences of many individuals within a single organization during a particular period in time. A career anchor reflects what one would not give up—what is at base, such as technological competence, that an individual values most (Schein, 1978, 1985a, 1993; see also, DeLong, 1982). In contrast, a career imprint reflects what one takes along as one changes employers over time and is associated with an employer rather than an individual.

24. Some organizational scholars have treated newcomer orientation or "entry" as one part of organizational socialization (Van Maanen & Schein, 1979). In other work, scholars have put forth staged models of socialization (e.g., Schein, 1978), while still others have focused primarily upon entry and have identified staged models regarding the entry period alone (Feldman, 1976; Porter, Lawler, & Hackman, 1975). In most instances, the emphasis of the socialization literature has been on the earliest kinds of role transitions—when individuals transition into organizations as new-hires.

25. Schein (1978).

26. Wanous (1980).

27. Bossidy and Charan (2002).

28. See Rousseau and Schalk (2000) and Rousseau (1985) for a discussion.

29. Prior organizational research, and career research in particular, has often excluded from analysis the role of the larger social context in understanding the antecedents to management development (Rousseau & Fried, 2000). Consider the following quote in a seminal paper by Van Maanen and Schein (1979, pp. 229–230): "It is true that changes in the larger environment within which organizationally defined roles are played out may force certain changes upon role occupants despite perhaps vehement resistance . . . but these fac-

tors go well beyond our interests here for they essentially lie outside an organizational analysis. The causal mechanism we seek to examine here is the organizational socialization process itself." This focused view reflects the context in which theory on organizational socialization was originally developed, an era in which careers were largely experienced within a single employer (Whyte, 1956). More recently, the notion of the career as "boundaryless" (Arthur & Rousseau, 1996) has emerged in career research, which has opened up inquiry into the role of the larger social context in which organizations and careers are situated. In the present research, I consider both the larger social psychological context as well as the competitive business environment in which careers at Baxter unfolded. Here, I adopt the assumption that the environment is not fixed and the organization's response to that changing environment in terms of its strategy and structure is also an important ingredient to consider in understanding the developmental context in which career imprints are cultivated.

30. Hall and Mirvis (1996).

31. The following are the underlying assumptions behind the development of career imprinting theory:

(1) Organizations are not stable entities. Therefore, one must consider the larger environmental, business, and social psychological context when studying the process of career imprinting. For example, when considering the place (the organization as a developmental context), it is not sufficient to consider organizational culture or intraorganizational systems such as socialization to understand the origins of career imprints. Rather, the business strategy, for example, determines the opportunity structure in which careers unfold. This view differs from traditional literature on organizational socialization in which the assumption is that organizations are relatively stable and, moreover, that understanding the environmental context is beyond organizational analysis and hence the study of career development in organizations.

(2) People are active participants in their career development (vs. passive). Therefore, paths do not originate from the organization irrespective of individuals' backgrounds and stage of career/adult development. These are key factors in determining how much "say" an individual has in his/her career development, how open or ready he or she is to such paths, and what the course of such paths may look like. It is the interaction between these two (people and place) that produces the paths that drive a specific imprint. This also runs counter to some of the traditional literature on socialization and careers more broadly. Prior research has suggested that "like a sculptor's mold, certain forms of socialization can produce remarkably similar outcomes no matter what individual ingredients are used to fill the mold or no matter where the mold is typically set down" (Van Maanen & Schein, 1979, p. 231). The perspective taken here is quite different; both place and people are investigated as important factors in the career imprinting process.

I make no functional assumptions about the necessity of organizations to hire certain individuals to meet specific needs in the organization, nor do I assume that industries "need" certain individuals to fulfill certain roles. Rather, the matching of people to organizations occurs through a human level of analysis, not a purely functional level. This is a social process. This view is consistent with organizational theory's interactionist view of social life, which says that individuals and not organizations create and sustain beliefs about what is and is not functional (Weick, 1979).

(3) Transitions of any kind are marked by anxiety that individuals want to reduce as they extend themselves into new roles, new identities. Various means of reducing such anxiety, including looking to peers, to mentors, to leaders, can provide powerful cues as to how to behave. Such vulnerable times amplify the potential for imprinting. This is consistent with adult development theory—being in between stages of devel-

opment and experiencing tension one wants to resolve. This is also consistent with career development theory and analyses of entry-level positions and identity (e.g., Berlew & Hall, 1966; Hall, 2004).

(4) Organizational life is only one opportunity for imprinting. Membership in any institution (e.g., Oxford) has the propensity to have such an effect. Here, I focus on organizational (employer) imprinting that stems from careers (hence, "career imprint") since work takes up significant time and energy in many adults' lives and is likely to affect individuals' choices when they move into leadership positions. Thus, when individuals move from one organization to another, they may take with them an organizational career imprint associated with their previous employers. Individuals' professional identities may be affected by prior career imprints as well as by other kinds of imprints (e.g., from an educational institution). Identity is a higher-level construct and sits at the individual level of analysis (vs. an organizational career imprint, which derives from interindividual career patterns).

(5) Imprints are not immutable to change in the sense that leaders can choose how to employ previous imprints, and they can affect the cultivation of an imprint in an organization they lead. Thus, career imprints may change within an organization over time (e.g., as leadership changes). Certain people may pick up or adapt an organizational imprint more strongly than others. Once an individual leaves an organization, he or she takes what was cultivated—the organizational career imprint—with himself or herself. How sticky that imprint is in terms of its effects on his or her choices as a leader and long-term professional development will depend upon his or her work situation, including the relational context of the organization he or she moves to. For example, individuals who move to new organizations with former colleagues are more likely to find that the previous employer's career imprint is related to subsequent leader design choices.

32. Focusing on the long-term career beyond a single employment relationship also contrasts with earlier research on organizational socialization and career development. Generally, the focus of much of the seminal work on careers has centered on how early career learning affects subsequent transitions within an organization. Here, the career imprinting concept focuses on implications for individual career development within an organization but also, as opportunities arise outside of the organization, for career changes and boundary transitions beyond intraorganizational role transitions. Using the typology of role responses provided by Van Maanen and Schein (1979), cultivating an organizational career imprint would be a custodial view, whereas leaving an organization would be an extreme form of rejection of a role, not "innovation" but rejection. Moving from one role within a well-established firm to another role within a start-up in a different industry falls outside their typology—what could be called a "radical" role transition since the boundary crossed was both organizational and industry-based.

33. See Dearborn and Simon (1958), Mason and Mitroff (1981), Cyert and March (1963), Beyer et al. (1997), and Walsh (1988).

34. This is not a book about Baxter's "success" or the "success" of those who left Baxter to start up, run, and/or take biotechnology firms public. The size and extent of Baxter's influence overall is difficult to ascertain since the biotechnology industry, with eight- to ten-year product development cycles, is still in its relative infancy. Therefore, for example, while Henri Termeer's leadership at Genzyme has been touted by many industry observers as exemplary, and the firm, Genzyme, has often been seen as a role model for other firms in the industry, for most biotechnology firms the jury is still out.

As a collective of firms, it would also be difficult with such long product-development horizons to assess whether Baxter-led firms have or have not been "successful" by some reliable measure of value. Even obvious indicators, such as whether or not a firm had a successful product in this industry, are difficult to assess because, although product ideas originate with small biotechnology firms, their revenue streams often travel as licensing agreements ensue. Thus, traditional "success" calculations such as return on investment become fraught with ambiguity. Therefore, the success of the industry or of Baxter alumni-led firms in the biotechnology industry is not examined here. Rather, I focus here on why Baxter had such a disproportionate influence on entrepreneurial activity in biotechnology, given the aforementioned patterns observed in the quantitative data.

35. Gompers, Lerner, and Scharfstein (2005).

Chapter 2

1. For an extensive review of Baxter's history, see Cody (1994).

Chapter 3

1. Bennis and Nanus (1985).
2. McCall, Lombardo, and Morrison (1988).
3. See, for example, Gabarro (1987).
4. Schein (1985b, p. 9).
5. Schein (1985b, 1999, 2004). See also Lorsch and Tierney (2002).
6. O'Reilly and Chatman (1996).
7. Ashmore, Deaux, and McLaughlin-Volpe (2004).
8. Tajfel (1981).
9. Rousseau (1995).
10. Whyte (1956).
11. For an in-depth review of the fundamental changes in relationships between employers and employees between the 1970s and 1990s, see Capelli (1999).
12. Hirakubo (1999) and Fingleton (1995).
13. Indeed, the organizational commitment of the 1960s and 1970s contrasts sharply with the career patterns of MBAs of the most

recent decade, the 1990s, in which individuals change careers and organizations often (Higgins, 2001a, 2001b). More recently, MBAs construct what organizational scholar Denise Rousseau (2001a) has termed "I-deals," which are idiosyncratic deals with an employer that are unique and well-tailored to suit individuals' needs. At the time the first wave of Baxter managers joined Baxter, loyalty to the firm was clearly expected and flexibility around benefits and work schedule was not negotiated—not at Baxter, not at IBM, and not at most established firms of that time.

14. In this sense, Baxter's selection mechanisms reflected Rosabeth Moss Kanter's (1977) account of "homosocial reproduction" in the 1950s-1960s-style corporation, which included selecting people who resembled those in power, particularly in the context of placing people into high-risk jobs that entailed significant amounts of discretion.

15. See also, Rosenbaum (1979) on "tournament mobility" and the extent to which organizations generate contests or "tournaments" among employees by rewarding satisfactory performance with challenging assignments at the next level (rather than with traditional rewards such as pay).

16. Reichers (1987).

17. Van Maanen (1976).

18. Van Maanen and Schein (1979).

19. Pfeffer (1981). See also, O'Reilly and Chatman (1996).

20. In addition, see Kanter (2001, p. 204–216) in which she proposes three ways that an organization can satisfy the cognitive, emotional, and moral needs of its employees, respectively: by offering assignments that yield a sense of mastery; by offering membership in a group characterized by mutual respect; and by offering employees the opportunity to find meaning through their work.

21. Alderfer (1972).

22. For example, see Berlew and Hall (1966).

23. Thompson, Hochwarter, and Mathys (1997).

24. Kahn, Wolfe, Snoek, and Rosenthal (1964) and Hall, Zhu, and Yan (2001).

25. Substantial research has shown that newcomers are especially susceptible to strong organizational contexts and cultures. Not only do they want to find task and normative information to reduce their anxiety associated with just joining the organization (Morrison, 1993), they also are more likely to be open to what they hear and see when they first join (Chatman, 1991; O'Reilly & Chatman, 1996).

26. Often, social scientists fail to recognize the significance of the broader context in which intriguing phenomena are located. We fail to take into account the period in time in which our data, such as individuals' accounts of their career experiences, played out. As qualitative researchers in particular, it is important to situate data in a historical context. In this way, we adopt an emic perspective and attempt to understand how individuals understand their world, rather than simply an etic perspective, which is the realist perspective of how individuals' activities are structured. Both the emic, the social construction of individuals' experiences, as well as the etic, the more objective patterns that emerge, are important to consider.

    Historically, career research has recognized the value of the emic and the etic perspectives. As career scholars of the Chicago School suggested decades ago, careers are not simply the easily identified positions and salary levels associated with one's work life; careers are also internally and subjectively determined by the sense we make of that sequence of experiences.

    For a review of these perspectives, see Barley (1989).

27. Cody (1994). The "Wee Willie" Keeler strategy ("I keep my eyes clear, and I hit 'em where they ain't") is a reference to the Hall of Fame baseball player from the late nineteenth and early twentieth centuries who used the phrase to describe the philosophy behind his success. The phrase is engraved on Keeler's plaque at the National Baseball Hall of Fame.

28. Cody (1994).
29. In 1980, 55 cents of every dollar paid to hospitals was supplied by the government (Aguilar & Bhambri, 1983).
30. Aguilar and Bhambri (1983).
31. Thomas and Bennis (2002, p. 4); see also Bennis and Thomas (2002a) for a fuller treatment.
32. See Baruch and Altman (2002) and Hall, Zhu, and Yan (2001).
33. Small-volume parenterals are the little vials that are added on to the large volume. Large-volume parenterals are the half-liter and liter solutions of water and sugar or salt.
34. Hawthorne (2003).
35. Kanter (2004).
36. Higgins (2001c).
37. Sanna (1992). See also Sanna and Pusecker (1994).
38. Roberts, Dutton, Spreitzer, Heaphy, and Quinn (2005) and Roberts (2005).
39. This is particularly interesting since, apart from this blip in history, Abbott's financial performance was also strong. Baxter's average annual growth in sales during the 1970s was approximately 21.6 percent, whereas Abbott's (not including 1971, the year of the recall) was approximately 17.2 percent (Abbott Laboratories, 2004; Baxter International, 2004a).
40. Bennis and Biederman (1997, p. 208).

Chapter 4

1. Ross and Nisbett (1991).
2. O'Reilly and Chatman (1996).
3. See Langer (1989) for a discussion of mindfulness. Further, those who are high in growth orientation are also more open to new experiences (Pichanic, 2003), which should increase the likelihood of cultivating a strong career imprint.
4. Levinson, Darrow, Klein, Levinson, and McKee (1978). See also Levinson (1986).

5. Levinson, Darrow, Klein, Levinson, and McKee (1978).

6. Analysis of the age data using coefficients of variation and analyses of variance (ANOVAs) reveal a statistically significant age difference between Baxter and the rest of the individuals in the dataset—that is, Baxter alumni are significantly younger than the alumni of other companies in the rest of the dataset.

7. See, for example, Super (1957) and Brown and Brooks (1996).

8. Hall (2002). See also Ibarra (1999).

9. See for example, Berlew and Hall (1966) and Ibarra (2003).

10. Berlew and Hall (1966), Ibarra (2003), and O'Reilly and Chatman (1996).

11. Ashforth (2001) and Hill (1992).

12. See for example, Louis (1980a). See also Louis (1980b).

13. Higgins (2001a).

14. Karaevli and Hall (2004).

15. Kegan (1982).

16. Kegan and Lahey (1984, p. 203).

17. Kegan and Lahey (1984, p. 204).

18. Beginning with Lawrence and Lorsch (1967/1986). See also Nadler and Tushman (1980).

19. Hackman and Oldham (1980).

20. Mobley (1977). See also Hom, Griffeth, and Sellaro (1984). For a recent review, see Maertz and Campion (1998).

21. O'Reilly, Chatman, and Caldwell (1991).

22. Nearly 30 percent of the individuals who came from Baxter reported having received their MBA; this is likely a conservative number since many people don't report educational background nor are required to do so by the SEC. Chi-square analyses were used to compare the educational backgrounds of individuals in the dataset with the six most-represented, pharmaceutical-company employment affiliations. These analyses provide the expected count of different educational degrees within this population if the distribution were even across the companies to the actual count of these degrees observed in the dataset. While the distribution of degrees was

not statistically significantly different than a normal distribution, Baxter's actual count of MBAs was the most in excess, compared to the other five companies, of its expected count of MBAs. Likewise, Baxter's actual count of Ph.D.s and M.D.s was the most in deficit, compared to the other five companies, of its expected count of Ph.D.s and M.D.s.

23. Muchinsky and Monahan (1987).

24. For a discussion of the psychological term *egosyntonic*, which refers to the extent to which an individual's behavior, thoughts, and attitudes are seen by the self as acceptable, see Edgerton and Campbell (1994). Here, the term is used to refer to congruence between an individual's values and those shared within an organization.

25. Kegan (1982).

26. Pinker (1995).

Chapter 5

1. As an example of a psychological approach, see Betz, Fitzgerald, and Hill (1989); for a sociological approach, see Barley (1989); for an anthropological approach, see Bateson (1989); and for career research in labor economics, see Becker (1975), and in organizational behavior, see Hackett, Lent, and Greenhaus (1991).

2. For example, see research on occupations by Rhodes and Doering (1993) and/or on work roles by Hall (1976).

3. Arthur, Hall, and Lawrence (1989, p. 8). See also Cochran (1994).

4. Hughes (1958) and Van Maanen (1977). Still, the vast majority of career research has been devoted to understanding the more objective side (for example, looking at outcomes such as rate of advancement). An examination of the subjective side of careers is rare in career research (Evetts, 1992; Stephens, 1994). For recent exceptions, see Heslin (2004) and Higgins (2001a).

5. It is important to clarify that an "assistant-to" position is not an administrative job; it is a management growth position.

6. Indeed, substantial research done by Gary Pisano (1996) in the area of management technology suggests that a critical competence for healthcare companies is learning by doing.

7. Tim Hall, a preeminent scholar in career theory, has done research showing that learning how to learn is indeed a critical competency in highly uncertain environments (see, e.g., Hall & Mirvis, 1996). While much of his research in this area has focused on the 1990s and beyond, there are implications for understanding earlier time periods as well—particularly in contexts in which there is a notable amount of uncertainty, as was the case when Baxter was building markets during the 1960s and 1970s.

8. Hill (1992).

9. Leadership scholar John Kotter's research shows that while general managers tend to view themselves as "generalists," this is not to say that they don't have particular skills. In his study, general managers had acquired specific skills in business, management, and across particular functional areas—all of which led them to feel they could "manage nearly anything well" (Kotter, 1982, p. 8). So too was the case at Baxter.

10. Boje (1991, p. 106).

11. Eccles and Nohria (1992, p. 29).

12. See also McAdams (2001).

13. Research by organization and management scholar Rosabeth Moss Kanter (2004) suggests that building, maintaining, and restoring confidence is a fundamental task of leaders. This task is particularly acute for leaders who are engaged in turnarounds, where the key challenge is to unravel negative spirals that have already been set in motion. She also notes that engendering overconfidence can yield unethical behavior, such as in the Enron accounting scandal.

At Baxter, given the tremendous amounts of responsibility that were doled out at such a young age, one could argue that there was the possibility for overconfidence, as Kanter's research warns. The interview data reveal how Baxter kept this in line.

As described in prior accounts, "Mr. Graham" was perceived as everywhere and as all-knowing, and he oversaw decisions made by senior managers such as Bill Gantz. Therefore, as far away as Bill Graham, Bill Gantz, Gabe Schmergel, and other corporate officers were from the subsidiaries, their oversight and the project teams that were often sent out to monitor inventories and accounts receivable helped keep confidence-building in check as individuals strove to hit their *20/20* targets at Baxter.

14. The details of the Abbott recall of 1971 and consequences are reported in Pratt (1987, p. 181), and newspaper articles at the time (e.g., Vartanig, 1971) suggest that the contamination caused infections in as many as five thousand hospital patients, which allegedly resulted in two deaths.

15. A reasonable question to ask is, "Is this unusual? Don't all smart business people go to war with their competitors?" Or, if not "war," then, similar contemporary phrases might be used, as in sports analogies. Certainly, the metaphor of war was top-of-mind for many of these veterans. Here, I would argue two points. First, this sort of ruthless competitive behavior had a pattern to it: generally, Baxter was taking market share. By the 1960s and 1970s, the innovations at Baxter had already occurred and now the challenge was to get customers to switch to Baxter's products, as was the case with the battle with Abbott. Therefore, the "hit 'em where they ain't" aspect of Baxter's strategy revolved around getting a foothold in a market, generally on the basis of superior quality, pricing high, based upon that quality proposition, and then, as competitors (re)entered, cutting costs to undermine their ability to (re)enter the marketplace. One alumnus described the strategy this way:

> The marketing philosophy—which I've never forgotten to this day—was "segment and dominate." That was [the] golden rule. In other words, every business you're in, you've got to pick out the discrete market segments by customer, by product type, by whatever it is, and then you've got to be the dominant player in that segment.

Second, these battles fought by Baxter managers were often operational, rather than strategic in nature: building a plant in a foreign subsidiary, bringing a plant in line with high quality standards, or closing a plant that was not efficient. As mentioned, Graham held the reigns when it came to strategy. Thus, Baxter middle managers were responsible for implementation. As the Abbott recall story as well as the Dutch Red Cross story showed, Baxter managers were prepared to produce high-quality products to take advantage when their competitor was down. Further, as this was the time period that preceded the Total Quality Management movement, when Good Manufacturing Practices were just taking hold, ensuring that Baxter products were produced with maximum safety (e.g., no leakage in the solutions packaging) was of critical importance.

16. For details on this incident from Abbott's perspective, see Pratt (1987). For details on the Abbott recall of 1971 from Baxter's perspective, see Cody (1994).

17. This stands in some contrast to social network research, in which tie strength is generally gauged by frequency of communication and/or by emotional closeness. Here, these connections with "comrades" were perceptual as well. As Barbara Lawrence's (2004) research suggests, individuals are powerfully influenced by those they regard as organizational reference group members.

18. Unfortunately, Bill Graham was not able to be interviewed at the time of this study. However, Baxter senior managers—including Ray Oddi (Graham's former assistant), Gabe Schmergel, Bill Gantz, and Jim Tobin, among many others—were interviewed extensively.

19. Goffman (1961) defines a "total institution" as "a place of residence and work where a large number of like-situated individuals, cut off from the wider society for an appreciable period of time, together lead an enclosed, formally administered round of life" (p. xiii).

20. Research by Laura Morgan Roberts (2005) suggests that impression management is critical to career success, particularly early on in one's career.
21. Resilience refers to how individuals, groups, or organizations are able to adjust, in a positive fashion, when facing challenge (Masten & Reed, 2002; see also Sutcliffe & Vogus, 2003).
22. For example, see Ropo and Hunt (1995) and Stevensen, Roberts, and Grousbeck (1989).

Chapter 6

1. One way to think of this is as an implicit event history analysis. All of these firms were essentially "at risk" for producing top managers for new biotech ventures. The question is, "Why did Baxter incubate so many?" Part of this answer, as described in Chapter Seven, lies in the kinds of career imprints these firms generated.
2. To determine which healthcare and pharmaceutical companies were prominent, a list of the top pharmaceutical and healthcare organizations by sales since 1979 was generated, using Standard & Poor's Compustat data. International companies are only ranked by Compustat beginning at 1988, so the rankings are based on the top thirty U.S. organizations from 1979 to 1987 and the top thirty U.S. and international organizations from 1988 to 1996. This list was supplemented with major pharmaceutical and healthcare companies that were private or based in Europe or Japan that were not listed in Compustat but were listed in PharmaBusiness and had comparable sales, since many young biotechnology firms rely on international resources for support and talent. Organizations were classified as prominent that appeared on these lists for any year that a firm in the dataset went public. A total of fifty-six pharmaceutical and healthcare companies were thus considered prominent.
3. Of course, there are sample selection problems associated with comparing the positions of people who all left major healthcare

firms to enter biotechnology. That is why these data are simply a "good place to start." When we explore the VC data, in the following chapter, we will be able to discern the extent to which VCs made attributions about firm-level differences that reflect what we see here with these data.

4. For further detail on Merck's leadership and organization, see Hawthorne (2003), Austin, Barrett, and Weber (2001), and Nichols (1994).

5. Hawthorne (2003, p. 33).

6. This is similar to what social psychologists call "transactive memory systems," in which people may not know the answer to a particular question but, with close relationships, they know who might know, which gives them an advantage. See Hollingshead (1998) and Wegner, Erber, and Raymond (1991).

7. Hawthorne (2003, p. 51).

8. Simons (1991).

9. Foster (1986).

10. Tedlow and Smith (1998, p. 7).

11. Johnson & Johnson (1972, pp. 9, 21). Nearly identical language is used in various annual reports throughout the 1970s as well.

12. Johnson & Johnson (1979, p. 46) and Foster (1986, p. 144).

13. Foster (1986, p. 150–151).

14. Indeed, J&J managed to continue this trend through the Tylenol recall of 1986, which cost it hundreds of millions of dollars and reduced by half—but did not erase—J&J's earnings that year (Johnson & Johnson, 2004). See also Jasinowski and Hamrin (1995, p. 177).

15. Kotter (1988, p. 89).

16. Simons (1987, p. 357).

17. Simons (2000).

18. See Kotter (1988, pp. 90–91) for another example of young J&J managers giving presentations to senior management.

19. As quoted in Simons (1987, p. 348).

20. Simons (1987, p. 351).

21. Beginning even before he became CEO, Burke "suspected that managers were only paying lip service" to the credo and started pressing to make it more relevant to the organization; he initiated a series of worldwide "'Credo Challenge' meetings," which took place over a three-year period and culminated in a revised credo, updated for the modern era, which was reissued in 1979 (Foster, 1986, pp. 138–139). Insisting that managers "challenge it, get rid of it, change it, or commit to it," Burke remained a champion of the credo throughout his tenure with Johnson & Johnson and felt the company's response to the Tylenol tampering incidents was the best proof of J&J's renewed, collective commitment to its values (Aguilar, 1984).

22. Johnson & Johnson's Tylenol product held a dominant share of the analgesic market in the early 1980s when, in 1982, several bottles of Tylenol were tampered with, poisoned with cyanide, and replaced on retail shelves by an unknown individual. The incident resulted in the deaths of seven people and a nationwide public-relations crisis for Johnson & Johnson. Although the incident had occurred after the products left the J&J factory and the company was absolved of any wrongdoing, CEO Burke was determined to live up to the credo's commitment to community. J&J quickly regained consumer confidence when it voluntarily recalled Tylenol capsules from stores nationwide—at a cost of $100 million—then reintroduced Tylenol using the industry's first tamper-evident packaging and issued coupons for free replacement of any Tylenol products that consumers may have discarded during the poisoning incident. Within months of the poisonings, J&J had regained its previous share of the analgesic market. When an additional tampering incident occurred in 1986, J&J discontinued the capsule form of Tylenol, replacing it with the safer caplet product, and pioneered additional safety measures in its packaging, again regaining market share within an amazingly short time period.

23. Note, however, that these biotech entrepreneurial activities were for the most part much later than the first wave of Baxter

Boys. With the exception of Vincent, Raab, and Rathmann, all of these transitions occurred during the 1990s. See Lamb (1987) for details on some of the transitions.

24. I note that these small numbers for international experience were also characteristic of both Merck and J&J positions—J&J probably due to its policy of hiring local nationals for overseas operations, making it perhaps less likely they would "return" to the United States to run a young biotechnology venture.

Chapter 7

1. Schaubert left to join Bill Bain in starting Bain & Company, a strategic management consulting company headquartered in Boston, Massachusetts.

2. For a review of the major milestones in the industry, see a timeline published by the Biotechnology Industry Organization (2004). See also Barley, Freeman, and Hybels (1992), Kornberg (1995), Robbins-Roth (2000), and Pisano (1996).

3. For an excellent review, see Henderson, Orsenigo, and Pisano (1999).

4. Robbins-Roth (2000, p. 7).

5. Saxenian (1994).

6. Gompers, Lerner, and Scharfstein (2005).

7. Social network research generally studies not the origins of social networks but rather the consequences, and in some instances the dynamics, of networks over time. For an exception and review, see Gulati and Gargiulo (1999).

8. When historicist explanations are offered in which one effect is attributed as the cause for another effect in a subsequent period, we are left with a question as to how that effect arose in the first instance (Stinchcombe, 1968). Other kinds of explanations, such as equifinality (Heider, 1958), suggest that many different factors arose to yield one consequence. Again, this functional kind of explanation begs the question of how this whole combination of factors got started. That is the focus here.

9. Gompers, Lerner, and Scharfstein (2005).

10. Gulati and Higgins (2003). See also Zacharakis and Shepherd (2001) and Zacharakis and Meyer (1998).

11. Higgins and Gulati (2003) and Higgins and Gulati (2004).

12. See, for example, Reuber and Fischer (1999).

13. Although there is very limited research on the cognitive dimensions of VC decision making, research shows that managerial capabilities are one of the most important characteristics of the entrepreneur or team (Boocock and Woods, 1994). Other reviews (Shepherd, Ettenson, and Crouch, 2000) suggest that industry-related competence is most significant. Here, as the quote suggests, I propose that VCs attend to signals associated with employment affiliations that affect their decision-making process.

14. In contrast to companies that spun out of Xerox, for example (see Chesbrough, 2002). See also Freeman's (1986) case studies of the semiconductor industry.

15. In the case of Baxter alumni, there was one possible exception to this pattern: Ted Greene. Greene is not a Ph.D.-trained scientist. However, he has several patents under his own name and was personally pursuing a scientific area he and just a few others had identified. Indeed, he described himself as more of a technology-driven entrepreneur than most of his colleagues at Baxter. Top VCs described Greene similarly—as "an entrepreneur who was going to start a firm in monoclonals all on his own until Hybritech came along and asked him to join them." Still, even in Greene's case, he did not try to single-handedly start a company; rather, from the very start, he partnered with two scientists.

16. In the case of Baxter's first wave, it was often the case that managers joined when the businesses were small—only a handful of people. Still, the point that these VCs make—that businesspeople were teaming up with scientist-founders—was true for Baxter alumni as it was for others coming from healthcare companies. One important and notable exception to this was

Genentech, which was founded by Boyer, a biochemist based at the University of California at San Francisco (who had, with Cohen at Stanford, developed the first recombinant DNA technology), and Swanson, who had worked with Kleiner & Perkins to start Genentech. Cetus also preceded the Baxter first wave and, like Genentech, was started by scientists, but, unlike Genentech, did not have a focused approach to the new science. Indeed, Swanson was frustrated by Cetus's "all over the map approach" (Robbins-Roth, 2000, p. 14).

17. For details on the product development process, see Pisano (1996).

18. Longman (1999).

19. Cohen, Cheng, Boyer, and Helling (1973).

20. Kohler and Milstein (1975).

21. Note that Greene did not follow in this path but instead pursued monoclonals.

22. As Pisano's (1994, 1996) research showed, biotech process development required a "learn by doing" orientation for protein molecules, whereas small molecule pharmaceutical process development built on lab research and chemistry knowledge and so required a "learn before doing" orientation. These two approaches parallel the "learning-based efficacy" found among Baxter managers, versus the "expertise-based efficacy" found at big pharmaceuticals such as Merck and J&J.

23. Griffeth, Hom, and Gaertner (2000).

24. Greenhaus and Callanan (1987).

25. Of course, the same was true at the other companies, such as J&J. However, in that instance, given the significantly greater number of divisions, it is possible that the narrowing of the pyramid was less apparent.

26. Organizational commitment and job involvement are two factors that affect turnover (Mitchell, Holten, Lee, Sablynski, and Erez, 2001).

27. For research on psychological contracts and breeches, see Rousseau (2001a, 2001b).

28. Research shows that during this timeframe Merck's letters to stockholders made little mention of biotechnology. For a discussion of Merck's and other pharmaceuticals' responses, see Kaplan, Murray, and Henderson (2003).

29. Spence's (1973) seminal research on signaling suggests that certain factors, such as an individual's educational background, can serve as a signal of an individual's capability, affecting the choice of hire. Here, it appears that taking a firm public was a sign of success that served similarly as a form of credentialing that affected the hiring process out of Baxter. For research on certification contests and how reputations for competence emerge in an industry (at the level of the organization), see Rao (1994).

30. Ashmore, Deaux, and McLaughlin-Volpe (2004).

31. The behavior of social comparison others can be a very powerful form of social influence. Research on career decision making has shown that individuals can be particularly vulnerable to the career moves of those with whom they socially compare themselves to during early career. Thus, they are more likely to follow the leader of those they role-model (Higgins, 2001b). Indeed, some interviewees talked explicitly about those in the first wave as "role models," whereas others simply described how the departure of those they considered peers prompted them to pick their heads up from their desks at Baxter and consider a move into biotech.

32. By 1983, two of the five members of the first wave had taken their firms public and by 1986, all of the first wave had taken firms public.

33. Rosen (1981). See also Lucas (1978).

34. See, e.g., Fernandez and Weinberg (1997).

35. Gompers, Lerner, and Scharfstein. (2005).

36. It is important to note, given the time period of these data (1980–2002), that the deals done between Baxter-led biotech firms and Baxter did not include the fourteen or so individuals who came on board at Baxter after Baxter acquired American

Hospital Supply. During this period, Baxter did $234.7 million in deals with Baxter alumni-led public biotech firms, whereas Abbott did only $53.7 million in deals with its alumni (Recombinant Capital, 2004). Even after accounting for firm size and the acquisition of American Hospital Supply, Baxter deals outstrip Abbott deals. In some respects, this may be a conservative estimate since some of the most important deals are likely those that predate a company's public offering, as the story in the Preface to this book suggests.

Chapter 8

1. March and Olsen (1976), Simon (1947/1997), and Thornton and Ocasio (1999).
2. For foundational organizational and psychological research on cognition, see Abelson (1976) and Neisser (1976). See also Calder and Schurr (1981).
3. Arnstein (2002).
4. Eccles and Nohria (1992).
5. Quirk and R.B.C. Capital Markets (2003, p. 7).
6. Papadopoulos and Donaldson, Lufkin & Jenrette Securities Corp. (1986).
7. Papadopoulos and Donaldson, Lufkin & Jenrette Securities Corp. (1986).
8. Weisbrod and Prudential-Bache Securities (1986).
9. Chandler (1962).
10. For an overview of the early years of Genzyme, see Bartlett and McLean (2002).
11. Since the government did not want to encourage further research in this area, Genzyme faced no patent barriers or licensing costs and enjoyed some tax breaks.
12. Bartlett and McLean (2002, p. 4). See also Arnstein (2002), Sawyer (2001), Teisberg (1994), Stipp (1992).
13. See "Genzyme Reports Fifth Profitable Quarter" (1987) on PR Newswire.

14. Specifically, Genzyme employed two research and development limited partnerships (RDLPs), one called Genzyme Clinical Partners (which was rolled out in 1987 and used to finance the development of Ceredase), and a second, Genzyme Development Partners (which was used to fund the development of HA products in 1989); two stock warrant off-balance-sheet research and development (SWORDs); and two carve-out deals (in the early 1990s). Each of these financing arrangements came with its own benefits and costs. For example, the RDLPs allowed Genzyme to maintain control over the projects' revenues but also allowed partners to cash in on a high rate of return and offered no secondary market. SWORDs did include a buyout price and so were more easily liquidated, but the cost to Genzyme was high since partners were promised high yearly returns. And carve-outs, another way to raise money by offering up parts of Genzyme's business (e.g., IG Labs), provided financing but also came with high administrative burden since each carve-out required its own board that needed to be coordinated with Genzyme's board. Eventually, in 1994, Termeer pioneered the use of tracking stocks in biotechnology. Tracking stocks (also known as "targeted" or "lettered" stocks) are traded independently from the corporation's stock. Revenues and costs are assigned to the division responsible for them, and (unlike carve-outs), since tracking stocks are not separate legal entities, they do not require a separate board or corporate charter. As such, the corporation retains much of the legal rights to the division's assets, proceeds from the tracking stock issue are tax free, and debt is available to the division at the corporate rate. For a discussion, see Salter (2002).

15. Weisbrod and Prudential-Bache Securities (1988, p. 8).

16. Buell and Kidder, Peabody & Company (1988, p. 2).

17. McGeorge and Sutro & Co. (1988, p. 3).

18. Miller and PaineWebber (1988, p. 17).

19. This story appeared after this book was in final stages of preparation for publication. See, Krasner (2005, p. D4).

20. Biogen's product and market focus is described in its annual reports; see for example, Biogen (1987).
21. Biogen (1987, p. i).
22. Buell and E. F. Hutton & Co. (1987, p. 1).
23. For further discussion and research on the collaborative arrangements between young biotech firms and big pharma, see Pisano (1990, 1991) and Pisano and Mang (1993).
24. Litwack and Becker W. Paribas Co. (1984, p. 2).
25. The diversity of Abbott's product lines is evident in its annual reports. In 1979, for example, Abbott's revenues were earned in the following proportions: pharmaceuticals and nutritionals, 49 percent; hospital and laboratory products, 41 percent; and consumer products, 10 percent (Abbott Laboratories, 1979).
26. Arnstein (2002, p. 32).
27. Arnstein (2002, p. 32).
28. Salter (2002, p. 13).
29. Bartlett and McLean (2002, p. 6).
30. Schein (1985b). Schein treats values and behaviors as observed manifestations of the cultural essence; they are levels of the culture but not what culture "really is" (p. 14).
31. Schein (1999, 2004).
32. The major exception to this rule is the company's lead proprietary therapeutic drug, Ceradase, which was developed internally and funded through a research and development limited partnership.
33. Arnstein (2002, p. 36).
34. Pollack (1998, p. C1).
35. Amgen (2003, p. 33) and Weintraub and Barrett (2002).
36. Adelson (1987).
37. Miller and PaineWebber (1988, p. 5) and Bartlett (2002, p. 11).

Chapter 9

1. Chi-square analyses were used to compare the roles that the alumni of these four major pharmaceutical companies entered at

the biotechnology firms they joined. The analyses revealed that there is a significant company effect on the distribution of these alumni into each of science, management, top management, board, and venture capital roles (p < .01 in each case). Looking at the actual counts of these distributions, compared to the expected counts if the distribution were normal, reveals how Baxter differs from these other companies. Baxter is the only overrepresented company of the four when it comes to having its alumni in management positions, and the only under represented company of the four when it comes to having its alumni in board positions. (Baxter and Johnson & Johnson are both overrepresented in top management positions, about equally.) Johnson & Johnson is the only overrepresented company when it comes to affiliations with biotechnology companies through venture capital firms. Merck is overrepresented only in science positions and very underrepresented in management (top and middle), while Abbott is almost entirely in line with the expected values for all of these types of positions.

2. March and Simon (1958).

3. Over the years, researchers have proposed different mental methods of information processing that might be used by an individual: (a) a "top-down" or "theory-driven" process, in which past experience shapes cognitive structures that, in turn, guides current perception and thought; and (b) a "bottom up" or "data driven" process, in which the current context of information drives thought patterns. Scholars now generally agree that theory-driven processing is employed in most settings. See Walsh (1995, pp. 281–282) for a review.

4. Dearborn and Simon (1958), Walsh (1988), and Beyer, Chattopadhyay, George, Glick, Olgilvie, and Pugliese (1997). For research examining specific linkages between CEO/Entrepreneur functional background and firm structure, see Boeker (1989); and firm capabilities, see Kazanjion and Rao (1999); and reactions to strategic stimuli, see Finkelstein and Hambrick (1995). For research linking founding team

characteristics to new venture growth and strategy, see Eisenhardt and Schoonhoven (1990).

5. Chattopadhyay, Glick, Miller, and Huber (1999).

6. Although I did hear of one person who made such a move.

7. Anders (2003).

8. Kotter (1982, pp. 8, 34–35).

9. Anders (2003).

10. Plotz (1997).

11. Connor (1998).

12. Beam (2000), Connor (1998), Plotz (1997), and Pogash (1995).

13. For a recent exception, see Datta, Guthrie, and Rajagopalan (2002).

14. Ibarra (2003, p. 133).

15. For recent research on developmental networks, see Higgins and Kram (2001), and for a self-assessment instrument that evaluates the structure of one's developmental network, see Higgins (2004).

16. IBM was long known for its focus on customer relationships and its emphasis on sales and marketing. Many senior executives had their start in the sales organization, and IBM regularly involved senior managers in making important customer sales, believing that it kept them fresh and in tune with the market for their products (Rodgers, 1986).

   Beginning in the 1990s, and driven by the dramatic financial setbacks IBM suffered in the competitive hardware marketplace as well as by Lou Gerster's influence, IBM experienced a dramatic shift to being a technology-driven company. During the 1990s, for example, IBM's new-found focus on product innovation earned the company more patents annually than any other company worldwide (International Business Machines, 2004).

Chapter 10

1. For exceptions, see Gunz and Jalland (1996) and Gunz, Jalland, and Martin (1998). These theoretical pieces on "career

streams" are consistent with the perspective presented here. See also Jones (2001).

2. See, for example, Haveman (1995). For a review and suggestions for mesolevel organizational research, see Rousseau and House (1994).

3. Schein (1993).

4. By the end of the year 2000, at which point Genzyme and Biogen had market values in the billions of dollars ($7.8 billion and $8.6 billion, respectively), Genzyme had engaged in $1.1 billion in deals with Genzyme alumni-led firms, compared to only $140 million in deals that Biogen completed with Biogen alumni-led firms (Thompson Financial, 2004).

5. For years, people have talked about the opportunities for consolidation in the biotech industry. Venture capitalists and industry specialists have called for "forced consolidation," as companies merge to gain mass and share resources during this down market. One of the most promising arenas for such consolidation appears to be biotech to biotech transactions, as opposed to the more traditional kinds of deals seen between pharmaceutical companies and biotech firms. Genzyme, with its ecosystem perspective, should be well-poised to take advantage of such opportunities.

Industry analysts point to other arenas such as the automobile industry, which at one point had 280 firms and now has only a handful in the United States. Likewise, the United States had 190 television-set manufacturers and now only has one. The point these analysts make is that biotech, like any industry, will experience winnowing out as a function of the industry's maturity (Ernst & Young, 2003). Companies that foster the development of an ecosystem perspective may be better positioned to cultivate deals between firms as this process unfolds.

6. March (1991).

7. Christensen (1998).

8. Tushman and O'Reilly (1996) and Tushman and Smith (2002). In a related fashion, research by Cockburn and Henderson

(1998) suggests that "connectedness" between pharmaceutical companies and the wider scientific community improves firm performance in drug discovery.

9. See also Chesbrough (2002).
10. Stinchcombe (1965).
11. Organizational scholars have referred to such patterns, in which organizations copy structures that successful organizations adopt, particularly under conditions of uncertainty, as "institutional isomorphism." For a full discussion, see Powell and DiMaggio (1991).

    Scholars have also differentiated among coercive, mimetic, and normative forms of institutional isomorphism. In the case of other companies copying Genzyme's structure, this would be a case of "mimetic isomorphism," whereas the case of influencing other organizations through professional associations would be a case of "normative isomorphism" (DiMaggio & Powell, 1983).
12. Assimakopoulos, Everton, and Tsutsui (2003).
13. Saxenian (1994).
14. Wayne (1983, p. F6).
15. In Bennis's research, he observed that successful professionals were often skilled at adapting across establishments (Bennis & Slater, 1968/1998, p. 17; Bennis & Nanus, 1985). See also Bennis and Thomas (2002b).

References

Abbott Laboratories. (1970). *Annual Report, December 31, 1970.* Abbott Park, IL: Abbott Laboratories, Inc.

Abbott Laboratories. (1979). *Annual Report, December 31, 1979.* Abbott Park, IL: Abbott Laboratories, Inc.

Abbott Laboratories. (2004). Abbott Laboratories, Net Sales, December 31, 1970–December 31, 1979. *Standard & Poor's Compustat.* Data retrieved July 2004.

Abelson, R. P. (1976). Script processing in attitude formation and decision making. In J. Carroll & J. Payne (Eds.), *Cognition and Social Behavior* (pp. 33–45). Hillsdale, NJ: Erlbaum Associates.

Adelson, A. (1987, November 2). Amgen chief confident on biotechnology gains. *The New York Times,* p. D2.

Aguilar, F. J. (1984). Johnson & Johnson (A): Philosophy & culture. *Harvard Business School Case Video No. 9–884–525.* Boston: Harvard Business School Publishing.

Aguilar, F. J., & Bhambri, A. (1983). Johnson & Johnson (B): Hospital services. *Harvard Business School Case No. 9–384–054.* Boston: Harvard Business School Press.

Amgen. (2003). *10-K, December 31, 2003.* Thousand Oaks, CA: Amgen, Inc.

Anders, G. (2003, May 15). Great expectations: General Electric alumni find it harder to shine. *The Wall Street Journal,* p. A1.

Animal learning. *Encyclopedia Britannica* (online premium edition). Retrieved July 15, 2004 from http://www.britannica.com/eb/article?eu=109613.

Arnstein, C. (Ed.). (2002). *A Different Vision: The Making of Genzyme.* Cambridge, MA: Genzyme Corp.

Arthur, M. B., & Rousseau, D. M. (Eds.). (1996). *The Boundaryless Career: A New Employment Principle for a New Organizational Era.* New York: Oxford University Press.

Arthur, M. B., Hall, D. T., & Lawrence, B. S. (Eds.). (1989). *Handbook of Career Theory.* New York: Cambridge University Press.

Arthur, M. B., Claman, P. H., & DeFillippi, R. J. (1995). Intelligent enterprise, intelligent careers. *The Academy of Management Executive, 9*(4), 7–20.

Ashforth, B. (2001). *Role Transitions in Organizational Life: An Identity-Based Perspective.* Hillsdale, NJ: Erlbaum Associates.

Ashmore, R. D., Deaux, K., & McLaughlin-Volpe, T. (2004). An organizing framework for collective identity: Articulation and significance of multidimensionality. *Psychological Bulletin, 130*(1), 80–114.

Assimakopoulos, D., Everton, S., & Tsutsui, K. (2003). The semiconductor community in the Silicon Valley: A network analysis of the SEMI genealogy chart (1947–1986). *International Journal of Technology Management, 25*(1/2), 181–199.

Austin, J. E., Barrett, D., & Weber, J. B. (2001). Merck Global Health Initiatives (A). *Harvard Business School Case No. 9–301–088*. Boston: Harvard Business School Press.

Bae, S. C., Klein, D. P., & Bowyer, J. W. (1999). Determinants of underwriter participation in initial public offerings of common stock: An empirical study. *Journal of Business Finance and Accounting, 26*, 595–618.

Barley, S. R. (1989). Careers, identities, and institutions: The legacy of the Chicago School of Sociology. In M. Arthur, T. Hall, & B. Lawrence (Eds.), *The Handbook of Career Theory* (pp. 41–65). New York: Cambridge University Press.

Barley, S. R., Freeman, J., & Hybels, R. C. (1992). Strategic alliances in commercial biotechnology. In N. Nohria & R. G. Eccles (Eds.), *Networks and Organizations: Structure, Form, and Action* (pp. 311–348). Boston: Harvard Business School Press.

Bartlett, C. A., (2002). Genzyme's Gaucher initiative: Global risk and responsibility. *Harvard Business School Teaching Case No. 5–303–066*. Boston: Harvard Business School Publishing.

Bartlett, C. A., & McLean, A. N. (2002). Genzyme's Gaucher initiative: Global risk and responsibility. *Harvard Business School Case No. 9–303–048*. Boston: Harvard Business School Publishing.

Bartlett C., & McLean, A. N. (2004). GE's talent machine: The making of a CEO. *Harvard Business School Case No. 9–304–049*. Boston: Harvard Business School Publishing.

Baruch, Y., & Altman, Y. (2002). Expatriation and repatriation in MNCS: A taxonomy. *Human Resource Management, 41*(2), 239–259.

Bateson, M. C. (1989). *Composing a Life*. New York: Atlantic Monthly Press.

Baum, J. A. C., Calabrese, T., & Silverman, B. S. (2000). Don't go it alone: Alliance network composition and startups' performance in Canadian biotechnology. *Strategic Management Journal, 21*, 267–294.

Baxter International. (1970). *Annual Report, December 31, 1970*. Deerfield, IL: Baxter International, Inc.

Baxter International. (1979). *Annual Report, December 31, 1979*. Deerfield, IL: Baxter International, Inc.

Baxter International. (2004a). Baxter International, Net Sales, December 31, 1970–December 31, 1979. *Standard & Poor's Compustat*. Data retrieved July 2004.

Baxter International. (2004b). *Company Profile: History*. Retrieved December, 2004 from http://www.baxter.com/about_baxter/company_profile/sub/history.html.

Beam, A. (2000, July/August). The last great newspaperman. *Stanford Magazine*. Retrieved July 8, 2004 from http://www.stanfordalumni.org/news/magazine/.

Becker, G. S. (1975). *Human Capital: A Theoretical and Empirical Analysis, with Special Reference to Education* (2nd ed.). New York: National Bureau of Economic Research.

Bennis, W. G., & Biederman, P. W. (1977). *Organizing Genius: The Secrets of Creative Collaboration*. Reading, MA: Addison-Wesley.

Bennis, W. G., & Nanus, B. (1985). *Leaders: The Strategies for Taking Charge*. New York: Harper & Row.

Bennis, W. G., & Slater, P. (1998). *The Temporary Society* (2nd ed.). San Francisco: Jossey-Bass. (Original work published 1968.)

Bennis, W. G., & Thomas, R. J. (2002a). Crucibles of leadership. *Harvard Business Review, 80*(9), 39–45.

Bennis, W. G., & Thomas, R. J. (2002b). *Geeks and Geezers: How Era, Values, and Defining Moments Shape Leaders*. Boston: Harvard Business School Press.

Berlew, D. E., & Hall, D. T. (1966). The socialization of managers: Effects of expectations on performance. *Administrative Science Quarterly, 11*(2) 207–223.

Betz, N. E., Fitzgerald, L. F., & Hill, R. E. (1989). Trait-factor theories: Traditional cornerstone of career theory. In M. B. Arthur, D. T. Hall, & B. S. Lawrence (Eds.), *Handbook of Career Theory* (pp. 26–40). New York: Cambridge University Press.

Beyer, J. M., Chattopadhyay, P., George, E., Glick, W. H., Olgilvie, D., & Pugliese, D. (1997). The selective perception of managers revisited. *Academy of Management Journal, 40*(3), 716–737.

Biogen. (1987). *Annual Report, December 31, 1987*. Cambridge, MA: Biogen, Inc.

Biotechnology Industry Organization. (2004). *Editors' and Reporters' Guide to Biotechnology: Time Line*. Retrieved August 17, 2004 from www.bio.org/speeches/pubs/er/timeline.asp.

Boeker, W. (1989). The development and institutionalization of subunit power in organizations. *Adminstrative Science Quarterly, 34*(3), 388–410.

Boje, D. M. (1991). The storytelling organization: A study of story performance in an office-supply firm. *Administrative Science Quarterly, 36*(1), 106–126.

Boocock, G., & Woods, M. (1994). The evaluation criteria used by venture capitalists: Evidence from a UK venture fund. *International Small Business Journal, 16*(1), 36–57.

Bossidy, L., & Charan, R. (2002). *Execution: The Discipline of Getting Things Done*. New York: Crown Business.

Brown, D., & Brooks, L. (Eds.). (1996). *Career Choice and Development* (3rd ed.). San Francisco: Jossey-Bass.

Buell, S., & E. F. Hutton & Co. (1987). *Biogen N.V.—Company Report, January 27, 1987*. Available from The Investext Group, www.investext.com.

Buell, S. J., & Kidder, Peabody & Co. (1988). *Genzyme Corporation–Company Report, October 26, 1988*. Available from The Investext Group, www.investext.com.

Burrill, G. S., & Lee, K. (1990). *Biotech 91: A Changing Environment*. San Francisco: Ernst & Young.

Burrill, G. S., & Lee, K. (1993). *Biotech 94*. San Francisco: Ernst & Young.

Burt, R. S. (1992). *Structural Holes: The Social Structure of Competition*. Cambridge, MA: Harvard University Press.

Bushee, B. J. (1998). The influence of institutional investors on myopic R&D investment behavior. *The Accounting Review, 73,* 305–333.

Bushee, B. J., & Noe, C. F. (2000). Corporate disclosure practices, institutional investors, and stock return volatility. *Journal of Accounting Research, 38,* 171–202.

Calder, B. J., & Schurr, P. H. (1981). Attitudinal processes in organizations. *Research in Organizational Behavior, 3,* 283–302.

Capelli, P. (1999). *The New Deal at Work: Managing the Market-Driven Workforce*. Boston: Harvard Business School Press.

Carter, R. B., & Dark, F. H. (1992). An empirical examination of investment banking reputation measures. *The Financial Review, 27,* 355–374.

Carter, R. B., Dark, F. H., & Singh, A. K. (1998). Underwriter reputation, initial returns and the long-run performance of IPO stocks. *The Journal of Finance, 53,* 285–311.

Carter, R. B., & Manaster, S. (1990). Initial public offerings and underwriter reputation. *The Journal of Finance, 45,* 1045–1067.

Chandler, A. (1962). *Strategy and Structure*. Cambridge, MA: MIT Press.

Chatman, J. A. (1991). Matching people and organizations: Selection and socialization in public accounting firms. *Administrative Science Quarterly, 36,* 459–484.

Chattopadhyay, P., Glick, W. H., Miller, C., & Huber, G. P. (1999). Determinants of executive beliefs: Comparing functional conditioning and social influence. *Strategic Management Journal, 20*(8), 763–789.

Chesbrough, H. W. (2002). Graceful exits and foregone opportunities: Xerox's management of its technology spinoff organizations. *Business History Review, 76*(4), 803–838.

Christensen, C. (1998). *The Innovator's Dilemma*. Boston: Harvard Business School Press.

Cochran, L. (1994). What is a career problem? *The Career Development Quarterly, 42,* 204–215.

Cockburn, I. M., & Henderson, R. M. (1998). Absorptive capacity, coauthoring behavior, and the organization of research in drug discovery. *Journal of Industrial Economics*, 46(2), 157–182.

Cody, T. (1994). *Innovating for Health: The Story of Baxter International*. Deerfield, IL: Baxter International.

Cohen, S. N., Cheng, A. C., Boyer, H. W., & Helling, R. B. (1973). Construction of biologically functional bacterial plasmids in vitro. *Proceedings of the National Academy of Sciences USA*, 70, 3240–3244.

Connor, C. (1998, Spring). Times Mirror CEO Mark Willes: Newspapers offers opportunities to MBAs. *The Bottom Line ONLINE* (Published at Columbia Business School). Retrieved July 8, 2004 from www.columbia.edu/cu/business/botline/spring98/3_5/willes.html.

Cyert, R. M., & March, J. G. (1963). *A Behavioral Theory of the Firm*. Englewood Cliffs, NJ: Prentice Hall.

Datta, D. K., Guthrie, J., & Rajagopalan, N. (2002). Different industries, different CEOs? A study of CEO career specialization. *Human Resources Planning*, 25(2), 14–25.

Dearborn, D. C., & Simon, H. A. (1958). Selective perception: A note on the departmental identifications of executives. *Sociometry*, 21, 140–144.

Deeds, D. L., DeCarolis, D. M., & Coombs, J. E. (1997). The impact of firm-specific capabilities on the amount of capital raised in an initial public offering: Evidence from the biotechnology industry. *Journal of Business Venturing*, 12, 31–46.

DeLong, T. J. (1982). The career orientation of MBA alumni: A multidimensional model. In R. Katz (Ed.), *Career Issues in Human Resource Management* (pp. 72–92). Englewood Cliffs, NJ: Prentice Hall.

Dibner, M. D. (1988). *Biotechnology Guide, U.S.A.* New York: Stockton Press.

Dibner, M. D. (1991). *Biotechnology Guide, U.S.A.* New York: Stockton Press.

Dibner, M. D. (1995). *Biotechnology Guide, U.S.A.* New York: Stockton Press.

DiMaggio, P. J., & Powell, W. W. (1983). The iron cage revisited: Institutional isomorphism and collective rationality in organizational fields. *American Sociological Review*, 48, 147–160.

Eccles, R. G., & Nohria, N. (1992). *Beyond the Hype*. Boston: Harvard Business School Press.

Edgerton, J. E., & Campbell, R. (Eds.). (1994). *American Psychiatric Glossary* (7th ed.). Washington, DC: American Psychiatric Press.

Eisenhardt, K. M. (1989). Building theories from case study research. *Academy of Management Review* 14(4), 532–550.

Eisenhardt, K. M., & Schoonhoven, C. B. (1990). Organizational growth: Linking founding team, strategy, environment, and growth among U.S. semiconductor ventures, 1978–1988. *Administrative Science Quarterly*, 35, 504–529.

Ernst & Young. (2003). *Beyond Borders: The Global Biotechnology Report*. New York: Ernst & Young, LLP.

Evetts, J. (1992). Dimensions of career: Avoiding reification in the analysis of change. *Sociology, 26,* 1–21.

Feldman, D. C. (1976). A contingency theory of socialization. *Administrative Science Quarterly, 21,* 433–452.

Fernandez, R. M., & Weinberg, N. (1997). Sifting and sorting: Personal contacts and hiring in a retail bank. *American Sociological Review, 62*(6), 883–902.

Fingleton, E. (1995, March 20). Jobs for life: Why Japan won't give them up. *Fortune,* 119–123.

Finkelstein, S., & Hambrick, D. (1995). *Strategic Leadership: Top Executives and Their Effects on Organizations.* Minneapolis, MN: West Publishing.

Florida, R. L., & Kenney, M. (1990). *The Breakthrough Illusion: Corporate America's Failure to Move from Innovation to Mass Production.* New York: Basic Books.

Freeman, J. (1986). Entrepreneurs as organizational products: Semiconductor firms and venture capital firms. *Advances in the Study of Entrepreneurship, Innovation, and Economic Growth, 1,* 33–52.

Foster, L. G. (1986). *A Company that Cares: One Hundred Year Illustrated History of Johnson & Johnson.* New Brunswick, NJ: Johnson & Johnson.

Gabarro, J. J. (1987). *The Dynamics of Taking Charge.* Boston: Harvard Business School Press.

Genzyme reports fifth profitable quarter (1987, November 4). *PR Newswire.* Available from LexisNexis.

Glaser, B. G., & Strauss, A. L. (1967). *The Discovery of Grounded Theory.* Hawthorne, NY: Aldine de Gruyter.

Glesne C. (1997). *Becoming Qualitative Researchers: An Introduction.* Boston: Longman.

Goffman, E. (1961). *Asylums: Essays on the Social Situation of Mental Patients and Other Inmates.* New York: Doubleday.

Gompers, P. A., Lerner, J., Blair, M. M., & Hellman, T. (1998). What drives venture capital fundraising? *Brookings Papers on Economic Activity,* 149–204.

Gompers, P. A., Lerner, J., & Scharfstein, D. S. (2005). Entrepreneurial spawning: Public corporations and the genesis of new ventures, 1986–1999. *Journal of Finance, 60*(2), forthcoming.

Gorman, M., & Sahlman, W. A. (1989). What Do Venture Capitalists Do? *Journal of Business Venturing, 4*(4), 231–247.

Greenhaus, J. H., & Callanan, G.A. (1987) *Career Management* (2nd ed.). Fort Worth, TX: Dryden Press.

Griffeth, R. W., Hom, P. W., & Gaertner, X. (2000). A meta-analysis of antecedents and correlates of employee turnover: Update, moderator tests, and research implications for the millennium. *Journal of Management, 26,* 463–488.

Gulati, R., & Gargiulo, M. (1999). Where do interorganizational networks come from? *American Journal of Sociology, 104*(5), 1439–1493.

Gulati, R., & Higgins, M. C. (2003). Which ties matter when? The contingent effects of interorganizational partnerships and IPO success. *Strategic Management Journal, 24*, 127–144.

Gunz, H. P., & Jalland, R. M. (1996). Managerial careers and business strategies. *Academy of Management Review, 21*(3), 718–756.

Gunz, H. P., Jalland, R. M., & Martin, E. G. (1998). New strategy, wrong managers? What you need to know about career streams. *Academy of Management Executive, 12*(2), 21–37.

Hackett, G., Lent, R. W., & Greenhaus, J. H. (1991). Advances in vocational theory and research: A 20-year retrospective. *Journal of Vocational Behavior, 38*, 3–38.

Hackman, J. R., & Oldham, G. R. (1980). *Work Redesign.* Reading, MA: Addison-Wesley.

Hall, D. T. (1976). *Careers in Organizations.* Glenview, IL: Scott, Foresman.

Hall, D. T. (2002). *Careers in and out of Organizations.* Thousand Oaks, CA: Sage.

Hall, D. T. (2004). Self-awareness, identity, and leader development. In D.V. Day, S. J. Zaccaro, and S. M. Halpin (Eds.), *Leader Development for Transforming Organizations: Growing Leaders for Tomorrow* (pp. 153–170). Mahwah, NJ: Erlbaum.

Hall, D. T., & Mirvis, P. H. (1996). The new protean career: Psychological success and the path with a heart. In D. T. Hall (Ed.), *The Career Is Dead—Long Live the Career: A Relational Approach to Careers* (pp. 15–45). San Francisco: Jossey-Bass.

Hall, D. T., Zhu, G., & Yan, A. (2001). Developing global leaders: To hold on to them, let them go! *Advances in Global Leadership, 2*, 327–349.

Haveman, H. A. (1995). The demographic metabolism of organizations: Industry dynamics, turnover, and tenure distributions, *Administrative Science Quarterly, 40*, 586–592.

Hawthorne, F. (2003). *The Merck Druggernaut: The Inside Story of a Pharmaceutical Giant.* Hoboken, NJ: John Wiley.

Heckman, J. J. (1979). Sample selection bias as a specification error. *Econometrica, 45*, 153–161.

Heider, F. (1958). *The Psychology of Interpersonal Relations.* New York: Wiley.

Helyar, J. (1998, August 10). Solo flight: A Jack Welch disciple finds the GE mystique only takes you so far. *The Wall Street Journal*, p. A1.

Henderson, R., Orsenigo, L., & Pisano, G. P. (1999). The pharmaceutical industry and the revolution in molecular biology: Interactions among scientific, institutional, and organizational change." In D. Mowery & R. Nelson (Eds.), *Sources of Industrial Leadership* (pp. 267–311). New York: Cambridge University Press.

Heslin, P. (2004). Conceptualizing and evaluating career success. *Journal of Organizational Behavior, 25*, 1–24.

Higgins, M. C. (2001a). Changing careers: The effects of social context. *Journal of Organizational Behavior, 22*, 595–618.

Higgins, M. C. (2001b). Follow the leader? The effects of social influence on employer choice. *Group and Organization Management, 26*(3), 255–282.

Higgins, M. C. (2001c). When is helping helpful? Effects of evaluation and intervention timing on individual task performance. *Journal of Applied Behavioral Sciences, 37*(3), 280–298.

Higgins, M. C. (2004). Developmental network questionnaire. *Multimedia Product No. 9–405–701.* Boston: Harvard Business School Publishing.

Higgins, M. C., & Gulati, R. (2003). Getting off to a good start: The effects of upper echelon affiliations on underwriter prestige. *Organization Science, 14*(3), 244–263.

Higgins, M. C., & Gulati, R. (2004) Stacking the deck: The effects of top management backgrounds on investor decisions. Harvard Business School Working Paper number 05-046.

Higgins, M. C., & Kram, K. E. (2001). Reconceptualizing mentoring at work: A developmental network perspective. *Academy of Management Review, 26*(2), 264–288.

Higgins, M. C., & Thomas, D. A. (2001). Constellations and careers: Toward understanding the effects of multiple developmental relationships. *Journal of Organizational Behavior, 22*, 223–247.

Hill, L. A. (1992). *Becoming a Manager: Mastery of a New Identity.* Boston: Harvard Business School Press.

Hirakubo, N. (1999, November–December). The end of lifetime employment in Japan. *Business Horizons,* 41–46.

Hollingshead, A. B. (1998). Communication, learning and retrieval in transactive memory systems. *Journal of Experimental Social Psychology, 34*, 423–442.

Hom, P. W., Griffeth, R. W., & Sellaro, C. L. (1984). The validity of Mobley's 1977 model of employee turnover. *Organizational Behavior and Human Performance, 234*, 141–174.

Hughes, E. C. (1958). *Men and Their Work.* Glencoe, IL: The Free Press.

Ibarra, H. (1992). Homophily and differential returns: Sex differences in network structure and access in an advertising firm. *Administrative Science Quarterly, 37*, 422–447.

Ibarra, H. (1999). Provisional selves: Experimenting with image and identity in professional adaptation. *Administrative Science Quarterly, 44*(4): 764–791.

Ibarra, H. (2003). *Working Identity: Unconventional Strategies for Reinventing Your Career.* Boston: Harvard Business School Press.

Imprinting. (2004). *Dictionary of the History of Ideas* [electronic edition]. Retrieved July 15, 2004 from http://etext.lib.virginia.edu/cgi-local/DHI/dhi.cgi?id=dv2–64.

International Business Machines, Inc. (2004). *History of IBM*. Retrieved July 9, 2004 from http://www.ibm.com/ibm/history/history/year_2002.html.

Jasinowski, J., & Hamrin, R. (1995). *Making It in America: Proven Paths to Success from Fifty Top Companies*. New York: Simon & Schuster.

Johnson & Johnson. (1970). *Annual Report, December 31, 1970*. New Brunswick, NJ: Johnson & Johnson, Inc.

Johnson & Johnson. (1972). *Annual Report, December 31, 1972*. New Brunswick, NJ: Johnson & Johnson.

Johnson & Johnson. (1979). *Annual Report, December 31, 1979*. New Brunswick, NJ: Johnson & Johnson, Inc.

Johnson & Johnson. (2004). Johnson & Johnson, Net Income, December 31, 1960–December 31, 2002. *Standard & Poor's Compustat*. Data retrieved March 2004.

Jones, C. (2001). Coevolution of entrepreneurial careers, institutional rules, and competitive dynamics in American film, 1895-1920. *Organization Studies*, 6: 911–944.

Kahn, R. L., Wolfe, D. M., Snoek, J. D., & Rosenthal, R. A. (1964). *Organizational Stress: Studies in Role Conflict and Ambiguity*. New York: Wiley.

Kanter, R. M. (1977). *Men and Women of the Corporation*. New York: Basic Books.

Kanter, R. M. (2001). *Evolve! Succeeding in the Digital Culture of Tomorrow*. Boston: Harvard Business School Press.

Kanter, R. M. (2004). *Confidence: How Winning Streaks and Losing Streaks Begin and End*. New York: Crown.

Kaplan, S., Murray, F., & Henderson, R. (2003). Discontinuities and senior management: Addressing the role of recognition in pharmaceutical firm response to biotechnology. *Industrial and Corporate Change*, *12*(4), 185–233.

Karaevli, A., & Hall, D. T. (2004). Career variety and executive adaptability in turbulent environments. In R. J. Burke & C. L. Cooper (Eds.), *Leading in Truculent Times: Managing in the New World of Work* (pp. 54–74). Malden, MA: Blackwell.

Kazanjion, R. K., & Rao, H. (1999). Research note: The creation of capabilities in new ventures—A longitudinal study. *Organization Science*, *20*(1), 125–142.

Kegan, R. K. (1982). *The Evolving Self: Problem and Process in Human Development*. Cambridge, MA: Harvard University Press.

Kegan, R. K., & Lahey, L. L. (1984). Adult leadership and adult development: A constructivist view. In B. Kellerman (Ed.), *Leadership: Multidisciplinary Perspectives* (pp. 199–230). Englewood Cliffs, NJ: Prentice Hall.

Khurana, R. (2002). *Searching for a Corporate Savior: The Irrational Quest for Charismatic CEOs*. Princeton, NJ: Princeton University Press.

Kohler, G., & Milstein, C. (1975). Continuous cultures of fused cells secreting antibody of predefined specificity. *Nature*, *256*(5517), 495–497.

Konrad Lorenz. (2004). *Encyclopedia Britannica*. Retrieved July 15, 2004 from http://www.britannica.com/eb/article?eu=109613.

Kornberg, A. (1995). *The Golden Helix: Inside Biotech Ventures*. Sausalito, CA: University Science Books.

Kotter, J. P. (1982). *The General Managers*. New York: The Free Press.

Kotter, J. P. (1988). *The Leadership Factor*. New York: The Free Press.

Kram, K. E. (1985). *Mentoring at Work: Developmental Relationships in Organizational Life*. Glenview, IL: Scott Foresman.

Krasner, J. (2005, January 4). Genzyme banks its future on cancer drugs. *The Boston Globe*, pp. D1, D4.

Lamb, R. B. (1987). *Running American Business: Top CEOs Rethink Their Major Decisions*. New York: Basic Books.

Langer, E. J. (1989). *Mindfulness*. Reading, MA: Addison-Wesley.

Lawrence, B. S. (2004). Organizational reference groups: A missing perspective on social context. *Working paper, Anderson Graduate School of Management, University of California at Los Angeles*.

Lawrence, P. R., & Lorsch, J. W. (1986). *Organization and Environment: Managing Differentiation and Integration*. Boston: Harvard Business School Press. (Original work published 1967.)

Lee, K., & Burrill, G. S. (1995). *Biotech 96*. Palo Alto, CA: Ernst & Young, LLP.

Lent, R. W., & Brown, S. D. (1996). Social cognitive approach to career development: An overview. *The Career Development Quarterly, 44*(4), 310–321.

Lerner, J. (1994). Venture capitalists and the decision to go public. *Journal of Financial Economics, 35*, 293–316.

Levinson, D. J. (1986). A conception of adult development. *American Psychologist, 41*, 3–13.

Levinson, D. J., Darrow, C. N., Klein, E. B., Levinson, M. H., & McKee, B. (1978). *The Seasons of a Man's Life*. New York: Knopf.

Litwack, A. H., & Becker W. Paribas Co. (1984). *Biogen N.V.–Company Report, June 26, 1984*. Available from The Investext Group, www. investext.com.

Longman, R. (1999). Living with limits: Device and biotech venture capital. *IN VIVO: The Business and Medicine Report, 17*(7), 43–52.

Lorenz, K. (1935). Der Kumpan in der Umwelt des Vogels. Der Artgenosse als ausloesendes Moment sozialer Verhaltungsweisen [The companion in the bird's world. The fellow-member of the species as releasing factor of social behavior]. *Journal Für Ornithologie, 83*, 137–213.

Lorsch, J. W., & Tierney, T. J. (2002). *Aligning the Stars: How to Succeed When Professionals Drive Results*. Boston: Harvard Business School Press.

Louis, M. R. (1980a). Career transitions: Varieties and commonalities. *Academy of Management Review, 5*, 329–340.

Louis, M. R. (1980b). Surprise and sense making: What newcomers experience in entering unfamiliar organizational settings. *Administrative Science Quarterly, 25*, 226–251.

Lucas, R. E., Jr. (1978). On the size distribution of business firms. *The Bell Journal of Economics*, 9(2), 508–523.

Maertz, C. P., & Campion, M. A. (1998). 25 years of voluntary turnover research: A review and critique. In C. L. Cooper & I. T. Robertson (Eds.), *International Review of Industrial and Organizational Psychology*, 13, 49–81. New York: Wiley.

March, J. G., & Olsen, J. P. (1976). *Ambiguity and Choice in Organizations*. Bergen, Germany: Universitetsforlaget.

March, J. (1991). Exploration and exploitation in organizational learning, *Organization Science*, 2, 71–87.

March, J. G., & Simon, H. A. (1958). *Organizations*. New York: Wiley.

Mason, R. O., & Mitroff, I. I. (1981). *Challenging Strategic Planning Assumptions: Theory, Cases, and Techniques*. New York: Wiley.

Masten, A. S., & Reed, M. J. (2002). Resilience in development. In C. R. Snyder & S. J. Lopez (Eds.), *Handbook of Positive Psychology* (pp. 74–88). New York: Oxford University Press.

McAdams, D. P. (2001). The psychology of life stories. *Review of General Psychology*, 5(2), 100–122.

McCall, M. W., Lombardo, M. M., & Morrison, A. M. (1988). *The Lessons of Experience: How Successful Executives Develop on the Job*. New York: The Free Press.

McGeorge, M. B., & Sutro & Co. (1988). *Genzyme Corp–Company Report, November 9, 1988*. Available from The Investext Group, www.investext.com.

McLennan, N. A., & Arthur, N. (1999). Applying the cognitive information processing approach to career problem solving and decision making to women's career development. *Journal of Employment Counseling*, 36(2), 82–96.

Megginson, W. L., & Weiss, K. A. (1991). Venture capitalist certification in initial public offerings. *Journal of Finance*, 56, 879–903.

Merck & Company. (1970). *Annual Report, December 31, 1970*. Whitehouse Station, NJ: Merck & Company, Inc.

Merck & Company. (1979). *Annual Report, December 31, 1979*. Whitehouse Station, NJ: Merck & Company, Inc.

Miles, M. B., & Huberman, A. M. (1994). *Qualitative Data Analysis: An Expanded Sourcebook*. Thousand Oaks, CA: Sage.

Miller, L., & PaineWebber. (1988). *Genzyme Corporation–Company Report, Conference Call Transcript, October 13, 1988*. Available from The Investext Group, www.investext.com.

Mitchell, T. R., Holten, B. C., Lee, T. W., Sablynski, C. J., & Erez, M. (2001). Why people stay: Using job embeddedness to predict voluntary turnover. *Academy of Management Journal*, 44(6), 1102–1121.

Mobley, W. H. (1977). Intermediate linkages in the relationship between job satisfaction and employee turnover. *Journal of Applied Psychology*, 62, 237–240.

Morrison, E. (1993). Newcomer information seeking: Exploring types, modes, sources, and outcomes. *Academy of Management Journal, 36,* 557–589.

Muchinsky, H. A., & Monahan, C. J. (1987) What is person–environment congruence? Supplementary versus complementary models of fit. *Journal of Vocational Behavior, 31,* 268–277.

Nadler, D., & Tushman, M. (1980). A model for diagnosing organizational behavior: Applying a congruence perspective. *Organizational Dynamics,* 9(3), 35–51.

Neisser, U. (1976). *Cognition and Reality.* San Francisco: W. H. Freeman.

Nichols, N. A. (1994, November–December). Medicine, management, and mergers: Interview with Merck's P. Roy Vagelos. *Harvard Business Review,* 105–114.

Nohria, N., & Groysberg, B. (2003, October 25). Coming and going. *The Economist, 12–17.*

O'Reilly, C. A., & Chatman, J. A. (1996). Culture as social control: Corporations, cults, and commitment. *Research in Organizational Behavior, 18,* 157–200.

O'Reilly, C. A., Chatman, J. A., & Caldwell, D. F. (1991). People and organizational culture: A profile comparison approach to assessing person-organization fit. *Academy of Management Journal, 34*(3), 487–516.

Papadopoulos, S., & Donaldson, Lufkin & Jenrette Securities Corp. (1986). *Biogen–Company Report, April 29, 1986.* Available from The Investext Group, www.investext.com.

Pfeffer, J. (1981). Management as symbolic action: The creation and maintenance of organizational paradigms. In L. L. Cummings & B. M. Staw (Eds.), *Research in Organizational Behavior, 3,* 1052. Greenwich, CT: JAI Press.

Pichanic, J. (2003). The Regulation of Well-Being: Growth and Action Orientations. Organizational Behavior Doctoral Dissertation, Harvard University.

Pinker, S. (1995). *The Language Instinct.* New York: HarperPerennial.

Pisano, G. P. (1990). The R&D Boundaries of the firm: An empirical analysis. *Administrative Science Quarterly, 35,* 153–176.

Pisano, G. P. (1991). The governance of innovation: Vertical integration and collaborative arrangements in the biotechnology industry. *Research Policy, 20,* 237–249.

Pisano, G. P. (1994). Knowledge, integration, and the locus of learning: An empirical analysis of process development. *Strategic Management Journal, 15,* 85–100.

Pisano, G. P. (1996). *The Development Factory: Unlocking the Potential of Process Innovation.* Harvard Business School Press: Boston.

Pisano, G. P., & Mang, P. Y. (1993). Collaborative product development and the market for know-how: Strategies and structures in the biotechnology industry. *Research on Technology Innovation, Management and Policy, 5,* 109–136.

Pittinsky, T. L. (2001). Knowledge nomads: Commitment at work (Doctoral dissertation, Harvard University, 2001). *Dissertation Abstracts International, 62,* 2103. (UMI No. 3011460)

Plotz, David. (1997, October 19). Los Angeles Times Publisher Mark Willes: In praise of the "cereal killer." *Slate Magazine* [electronic version]. Retrieved July 8, 2004 from http://slate.msn.com/id/1836.

Podolny, J. M. (1993). A status-based model of market competition. *American Journal of Sociology, 98,* 829–72.

Podolny, J. M. (1994). Market uncertainty and the social character of economic exchange. *Administrative Science Quarterly, 39,* 458–483.

Podolny, J. M. (2001). Networks as the pipes and prisms of the market: A look at investment decisions in the venture capital industry. *American Journal of Sociology, 107*(1), 33–60.

Pogash, C. (1995, July/August). General Mills' Gift to Journalism. *American Journalism Review* [electronic version]. Retrieved July 8, 2004 from www.ajr.org/Article.asp?id=1500.

Pollack, A. (1998, December 24). An air of mystery surrounds the abrupt resignation of Biogen chief. *The New York Times,* p. C1.

Porter, L. W., Lawler, E. E., & Hackman, J. R. (1975). *Behavior in Organizations.* New York: McGraw-Hill.

Porter, M. E. (1992). *Capital Choices: Changing the Way America Invests in Industry.* Boston, MA: Council on Competitiveness/Harvard Business School.

Powell, W. W., & DiMaggio, P. J. (Eds.). (1991). *The New Institutionalism in Organizational Analysis.* Chicago, IL: University of Chicago Press.

Pratt, W. D. (1987). *The Abbott Almanac: 100 Years of Commitment to Quality Health Care.* Elmsford, NY: The Benjamin Company.

Quirk, W. R., & R.B.C. Capital Markets. (2003). *The In-Vitro Diagnostics Industry: Overview and Emerging Opportunities, December 5, 2003.* Available from The Investext Group, www.investext.com.

Rao, H. (1994). The social construction of reputation: Certification contests, legitimation, and the survival of organizations in the American automobile industry: 1895–1912. *Strategic Management Journal, 15,* 29–44.

Recombinant Capital. (2004). *Alliances database.* Available at www.recap.com.

Reichers, A. E. (1987). An interactionist perspective on newcomer socialization rates. *Academy of Management Review, 12,* 278–287.

Reuber, R. A., & Fischer, E. (1999). Understanding the consequences of founders' experience. *Journal of Small Business Management, 37*(2), 30–45.

Rhodes, S. R., & Doering, M. M. (1993). Intention to change careers: Determinants and process. *Career Development Quarterly, 42,* 74–92.

Robbins-Roth, C. (2000). *From Alchemy to IPO: The Business of Biotechnology.* Cambridge, MA: Perseus Publishing.

Roberts, L. M. (2005). Changing faces: Professional image construction in diverse organizational settings. *Academy of Management Review, 30*(4), forthcoming.

Roberts, L. M., Dutton, J., Spreitzer, G., Heaphy, E. D., & Quinn, R. E. (2005). Composing the reflected best-self portrait: Building pathways for becoming extraordinary in work organizations. *Academy of Management Review, 30*(4), forthcoming.

Rodgers, F. G. (1986). *The IBM Way: Insights into the World's Most Successful Marketing Organization.* New York: Harper & Row.

Ropo, A., & Hunt, J. G. (1995). Entrepreneurial processes as virtuous and vicious spirals in a changing opportunity structure: A paradoxical perspective. *Entrepreneurship Theory and Practice, 19*(3), 91–111.

Rosen, S. (1981). The economics of superstars. *American Economic Review, 71*(5), 845–858.

Rosenbaum, J. E. (1979). Tournament mobility: Career patterns in a corporation. *Administrative Science Quarterly, 24*(2), 220–241.

Ross, L., & Nisbett, R. (1991). *The Person and the Situation: Perspectives of Social Psychology.* New York: McGraw-Hill.

Rousseau, D. M. (1985). Issues of level in organizational research: Multi-level and cross-level perspectives. *Research in Organizational Behavior, 7,* 1–37.

Rousseau, D. M. (1995). *Psychological Contracts in Organizations.* Newbury Park, CA: Sage.

Rousseau, D. M. (2001a). Idiosyncratic psychological contacts: Are flexibility and consistency mutually exclusive? *Organizational Dynamics, 29,* 260–273.

Rousseau, D. M. (2001b). Schema, promises, and mutuality: The psychology of the psychological contract. *Journal of Organizational and Occupational Psychology, 24,* 511–541.

Rousseau, D. M., & Fried, Y. (2000). Location, location, location: Contextualizing organizational behavior. *Journal of Organizational Behavior, 22,* 1–15.

Rousseau, D. M., & House, R. J. (1994). MESO organizational behavior: Avoiding three fundamental biases. In C. Cooper & D. M. Rousseau (Eds.), *Trends in Organizational Behavior, 1,* 13–30.

Rousseau, D. M., & Schalk, R. (Eds.). (2000). *Psychological Contracts in Employment: Cross-National Perspectives.* Newbury Park, CA: Sage.

Sahlman, W. A. (1990). The structure and governance of venture-capital organizations. *Journal of Financial Economics, 27*(2), 473–521.

Salter, M. S. (2002). Tracking stocks at Genzyme (A). *Harvard Business School Case No. 9–902–023.* Boston: Harvard Business School Press.

Sanna, L. (1992). Self-efficacy theory: Implications for social facilitation and social loafing. *Journal of Personality and Social Psychology, 62,* 774–786.

Sanna, L., & Pusecker, P. (1994). Self-efficacy, valence of self-evaluation, and performance. *Journal of Personality and Social Psychology, 20*(1), 82–92.

Sawyer, J. (2001). The house that Henri built. *Pharmaceutical Executive,* 30–42. Available online at www.pharmexec.com.

Saxenian, A. (1994). *Regional Advantage: Culture and Competition in Silicon Valley and Route 128.* Cambridge, MA: Harvard University Press.

Schein, E. H. (1978). *Career Dynamics: Matching Individual and Organizational Needs.* Reading, MA: Addison-Wesley.

Schein, E. H. (1985a). *Career Anchors.* San Diego, CA: University Associates.

Schein, E. H. (1985b). *Organizational Culture and Leadership.* San Francisco: Jossey-Bass.

Schein, E. H. (1993). *Career Anchors* (2nd ed.). San Diego, CA: Pfeiffer (Jossey-Bass).

Schein, E. H. (1999). *The Corporate Culture Survival Guide.* San Francisco: Jossey-Bass.

Schein, E. H. (2003). *DEC Is Dead, Long Live DEC: The Lasting Legacy of Digital Equipment Corporation.* San Francisco: Berrett-Koehler.

Schein, E. H. (2004). *Organizational Culture and Leadership* (3rd ed.). San Francisco: Jossey-Bass.

Shepherd, D., Ettenson, R., & Crouch, A. (2000). New venture strategy and profitability: A venture capitalist's assessment. *Journal of Business Venturing, 15,* 449–467.

Simon, H. A. (1997). *Administrative Behavior: A Study of Decision-Making Processes in Administrative Organizations.* New York: The Free Press. (Original work published 1947.)

Simons, R. (1987). Planning, control and uncertainty: A process view. In W. J. Bruns & R. S. Kaplan (Eds.), *Accounting & Management: Field Study Perspectives* (pp. 339–362). Boston: Harvard Business School Press.

Simons, R. (1991). Strategic orientation and top management attention to control systems. *Strategic Management Journal, 12*(1), 49–62.

Simons, R. (2000). Codman & Shurtleff, Inc.: Planning and control system. *Harvard Business School Case No. 9–187–081.* Boston: Harvard Business School Publishing.

Spence, M. (1973). Job market signaling. *Quarterly Journal of Economics, 87,* 355–375.

Stephens, G. K. (1994). Crossing internal career boundaries: The state of research on subjective career transitions. *Journal of Management, 20,* 479–501.

Stevensen, H. H., Roberts, M. J., & Grousbeck, H. I. (1989). *New Business Ventures and the Entrepreneur.* Homewood, IL: Irwin.

Stinchcombe, A. L. (1965). Social structure and organizations. In J. G. March (Ed.), *Handbook of Organizations.* Chicago: Rand McNally.

Stinchcombe, A. L. (1968). *Constructing Social Theories*. Chicago, IL: University of Chicago Press.

Stipp, D. (1992, June 23). Genzyme counters criticism over high cost of drug. *The Wall Street Journal*, p. B4. (Available from Factiva.com)

Strauss, A., & Corbin, J. (1998). *Basics of Qualitative Research: Techniques and Procedures for Developing Grounded Theory* (2nd ed.). Thousand Oaks, CA: Sage Publications.

Stuart, T. E., Hoang, H., & Hybels, R. C. (1999). Interorganizational endorsements and the performance of entrepreneurial ventures. *Administrative Science Quarterly, 44*, 315–349.

Super, D. E. (1957). *The Psychology of Careers*. New York: Harper.

Sutcliffe, K. M., & Vogus, T. J. (2003) Organizing for resilience. In K. Cameron, J. E. Dutton, & R. E. Quinn (Eds.), *Positive Organizational Scholarship: Foundations of New Discipline* (pp. 94–110). San Francisco: Berrett-Koehler.

Tajfel, H. (1981). *Human Groups and Social Categories*. New York: Cambridge University Press.

Tedlow, R. S., & Smith, W. K. (1998). James Burke: A Career in American Business (A). *Harvard Business School Case No. 9–389–177*. Boston: Harvard Business School Publishing.

Teisberg, E. O. (1994). Genzyme Corp.: Strategic challenges with Ceradase. *Harvard Business School Case No. 9–793–120*. Boston: Harvard Business School Publishing.

Thomas, D. A., & Gabarro, J. J. (1999). *Breaking Through: The Making of Minority Executives in Corporate America*. Boston: Harvard Business School Press.

Thomas, R. J., & Bennis, W. G. (2002). Leadership crucibles. *Executive Excellence, 19*(11), 3–4.

Thompson, K. R., Hochwarter, W. A., & Mathys, N. J. (1997). Stretch targets: What makes them effective? *Academy of Management Executive, 11*(3), 48–60.

Thompson Financial. (2004). Joint ventures & strategic alliances database. *Thomson Financial Securities Data*. Data retrieved February 2004.

Thornton, P. H. (1999). The sociology of entrepreneurship. *Annual Review of Sociology, 25*, 19–46.

Thornton, P. H., & Ocasio, W. (1999). Institutional logics and the historical contingency of power in organizations: Executive succession in the higher education publishing industry, 1958–1990. *American Journal of Sociology, 105*(3), 801–843.

Tushman, M. L., & O'Reilly, C. A. I. (1996). Ambidextrous organizations: Managing evolutionary and revolutionary change. *California Management Review, 38*(4), 8.

Tushman, M. L., & Smith, W. K. (2002). Organizational technology. In J. Baum (Ed.), *Companion to Organizations* (pp. 386–414). Malden, MA: Blackwell.

Van de Ven, W., & van Praag, B. (1981). The demand for deductibles in private health insurance. *Journal of Econometrics, 17,* 229–252.

Van Maanen, J. (1976). Breaking-in: Socialization to work. In R. Dubin (Ed.), *Handbook of Work, Organization, and Society* (pp. 67–130). Chicago: Rand McNally.

Van Maanen, J. (1977). Toward a theory of the career. In J. Van Maanen (Ed.), *Organizational Careers: Some New Perspectives* (pp. 161–179). New York: Wiley.

Van Maanen, J., & Schein, E. H. (1979). Toward a theory of organizational socialization. *Research in Organizational Behavior, 1,* pp. 209–264.

Vartanig, V. G. (1971, July 24). Stocks decline in slow trading. *The New York Times,* pp. 43, 46.

Walsh, J. P. (1988). Selectivity and selective perception: An investigation of managers' belief structures and information processing. *Academy of Management Journal, 31,* 873–896.

Walsh, J. P. (1995). Managerial and organizational cognition: Notes from a trip down memory lane. *Organization Science, 6*(3), 280–321.

Wanous, J. P. (1980). *Organizational Entry: Recruitment, Selection, and Socialization of Newcomers.* Reading, MA: Addison-Wesley.

Wayne, L. (1983, October 23). A GE alumnus shakes up Rubbermaid. *The New York Times,* p. F6.

Wegner, D. M., Erber, R., & Raymond, P. (1991). Transactive memory in close relationships. *Journal of Personality & Social Psychology, 61*(6), 923–929.

Weick, K. E. (1979). *The Social Psychology of Organizing* (2nd ed.). New York: McGraw-Hill.

Weintraub, A., & Barrett, A. (2002, September 18). Amgen vs. J&J: Will it ever end? *Business Week Online.* Available from LexisNexis.

Weisbrod, S., & Prudential-Bache Securities. (1986). *Biogen N.V.–Company Report, December 24, 1986.* Available from The Investext Group, www.investext.com.

Weisbrod, S., & Prudential-Bache Securities. (1988). *Genzyme Corp.–Company Report, June 1, 1988.* Available from The Investext Group, www.investext.com.

Whyte, W. H. (1956). *The Organization Man.* New York: Simon & Schuster.

Winship, C., & Mare, R. D. (1992). Models for sample selection bias. *Annual Review of Sociology, 18,* 327–350.

Zacharakis, A. L., & Meyer, G. D. (1998). A Lack of Insight. *Journal of Business Venturing, 13,* 57–76.

Zacharakis, A. L., & Shepherd, D. L. (2001). The nature of information and overconfidence on venture capitalist's decision making. *Journal of Business Venturing, 16*(4), 311–332.

Zucker, L. G., Darby, M. R., & Brewer, M. B. (1998). *Intellectual capital and the birth of US biotechnology enterprises.* Washington, DC: National Bureau of Economic Research.

Index